person to person

person to person

THE GOSPEL OF MARK

Paul V. Vickers

ff

Swedenborg Foundation Publishers
West Chester, Pennsylvania

Library of Congress Cataloging-in-Publication Data
Vickers, Paul V.
        Person to person : the Gospel of Mark / Paul V. Vickers.
        p.   cm.
        ISBN 0-87785-380-0
        1. Bible. N.T. Mark—Criticism, interpretation, etc.
        2. New Jerusalem Church—Doctrines. I. Title.
BS2585.2.V465 1998   98–13695
226.3'077—dc21   CIP

Cover Art: Detail from "St. Mark Writing the Gospel."
Greek manuscript, Constantinople, second half of 11th century.
The Pierpont Morgan Library/Art Resource, NY

Edited by Stuart Shotwell
Designed by Helene Krasney
Set in Garamond by Sans Serif, Inc., Saline, Michigan
Printed in the United States of America

For more information on Swedenborg Foundation Publishers, contact:
Swedenborg Foundation
320 North Church Street
West Chester, PA 19380 or
http://www.swedenborg.com.

1 2 3 4 5

To my masters,
my colleagues,
and, especially,
my students,
in gratitude for
my instruction

CONTENTS

Introduction ix

One: Jesus begins his ministry 1

Two: Sinners and forgiveness 27

Three: Crowds and critics 39

Four: Parables of change 51

Five: Healing 65

Six: Miracles and apostles 79

Seven: Jews and Gentiles 99

Eight: Blind disciples 115

Nine: Transfiguration and failure 133

Ten: To Jerusalem 151

Eleven: Entry into Jerusalem 167

Twelve: Jesus rejected 181

Thirteen: Things to come 201

Fourteen: Supper and betrayal 217

Fifteen: Pilate and crucifixion 249

Sixteen: Resurrection 273

INTRODUCTION

READING THE GOSPEL

To speak to God "person to person" would provide a firm foundation for anyone's life. Many wonder if it is possible. Yet the Gospels were provided as a word from God to tell us the good news about his coming to us in Jesus Christ, and in them we should find the contact we need. But we shall only make such contact if we read in a way that makes it possible. The Gospels can be read merely as ancient documents, or the history of an amazing life, or a source of creeds and contention. Many have used them to control and to condemn other people. The purpose of this commentary is to show a way that makes them a word from God to each individual.

If God is to speak to us in the Gospels we must approach him as his children. We must not look for a record of past history or a way of judging other people or a commentary on church politics and worldwide events. We must think of the meaning for our life in each verse we read, finding all of it in our own life and not directing it onto other people or other problems. Then we must think about the way our life falls short of God's hope for us and begin to change our life to accept his love. Remember that God gives us life moment by moment, and so what he provides for our instruction he himself can use in our mind, showing its meaning for us. The Gospels are a revelation from God; thus, he can reveal to us from them what we need personally to receive his love into our life.

This book is written to illustrate a way of reading the Gospel that each of us can undertake and understand individually, and in so doing find a personal relationship with God. Down the ages, most interpretation of the four gospels has looked for teaching or fulfillment in the history of nations and churches, and in the propounding of moral codes to govern and demand obedience from people at large. It seems to me that this is quite against the spirit of the Gospel. Jesus is always challenging individuals. They may come to him in crowds, but his message confronts each individual as a personal challenge. He asks for personal change in behavior, for individual repentance and new life. There is no sign of any effort to formulate organizations under moral or administrative banners. Jesus calls for individuals to change their way of life. He leaves us to draw the corollary that, if enough people change themselves, then their changed lives will change the world. The Gospels should be read, therefore, by each one of us as a personal challenge to see life in a new way and change it for the better. This book is an effort to help individuals seek in Mark's gospel for such vision and its consequent challenge to life. That does not ignore the universal effect of the coming of Jesus Christ, but it accepts that such cosmic change can only come about by spiritual change in individuals.

The purpose of such reading must be clearly understood. It will not be simply to acquire knowledge, and certainly not to instruct or direct other people. It will be to shed light on one's own behavior, to clarify personal thoughts and, above all, to enable us to see the motives that drive us on and to change them for the better. Such vision will be unique to each individual and directly applicable to his or her life.

However, talking to God personally can never be a matter of understanding alone, nor yet merely of a discipline for life from what we see. Affection and joy will be the mainstay of the conversation, as it is of any worthwhile human relationship. As soon as we read, we realize that we are approaching one whose love for us is immeasurable and unending. We read of the love of God acting in Jesus Christ in a particular place and time, but the Gospels emphasize that this is to give each one of us the opportunity to change in our place and time. We need to feel God's personal interest and love for each of us individually, which is the real meaning of salvation. It is not simply that God loves the whole human race. He loves each individual, with the commitment to sorrow or joy that a parent has with a child. All his action in the past and the present is simply to live with us in our life *now*. Thus, the relationship we seek in reading Scripture is more than a search for knowledge, wonderful as that might be. It is to live with God day by day.

PARABLE MEANING

To cast the whole scene of the Gospels in our own mind and life is easy enough when we are reading direct commands and appeals to us by the Lord. When we enter upon scenes of healing, or of confrontation with various factions, or teaching upon a problem of life long past in Palestine, we need to use the Lord's own method to arrive at a personal meaning. The Gospel assures us that "without a parable he did not speak to them," and we must use the method of parable to grasp the personal message to us. After all, the Lord is not interested in conveying to us how some one individual was cured of blindness, but in showing us how our eyes can be opened. There is no value for us in knowing about those who followed or betrayed him in the past; we need to see our betrayal or loyalty in the present and what makes such action happen for us.

The use of parable is not some invented crossword-puzzle method of reading the Scriptures. It depends on the way the world around us is linked to the world within us. Our minds—our thoughts and affections—have a pattern that makes them useful to us; that same pattern is carried into the use of our bodies, and then into the physical environment as earthly uses. The way God creates has the same pattern of being useful, whether it creates the souls of men and women, or their minds, or their bodies, or their physical environment.

We are aware of this parable link, and we use it in common speech. We "give birth" to a new idea; we "chew over" knowledge; we "breathe" a new spirit into an endeavor. We also "grow" in spirit, and our ideas "branch out" or "bear fruit"; we are as innocent as a lamb, as cunning as a fox, as harmless as a dove. This carries the linkage out from ourselves to the world created around us. These are not analogies we make for ourselves. They exist because God creates our inner world of mind by the same pattern that he creates our bodies and the physical world around them.

Therefore, we "think in parable." Wrong things are "dark." "Light is shed" on a problem. Important matters are "above" others or "deep within" them. Our thoughts "run on" or "wrestle" with each other. Our attitudes are "hard" or "soft" or "twisted." These are all patterns of bodily life. We think in images drawn from our bodies and the surrounding world. There is a common idea that really intellectual thinking removes itself from all such symbolism, but it usually conceals it, or produces an arid presentation of ideas that lacks reality and impact to other minds.

This built-in "parable" characteristic of human minds is the foundation of the parable in Scripture, and so the Gospels are full of illustrations from our bodies and the healing of them, and from the growth of the natural world and its behavior. Such illustrations are cast in the limited understanding people had then of the natural world and their own bodies, but their depth of meaning is not restricted. The field of parable is extended by the activities and the personalities of men and women whose lives are bound up in the life of Jesus, as he works for our redemption. Those involved in the story become part of the parable. Jesus points to this use of parable as he heals the blind man in John 9, or discusses food with his slow-witted disciples in Matthew 16:5–12 and warns them of "the leaven of the Pharisees."

The symbols in the parables are not a kind of fixed code to be decoded. In different contexts, their interplay varies; but it is remarkably easy to see the general pattern that unfolds. We cannot hope to see the whole message the Gospel conveys in this way, but we can see some of it and extend what the Lord is saying to us. As we use what we see, it will develop more and more. A parable approach to Scripture has colored the work of some commentators and more preachers, but few have sought for a coherent plan that enables a consistent approach to different stories. The only pioneer work I know is in the works of the eighteenth-century Swedish scholar Emanuel Swedenborg, and much of my attempt is indebted to his writing. Following the way Jesus himself uses parables, Swedenborg takes the uses things or people perform to characterize their parable meaning, and this enables understanding of them in different contexts. Thus, our minds are made to understand spiritual ideas in the worldly images of parables, miracles, and incidents in the Gospels. Swedenborg sees this internal sense in the Word as the way God can reveal himself and make a real second coming to men and women.

Moving beyond the literal meaning of the Gospels may seem risky, for we may see our own ideas rather than the Lord's light. We can prevent any such deviation if we keep in mind the general teaching of the whole of the Gospel. Nothing in the Gospels will contradict their own obvious teaching—that we are to love the Lord with all our powers and our neighbor as our selves. Their warnings not to judge or condemn others will prevent us from misusing the message. We shall not direct it against others, but onto our own life and our need for change.

None of us is able to use the whole of the truth that could shed light on our way of living. Many things must remain obscure. Indeed, until we can accept what we do see and use it in our life, we shall be blinded to many things by our own attitudes. So no one can offer to unfold the meaning of the Gospel in this sense. But this book attempts to use, and so illustrate, a way of thinking about the gospel of Mark that can bring the individual into a person-to-person way of listening to what is said. Then anything that is understood can be used to change personal life for the better. The method illustrated must be used and developed by each person for his or her own life. Every idea understood will demand changes in our way of living and thinking. We shall not only read, but we shall actively seek to change our lives by what we see. Seeking into Mark's gospel in this way will bring a presence of the Lord into our daily life. We shall live with a constant awareness of his love, and it will bring joy as well as illumination into all our efforts.

THE COMMENTARY

In the gospel of Mark, for the sake of easy reference I have maintained the accepted division into chapters, although it is arbitrary at times. At the beginning of each chapter, I have tried to explain the general development of this gospel and the impact its major themes have on our own lives. From this some overall view can be gained before entering into detail. Then, after each group of verses, I give sufficient background knowledge to make its meaning clear, and note any comparison with the other gospels that seems useful; but I have not followed speculations that do not seem to contribute to our personal understanding of the text.

Having tried to gain a clear view of the text, I have written, so far as I am able, what it shows me—first, of the Lord's own work on earth to redeem us and then of the meaning this has now in our own individual lives. My interpretation is not intended to lay down a vision for others. It is just the simplest way I can illustrate this "person-to-person" way of reading. I have no doubt that, in general ways, we shall see the same message in Mark's gospel; but the details of our vision, and the way we apply them to our own individual life must be seen by each person. Every idea understood will require changes in our way of living and thinking. If we make these changes, the Gospels will bring a presence of Jesus into our daily life. However poorly we understand at first, it will be personal to us. We shall be living with the love that made us and is there for our salvation, and this will bring a constant joy, even in our problems and difficulties.

At this point you can begin to read the commentary on the gospel. Further ideas on the origin and the writer of Mark's gospel follow below, but they are not essential to your reading and can be read later if you wish.

GOSPEL ORIGINS

The Gospels depend on the preaching and teaching of those who heard Jesus and saw his work, and then sought to convey the good news to others. Such teaching would settle into a pattern of words and incidents, remembered and retold by a disciple many times and in many places in the days after the resurrection. Mark's gospel is commonly dated around 64 A.D., during Nero's persecution of the Christians. At that time, witnesses to the life of Jesus were endangered, and Peter's death may have demanded a record of his preaching. A date twenty years earlier has also been argued, since those who could not hear disciples personally may have sought a written account before the persecution began. It is enough for us to realize that probably a generation of preaching preceded the written record, and it will have affected the content and style of the Gospels when others began to write.

I attempt no detailed analysis of the origins and transmission of this first gospel, nor seek to provide background knowledge other than is necessary to make its meaning clear. I acknowledge my debt to all those who have worked in such fields, but my purpose is to consider Mark in a particular way as it has come down to us. God's purpose in the Gospel was to have a channel to speak to each of us personally in this and every age. How his providence provided and preserved the text of the Gospel is wonderful and intriguing and worthy of study, but it fails its purpose unless we are using personally what he has given. The person who recalled incidents or preached the good news, or wrote down the story, or copied or amended it is not our essential study. The instruments God uses to formulate his Word to us are not, in themselves, important. What we read is not "Mark's" gospel. It never declares itself to be so. It is the good news about Jesus Christ.

We can never be certain which "Mark" was the author (and the name is the commonest Latin name in the Roman Empire). It may well be that we can build a good case for assuming John Mark to be the writer, as tradition asserts. His work with Peter would give him the substance as he heard the apostle preach and teach. There may be personal touches that support Mark's authorship. We know the disciples used Mark's mother's house in Jerusalem (Acts 12:12) and the personal reminiscence of the young man naked in the garden (Mark 14:51) could suggest Mark coming in haste from his home when he realized the dangers of that night's betrayal. The writer knows life in Palestine as it was lived at that time; and what seems to be occasional vagueness about topography may be because he is following the order of Peter's teaching, rather than rearranging it for a better chronology. We must remember that the aim at the beginning was to convey to others the importance and value of Jesus' work and teaching, and incidents were grouped in series that were never intended to be a detailed chronology of the Lord's life.

With every copy handwritten, we cannot rule out also occasional scribal errors, transpositions, or occasional later additions. It is possible to suggest that, as the gospel was used in the church, some additions may have been made to a simpler statement. But if we could confirm Mark's authorship of the whole without any shadow of doubt, surely we would only have pinpointed one of the agents God used to provide his Gospel. God must have used Mark's religious intention in writing the work to provide words that convey God's truth to us, as he used others like Peter to remember and describe and preach about what they had heard and seen. He will have used the same intention in others to copy it, preserve it, and (if it has happened) to add to it.

If it seems strange that providence could use so many factors to produce a word from God, think for a moment of the myriad factors in millions of human lives that God guides for the salvation of each individual. Concentrating on the accuracy and historicity of the text can lead us to forget that, whatever its development, at every stage it has been the gift of God.

For more than a hundred years, there has been a growing dismissal among scholars of any such use of the Gospels. Incidents of healing or behavior are treated as just incidents, with no more meaning than that they happened. Any idea that they might carry a spiritual message to later ages is dismissed. Any apparent interpretation of parables, as in Mark 4, has been declared the later addition of teachers not understanding the real purpose of parable. The parables themselves have been asserted to have only one restricted point to make, and anything that does not fit such a method has been declared a "late addition" to the Gospels. One can understand the reaction against the futile allegorizing of Scripture in past centuries from Origen onwards; the Gospels have been used by too many to provide authority for their own ideas. But the intertwining of stories and teaching, the constant emphasis that there are hidden things that will be revealed to the disciples, shows that those who had heard Jesus looked for more meaning than the literal stories and descriptions. Jesus lived and taught among people who were used to the parable method of teaching, for it is common in the Old Testament. The prophets tell and enact parables in their prophecies, and the style is integral to the Old Testament writers. The method was consequently used by Jewish teachers. It seems likely, therefore, that Jesus too was using the method and that it is embodied in the Gospels because it is inherent in the way men and women think, a provided way of divine illumination.

THE HISTORICAL EVENT

Much time and energy has been devoted to deciding what happened historically some two thousand years ago and whether the Gospels have preserved that accurately in their present form. Such an attitude sees the actual event as the revelation of God. I prefer to consider the Gospels as the revelation God has brought to us. The incarnation had its own importance in God's action to save humankind, and that would be so whether we knew about it or not. The real nature of such a work by God could never be revealed fully to our finite understanding. No record could provide a detailed description of Jesus' life; if it were attempted, it could only be given by eyewitnesses who did not understand what was really happening in Jesus and whose viewpoints would be varied. We need to know about his earthly life only so that we can use its revelation of the nature of God and make use of his saving power. The essential truth is not lost in the Gospel preserved for us, nor can it be separated from the message of the Gospel; but the way it is described is itself a divine action to give God a way to speak personally of his salvation to each one of us. It is shortsighted to see God acting powerfully in the event and then to deny him any power to provide the good news in such a form that it will serve men and women in later generations.

It has become customary to speak of God as beginning creation or acting at a particular time to provide a prophet or a savior or to perform a miracle; but we have lost the sense that he is continually alive in a creation that he continually makes, and therefore continually provides for. Things exist only because of God's love; therefore, they are always cared for by that love. This is the way we should think of the Word: as a gift continually preserved and continually used for our salvation.

The Gospels are not attempting to provide an accurate historical record to prove, in some way, that a divine act happened. The divine purpose was fulfilled as God acted, and humanity does not sit in judgment on that. The Gospels were provided so that we might know and make use of the salvation offered. It is often forgotten that truth can be conveyed by something that is not necessarily historically accurate. Most of us can see a truth in the story of the Good Samaritan, even if it is only the need for compassion; but that story, though based on a common occurrence, was invented by Jesus for his purpose and is not historical. The divine work of Jesus' coming to redeem the human race is the whole basis of the written gospel and is a historical event; but the varying remembrance of eyewitnesses, the stringing together of events to preach to others, of additions to explain and scriptural quotations to illustrate, is a process that God has used to fashion a revelation of the event useful to individuals down through the ages. It is not necessarily historically accurate in its details, which indeed differ in the four gospels. Nevertheless, in the way events are described, the Gospel reveals God's work for us and enables us to cooperate with him. This is always the attitude of Jesus to the Scriptures of his own day. My purpose here has been to try to use that approach to Mark's gospel.

THE TEXT AND TRANSLATION

The translation of Mark's gospel used here is not any one of the many valuable translations published in the last half century. They serve various purposes in providing readable translations in modern idiom, some seeking for more accuracy, others to provide a more polished translation, some to enhance the drama, others to simplify, and some to incorporate every alternative reading in ancient manuscripts to that "received text" that came to be used by the church. These alternative readings are mostly minor matters and would make little difference to the meaning of the text. Where such deviations existed, they could presumably be used by men and women for the purpose of a Word from God. I have preferred to follow the Received or Byzantine text, since it was the one divine providence left with the church for most of its existence, and in which therefore the essential message can be presumed to lie.

What use providence made of other forms of text, I do not attempt to discuss.

In the text of Mark's gospel, the ending from 16:9 shows signs of recommencement and a different style. This suggests that an ending has been provided to conclude an unfinished or mutilated work. The existence of early manuscripts with a different ending supports that idea. This may seem a radical variation in the text's origin, but that does not destroy the concept of providence governing the final form of the text. The whole gospel had to be built up from the recollections of people, probably remembered and preached by one person and written down and arranged by another, and the text that we have is formed for us under providence to convey the good news to us in a form we can use. I have used the whole of that text in the same way without distinction.

In this work, since the commentary follows the translation and can explain difficulties, there is no need to seek ways of translating ancient customs and measures in modern terms; nor do I seek a polished form attractive in public reading. We simply need to know what the text we have received in Greek is saying to us. I have translated it in that vein, making no attempt to polish it where it might seem clumsy and preserving characteristics that may not make for a good English style. Thus the frequent conjunctions—many sentences are connected to the previous one by "and" *(kai)*—are typical of Hebrew and Aramaic, where there seems to be a need to connect things closely together. The continual use of "immediately" *(euthus, eutheos)* gives the gospel the primitive style of a word-of-mouth storyteller; rather as a naive narrator in English might say, "And then we went to Paris and then we went to Berlin," where the adverb "then" is really used to ensure that the listener's attention is held to the importance of the story. The impression of a naive and unpracticed storyteller increases as emphasis is frequently made by adding redundant phrases. The language is unpolished, suggesting someone with a restricted knowledge of Greek and not a very large vocabulary—moreover someone who was probably more at home in Aramaic than Greek and accustomed to use "slang" and Latinized words. All this does not make for a stylish production, and it is probably a mistake to try to turn it into one. The original has an urgency and conviction in its drab featureless style that is best left alone for our purposes.

ACKNOWLEDGMENTS

My thanks are due to my wife Nita for enabling me to write. I am, as always grateful to my cousin the Rev. John E. Elliott, for his help and support, although I must bear responsibility for any opinions expressed here.

I would also like to thank the staff of the Swedenborg Foundation for their work on the production, especially Dr. Stuart Shotwell for his guidance on American publications and the senior editor, Mary Lou Bertucci, for her care at every stage.

person to person

Chapter One

JESUS BEGINS HIS MINISTRY

Once humanity had fallen into evil, the only way for God to reach people with his loving life was to bring it into their condition. Then, as they made each step away from evil, his power could sustain them. They needed love from God in every small step of their progress. But the infinite love of God that maintains the universe and every soul in it and their every thought and affection—this could not come directly into our restricted life. If it had come immediately in that fashion, it would have destroyed where it entered. It had to be born as a son and grow up as we do. It had to build up its presence here through all the stages of man's life, all coming alive steadily from the love of God until, as Jesus said at the end, "I and the Father are one." This presence of God brought into every stage of our life in Jesus Christ is our hope of salvation. This is the joy in our reading of Mark's gospel.

As we read and try to understand, there will be two aspects to our thought. We shall see something of the work going on in Jesus himself, and so understand his revelation of God's nature more clearly. However, the story that reveals this to us also shows how he helps us personally. It becomes the story of his power at work within us to change us individually. Such changes take time, a whole lifetime, and we may not be able to see them all in sequence in our personal life; but we shall understand what is meant to happen and know the joy of Jesus' presence in our lives as we strive to accept the power he offers.

1. The beginning of the good news of Jesus Christ, the Son of God.

This is not just a title or introductory phrase to be passed over lightly. Rather it sets the tone for all our reading. It puts us into a context with God, who is speaking to us about his way of saving us from our selfishness. From the beginning, we cannot think of ourselves and our concerns in an isolated way. The good news is of the power and influence of God, brought in Jesus Christ especially to us in our own particular sphere. Such a birth of divine love into our world follows the pattern of our existence. Its presence becomes a "Son," who can learn and experience in our fashion and can make decisions in life that enable that love to be established at our level. It will be formed in the true pattern of life that is the truth or the Word. That is the way God's life always works, and it has been since the beginning; but, in Jesus, it becomes flesh in this world. Except when Jesus is conscious of the divine life within him, this can place him in the same position as us, enduring temptation, praying to his Father. But the life coming alive in him is the love of God, "the Father" who sent him into the world. By the end of the process in this world, Jesus will be able to say, "He who has seen me has seen the Father." Yet that does not mean that we are back where we started from. God has achieved a real presence in this world in the same level of temptation and understanding that we use and will be able to sustain and enlighten us. This redemption is a permanent achievement. Divine love is not just active creating the universe and us; it lives with us in our need and offers us salvation from our selfishness. The gospel finds nothing strange in God's entering into our world for our salvation. We know that the love of God created us. We can only read correctly if we also know that the love of God does everything necessary to save every individual human being.

Already the emphasis is on our need to be saved from something that obsesses us, something that obstructs and turns our powers away from God. We need release from this, if we are to see our lives as God intended. We need a power from him that we can use. The name "Jesus" is derived from the Hebrew for "Jehovah saves" and declares that the action is from God himself, who is called Jehovah or Yahweh in the Old Testament. "Christ" stands for the Hebrew *Messiah,* "the anointed one." It is not primarily a thought of a new king to rule our lives, but rather of the anointing of earthly life with the love of God in Jesus Christ in such a way that his strength is available to us. This good news is the foundation of all that follows as Mark's gospel traces our salvation.

2–3. As it is written in the prophets, "Behold, I send my messenger before your face, who shall prepare your way before you; a voice crying in the wilderness: Prepare the way of the Lord, make his paths straight."

Now the Old Testament is quoted, a reminder that God's love is not given to sudden bursts of activity, but that he has been acting to reach us and help us throughout and before all time. The prophecy is in Malachi 3:1 and Isaiah 40:3. It was fulfilled as John the Baptist in the desert of Judea announced our Lord's coming at a point in time; but it is not simply a historical event. The power it brought is now available to save us in the time in which we are born. The prophecy is made to us in our own personal desert, where nothing good grows and where we wander without any real purpose. We need to grasp the nature of this, our own private wilderness, before we can begin to escape from it.

We need salvation because of the inherited tendency to be selfish that forms the groundwork of our lives. This is not to deny that we need to care for ourselves. There is a very proper love of self that is necessary if we are to be fit and able to be of use to anyone else. We need to preserve our health and strength, to be educated and trained and refreshed by leisure, or we shall be of little use to help our fellows. The problem lies in the reason that we do these things that care for ourselves. If it is for our own ease or that we may acquire wealth or power to use for ourselves, then our life is driven by the selfishness we all inherit. Any care we have for ourselves (and those closely bound to ourselves) has to be so that we can serve our neighbors, and so the Lord. The prime reason for our lives must be to find the happiness of returning the love of the Lord, who makes us. That we do by loving our neighbors as his children and sharing in their joy. The love of our self must be the servant to those higher loves by keeping us able to help our neighbor and our Lord. Inevitably it is not so at first, when we become increasingly aware of the sheer selfishness that the human race inherits from generations of evil in the world. That selfishness turns our proper life upside down, causing us to think of ourselves first, our fellows only as we can make them serve us, and knowledge about God only as a way of manipulating others.

Our mind may well seem to grow a multitude of desires, thoughts, activities that are not obviously harmful, but since these lack good intentions for others, they are barren. We need to go over the reason that we do our job, react to family and friends, enjoy life. If the answer is "for what we get out of it," then nothing really grows for others. And what we get out of it does not last, so that we need a further achievement, another domination of others, another pleasure, to make a barren life seem worthwhile. In such a state we have no aim in life that goes beyond our own momentary satisfaction, nothing that goes by a "straight path" for someone else's good. We need to prepare a way in our mind for the Lord to enter. In our wilderness of selfish living, we must cease to love ourselves and find a way to help others as the mainspring of our lives. Each of us must gain a personal realization of this fallen state of our mind. We must study our own wilderness and admit its existence before we can go any further. Then in our desert of living for ourselves, we have to cease to love ourselves alone and look for some way to love and help another person.

4–6. John arose baptizing in the wilderness and proclaiming a baptism of repentance to send away sins. And all the country of Judea and they of Jerusalem went out to him and were all baptized by him in the river Jordan, confessing their sins. And John was clothed in camel hair and had a belt of leather about his loins, and he ate locusts and wild honey.

Presumably John baptized in the reaches of the lower Jordan, not far from Jericho. Since there was opposition to him, not all those in Judea and Jerusalem can have tramped eastward to the river, but they must have thronged to him in such numbers that it seemed as if all the country was on the move. 2 Kings 1:8 and Zechariah 13:4 suggest that John's clothing was traditional for a prophet, probably consisting of a leather loincloth with a coat woven from camel's hair over it, or possibly the skin with the hair still on it. His food suggests a wilderness bare of all but insects.

Our mind needs a baptism into a new way of life, a baptism that operates by repentance. Repentance is often misunderstood as feeling sorry for one's sins. No doubt that will be in mind, for we cannot ignore our selfish past, but repentance is far more positive than that. We are confessing not just sins of the past, but the sin of the way we are living now. At the corresponding point in another gospel (Luke 3:10–14), various people ask what they should do, and in each case the command is to act in such a way that others are not harmed and may feel compassion and help. Only such a change in our way of living sends away the sin that is committed every time we live selfishly, without regard for others. To live this new life, we need ideas to wash out our self-centered ways and cleanse our lives. This is done with the "water of everlasting life," as the truth is called. At this stage, the water of truth for our baptizing comes from the River Jordan, which is on the very boundary of the Holy Land. We start with the most external and direct commands of the gospel about loving the neighbor and not stealing, lusting, hating. Only when the more obvious evils of our life are washed away can we begin to see the depth and love within the gospel. This rough-and-ready grasp of the obvious truths for life is typified in the messenger, for John is clothed in rough camel hair and leather, and eats locusts and wild honey. The first message to our mind speaks obviously in down-to-earth terms about the coarse self-love that shows in much of our life. No deep and elaborate ideas can be used, for in this state we feed on lowly general ideas of truth that hop and flutter through our minds like locusts. The change in our way of life will bring some help to others, but any sweetness we find in our new life is still spasmodic, like the occasional discovery of wild honey in a wilderness. Yet with obvious challenging truths we are baptized, and our reaction must be a personal repentance that changes our daily behavior, at home, work, and play.

This change occurs not just in the outward manner of our lives. We are mostly law-abiding and outwardly civil and helpful already. It may seem strange to speak of evil in the midst of normal, outwardly obedient lives; but unless our purpose is to love and help others, we may be simply using this facade to get our own way. We are all aware that loving words can have no real purpose behind them and that we perform a great many actions not because we want to help others, but because we want to maintain our place and have the benefits of our place in the world. The normal sequence of life has under it the basic evil that wants things for ourselves alone, and we see it break loose in times of stress in the mayhem of riot and violence. So it is the fundamental purpose behind our whole behavior that must accept the need to change and think of others and the Lord's purpose for us all.

This basic change in the way we live is essential. The gospel is not given merely to provide knowledge, but to change the way we live with others. The water of our baptism is not a pool of ideas to contemplate, but a dynamic flowing river of commands to change us. Unless we begin with real repentance to change our lives, nothing can be revealed to us of the joy we can find in knowing Jesus and his way. Every time we see some light on our nature and our behavior, we must use it to change the way we live, not merely delight in it as a good idea.

7–8. And he preached, saying, After me comes he who is mightier than I, the thong of whose sandals I am not fit to bend down and untie. I baptized you with water, but he will baptize you with the holy spirit.

In the message demanding a change of life, there is also a promise of a true relationship with God, of knowing his love in the heart and acting from that love and not mere obedience. The whole point of putting away the sinful life is to allow a new holy spirit from God to act in us, to baptize us with an inner power of truly loving others and rejoicing in their good. In a way, as John says, there is no relationship between the way of repentance and that of love, for repenting looks always at the evil to be resisted, whereas love looks always at the joy of serving. The one does not even touch the lowliest service, "the sandal thong," of the other; but we see the promise of this new power in our life, even while we are only cleaning up our obvious selfishness and evil.

It is important that we should always have this hope of eternal life in our living. A demand only for repentance and obedience would leave us constantly repressing selfishness that was not replaced in us by anything better. In the end, we would lose heart. We need to be able to suppress our selfishness by using a different power in our lives. The promise of new life from God, to save us and give us a new spirit, is an essential part of John's call to repentance.

9–11. And it happened in those days that Jesus came from Nazareth of Galilee and was baptized by John in the Jordan. And immediately going up from the water he saw the heavens opened, and the spirit as a dove descending on him. And a voice came out of the heavens, "You are my beloved son in whom I delight."

Mark tells us nothing of the birth and childhood of Jesus, only briefly that he came from a town in Galilee. So Jesus enters the story already able to do his work. Nevertheless, we need to remember the preceding years from his birth. Jesus had spent some thirty years growing up in a busy home in Nazareth, the eldest of seven, for we are later told he had four brothers and at least two sisters. He had taken his part in the life of the community, presumably working as a carpenter, experiencing our natural life and the power of selfishness in the human mind he took from Mary. He had been fighting this evil in daily life and putting it away, replacing it with the love from God that was his soul. The work was not entirely completed, for there were still some dire temptations to be faced, but to a large extent he had put on in this world a life directly powered by the love of God. This enables the divine declaration at this point and explains the vision from which he taught the truth and his power to perform miracles that relate to the creative love of God.

John's baptizing culminates in the baptism of Jesus; and this answers a problem that now begins to trouble us. For how can we receive the love of God into our imperfect lives? There is no relationship between the infinite creative love of God and our limited earthly life, even with our faltering steps of repentance! But God has made such a relationship in Jesus. He was born like us, grew up like us, and now is baptized like us. He has entered into all the states we know and, just as we wash our lives clean by the water of truth, he has worked by truth and washed the selfishness from human life in a baptism like ours. Yet he is not like us in his being; for the spirit of God is his life, and we realize that the changes he made in his life drew down into earthly life the very life of God. This holy spirit that came by him, and that baptizes us spiritually, is shown at his baptism by the holy dove. He is "the beloved son" of God, as the voice from heaven declares. So we know the love of God is present in our earthly state at every step along the way. He has filled each truth we may learn with the power of love at our level. The truth we learn is not just knowledge. It is dynamic with his unselfish love and can work to change us if we use the truth. We are not walking to him alone along a long lonely way with some possible hope at the end. Every step of the way he is holding our hand with the strength he brought to us.

12–13. And immediately the spirit drove him out into the wilderness. And he was there forty days in the wilderness tempted by Satan, and he was with the wild beasts; and the angels ministered to him.

"Forty" is the figure used in Scripture for something that must be endured to the end, as in the forty years Israel wandered in the wilderness, and the forty days and nights it rained upon the Ark, and the same time Elijah traveled to Horeb. "Satan" is, like the devil, the great adversary of humanity, and is prominent in the Book of Job.

Jesus' involvement with our experiences is immediately stressed, for the spirit which is acting in him reveals to him the same "wilderness" of emptiness and stress of self-love that we know. He comes under the challenge of a "Satan" of false attitudes to life's purpose, and the "beasts" of lust attack him. But he never accepts such evil when it attacks him. He resists and by so doing replaces the inhumanity he becomes aware of with a truly divine humanity of love for others. The Satan is the accuser of humankind who seeks their destruction by hatred and deception. Since God is the only creator, such a force must have arisen because humans distorted God's way of love to ways of hate. Jesus faces the false way of living that the concentrated evil of humankind has woven into life and rejects it, replacing it with God's unselfish love for others. The angels (literally "messengers") who aid him are indeed the messengers of God: the truths about life and its purpose that are in the Scripture. Jesus' use of these truths in resistance is stressed in Matthew 4 and Luke 4 where he quotes the Scripture in his temptations. This combat of temptation is not a single incident; it is "forty days" long, the figure always used for stress that lasts until its work is accomplished. He had been resisting since his childhood, and we shall find temptation attacking Jesus even to the passion on the cross.

The work of Jesus made the link that enables us to draw on his power of love, for in him love has been brought into the truth. We also can live our lives by the truth of God's Word, and in that truth receive the power of his love. Our awareness of his redeeming love is absolutely essential to us. We cannot change our lives of selfishness by our own self. Only by denying ourselves and using the truth into which Jesus has brought a new power of love can we really be changed. The way to resist our temptations is to use the truth that demands our service to others. We must accept the demand to serve others, for the commands of truth can be used to criticize others and excuse ourselves.

"The devil can quote Scripture for his own purpose," and the way this temptation is described in Matthew and Luke shows it.

There is a warning for our lives in this passage that we need to remember. As we start changing our way of life, we shall find we only see more and more of our selfishness at work. The beginning of our repentance will also bring greater conflict into our minds. We shall not immediately escape from the wilderness of our self-absorption, but will find that our efforts to clean up our life will draw on more attacks from false ways of living. The lusts of selfishness, the "wild beasts" in us, will become more obvious in their attacks. We have to listen to the truths that are messages from God and resist with their aid, for they have in them now all the love of God to strengthen us.

> *14–15. And after John was arrested Jesus came into Galilee declaring the good news of the kingdom of God and saying, "The time is fulfilled and the kingdom of God has drawn near; repent and believe in the good news."*

Mark assumes here that we know of John's arrest, and he later introduces the story about it in parenthesis in chapter 6:17–29. We must remember that we are hearing the good news, and this controls the order of the gospel. We have no idea what period elapsed from the time John baptized Jesus until he was imprisoned, but it cannot have been long. Luke tells us that John's work began in "the fifteenth year of Tiberias," 28–29 A.D., which would also mark the beginning of Jesus' ministry of some three years. Such dates can only be approximate, and it is impossible to date these events accurately. Jesus was born in the time of Herod the Great, which means 4 B.C. at the latest. A ministry beginning when he was about thirty would then give 26 A.D. as the date here. The impression from the gospel is that John died early in Jesus' ministry.

A change comes now, for John's influence ceases and that of Jesus takes over. In our personal lives, we are passing beyond the stage of mere obedience and are beginning to respond more from an affection for others and a willingness to serve them. The "kingdom of God" is nearer, when we shall be ruled by his love in the truth; but still there is the call to repentance. We still need to look constantly for the thoughts and desires that serve our greed and pride, and we need to prevent their controlling our life. Often, believing in the good news about Jesus Christ is identified with knowing about it and understanding it. Belief is a good deal more than this. Belief is an act of the will. It is a desire that the purposes of God shall be achieved, and not one's own. We are in Galilee, far away from the temple at Jerusalem, and that shows us engaged in living our earthly life and striving for obedience to the truth there. It will be some while before the scene can move to Jerusalem and a change to inner holiness can be made. But change at this outward level is still real change.

16–20. And walking by the sea of Galilee he saw Simon and his brother Andrew casting a net in the sea, for they were fishermen. And Jesus said to them, "Follow me, and I will make you become fishers of men." And immediately they left their nets and followed him. And going on a little way, he saw James the son of Zebedee and his brother John in the ship mending their nets. And immediately he called them, and leaving their father, Zebedee, in the ship with the hired men they went away after him.

The Sea of Galilee covers 112 square miles and is well stocked with fish, yielding in modern times over 1200 tons a year. The first disciples earned their living fishing the lake. Simon and Andrew were apparently using a cast net, dropped over fish by someone standing in the water; but they had a ship, as had Zebedee. It seems likely that those Jesus called had heard him teaching in Galilee, but it still required considerable determination to leave the settled lives they had known and follow Jesus.

It will require as much determination in us to leave our accustomed way of life and begin with a new motive. Clearly we are being called to become disciples of Jesus and we see, in the call of these disciples nearly two thousand years ago, our own call today. But the disciples are varied in type. If we are to learn about and use a new way of life from Jesus Christ, then there have to be various things in our mind that will follow him. Just as he called disciples in the world, Jesus calls certain powers in our mind. The transformation of the first disciples from catching fish to catching men depicts such a call in our mind. Fish are often described as cold-blooded, but the truth is that they take on the temperature of their surroundings. They have no source of warmth in themselves. The ideas of truth we understand are like that at first. We fish them out of the Bible, and they take their warmth of affection from the circumstances of the moment. Sometimes it is the cold light of mere knowing, sometimes it burns with criticism of someone else, sometimes it has the warmth of our fellowship with those from whom we learn. None of this provides an indwelling love that acts in the truth. But if we become a disciple of Jesus and follow his way, we concentrate on loving and helping others. The truths we know are no longer "cold fish," but become part of the way of loving. They have their own warmth from the love that works in them and become truly human in their nature. We shall "catch men." The life of our mind will change its concentration and follow Jesus. Not all our knowledge will be transformed at one time from mere cold knowing to warm and human understanding, but this is the process that will go on when we truly try to follow Jesus.

If we are to use the gospel in this personal way, we have now a number of things to identify in ourselves. Clearly the four disciples here are different aspects of our discipleship. The four gospels as a whole identify Simon, later called Peter, as the rock of faith on which the church is built. Our "Simon" is the way we believe the truth, which is the bedrock of all our living. This has a necessary brother, Andrew, in our obedience to what we believe. John is "the beloved disciple" of the gospel and typifies our love for the Lord that motivates us. He too has a brother in the acts of love and compassion that express that love to others. This is James. Note that the two sets of brothers are occupied at first in different ways. Faith and obedience, Peter and Andrew, are fishing with the net of intelligence for more ideas. Love and its acts of compassion, John and James, are mending nets, for it is love that strives to make sure that our intelligence catches ideas securely from love. It is more interested to make sure our thought is loving than in the number of ideas we actually catch on to. These "disciples" are not separate in our mind. They express the various aspects of our Christian life that work together in following our Lord. All such powers in us must accept the call to leave the old way of life and all that fathered it and follow the new way.

21–28. And they went into Capernaum; and immediately on the Sabbath he entered the synagogue and taught. And they were astonished at his teaching, for he taught them as one having authority and not as the scribes. And there was in their synagogue a man with an evil spirit, and he cried out saying, "Ah! What have you to do with us, Jesus of Nazareth? Have you come to destroy us? I know who you are, the holy one of God." But Jesus rebuked him, saying, "Be silent, and come out of him." And throwing him into convulsions, the evil spirit cried out with a loud voice and came out of him. And they were all astonished, so that they questioned among themselves, saying, "What is this? A new teaching such that he commands the evil spirits and they obey him!" And immediately his fame went out into all the surrounding country of Galilee.

Capernaum was on the northwest shore of the lake. The synagogue was a place for Jews to "come together" (for that is what the word means) to hear the Scriptures read and expounded, and to pray. Jewish worship had properly to take place at the temple in Jerusalem, but people could only travel there occasionally. At other times, the synagogue provided a religious center for them. The scribes played an important part in the synagogue, for they were responsible for preserving the written Scripture, and for explaining it to the people. Much of their teaching may have been derived from others; but, in any event, it arose from comparisons of Scripture rather than the dynamic teaching that seemed so startling in Jesus. It is noteworthy that Mark does not give us much record of Jesus' teaching, as the other gospels do, but concentrates more on its effect. The "evil spirit" that possesses the man is expressed by a word that means "unclean, filthy," and refers to the contamination of human affections by selfishness, which makes them evil instead of good. Such a spirit of evil has been generated by centuries of human lives that have misused life from God. It is as powerful to flow into us now as it was in Jesus' time, but now it cannot obsess us and can be resisted in his strength, whereas then it had begun to dominate the minds and bodies of certain men and women, regardless of their own efforts.

The scene here is set in a synagogue in Galilee, far away from the temple in Jerusalem, as a reminder that much needs to be changed in us of very earthly ways of thinking and behaving. Only much later will the work be done at the center in Jerusalem. There is a great deal of self-love in our minds that makes our outward lives unclean. Here we are subject to an influx of evil that is directly opposed to any holy love from Jesus. This will cry out against the presence of Jesus in our lives, as the evil spirit cries out here. As we strive to listen to his teaching, there are going to be great convulsions in our ways of thinking, and in the life we lead as it is changed. The presence of Jesus in our life convulses our old life because, like the man in the synagogue, it is possessed by a "devil" of evil.

It is intriguing that the evil spirit in the man recognizes Jesus for what he is, for the selfishness in us knows what it is opposing as it fights against the new spirit. But such knowledge is soon silenced in our mind. If we realized how far the Lord is going to lead us away from our old self-centered life and how much will be changed, we could not face it all at once. We often think of God's providence as a force controlling the accidents and happenings of worldly existence, but perhaps its greatest care for us is in understanding and controlling the action of our evil, so that it is only released as we can conquer and reject it. In us, as in the synagogue, Jesus silences the evil that would overwhelm us without his protection. He leads us step by step, so that we can fight each battle as it comes, and he silences the awareness of our deep evil. Again we have the emphasis that Jesus' power to help us is in the "new teaching." If we trust his truth, it can force our evil spirit of selfishness to leave us. The power is there because Jesus has brought love into the truth; but it will only work to heal us if we use the truth to change our lives and so accept his power.

Jesus now begins to show his power to help men and women. He has not yet wholly accomplished his work of redemption, which will only be completed at the resurrection. John is careful to remind us that "the holy spirit was not yet," because Jesus was "not yet glorified." Nevertheless, for some thirty years, he has been becoming aware of the evil that humanity has brought into life and has been forcing it out of his being and replacing it with the love of God. It is small wonder that the power of evil possessing the man knows the nature of Jesus and has to give way to his power. The whole power of the love of God was Jesus' life and was present now in most of Jesus' being, and it shows in the works that he can do. It is this that enables him to perform miracles and healings.

29–34. And leaving the synagogue they came immediately with James and John into the house of Simon and Andrew. And the mother-in-law of Simon was lying in a fever, and so they spoke immediately to him about her. And he came to her and took her hand and raised her up. And immediately the fever left her and she served them. When evening came and the sun went down, they brought to him all who were ill and those possessed by devils, and the whole city was gathered together at the door. And he healed many who were sick of various diseases, and cast out many devils, not allowing the devils to speak because they knew him.

John 1:44 tells us that Simon and Andrew were from Bethsaida; but by now they lived in Capernaum. Physical healing forms a major part of Jesus' ministry. Nothing shows the love of God so directly and obviously as the relief of pain and the removal of disability. Our own impulse to help the sick springs immediately from compassion, and we can see the love of God for each one of us most clearly in Jesus healing the people. Here he helps in two ways: he casts out devils and he heals diseases.

Reference to "devils" can conjure up in the mind ideas of hideous demons completely alien to human beings. When spoken of collectively as "the Devil," some second force opposed to God can be imagined. We need to realize that there is only one force in creation, and that is the love of God. But that love wants to give the joy of its life to men and women as though it were their own, and so it gives them the freedom to choose to accept that loving life. If in their freedom they do not choose to accept it, they live for themselves; and it is their selfishness that becomes this other force resisting God's love. This is the origin of all evil. Where it possesses human beings, it creates a "devil" of evil controlling them. Down the ages, men and women have rejected the way of love and created such devils, which have influenced the lives of succeeding generations. This is the origin of the devils that Jesus casts out with his love.

Such evil in men and women changes the nature of their community so that, in place of the freedom of loving service, there comes a constant effort to take from others and to control them for personal ends. As the structure of society is changed, so is the nature of the human mind. Made to use love from God to love and help others in earthly service, the mind becomes instead an instrument to take everything for oneself, and service to God and others is used to control others by hypocritical demands. Generations of such distortion gravely change the mind each human being inherits, so that it thinks first of self and only last of loving and helping others. It is worth realizing we have this built-in tendency to see everything as it affects us rather than others, to react for our own advantage rather than to help others. If Jesus is to heal us, we need to acknowledge this "devil" in our own mind, this inherited change in the nature of the human mind from which we all suffer, and from which we all need salvation.

It is important to realize that it is a *tendency* toward evil in the mind that is inherited. This inherited quality is often spoken of as "original sin," but no one can inherit sin. Sin is the deliberate commission of evil from self-love and can be committed only by an individual and can be repented by and forgiven only that individual. Nevertheless, quite apart from our own selfish acts, inheriting such a damaged mind means that we need healing in a very real and intimate way. We need a new loving life able to act into us from God, so that we can use our minds to love and serve others. God's coming in Jesus Christ is the way he reaches us again with his love and heals our souls.

As well as the devils of selfishness that possess and act in us, which must be cast out, there are long-term effects from evil that leave our mind diseased. If we look into ourselves, we can see these spiritual diseases. Because we have been used to living for ourselves, we are in a fever of worry about worldly problems. We have been so accustomed to think of our rights rather than of our responsibilities that as soon as a stress arises we are crippled in helping others, because we see what it will do to us rather than what it is doing to them. We weaken truth by learning what it will do for us, rather than what we are to do for others. Our pride in achievement cramps our acts of love. All of these long-term effects of our old selfishness exist as "diseases" in our spiritual darkness when "the sun goes down" and must be healed. Some of them are very closely related to our present effort to follow Jesus. The fever of Simon Peter's mother-in-law is a sign that a fever of pride will be very close to our new discipleship. Others are stirred up in many parts of our life by our efforts to follow Jesus. All of these need to be brought into the sphere of our new life and healed. The way this is done is by the hand of Jesus. The power of the hand enacts what love desires. Jesus' hand is the truth that he has filled with his power of love. We have to come to that power by constantly using the truth with the intention to love others. Then much sickness of self-love in our mind can be healed.

> *35–39. And very early, while it was still night, he got up and went out into a desert place and prayed there. And Simon and those with him followed, and when they found him they said to him, "Everyone is looking for you." And he said to them, "Let us go into the neighboring towns so that I can preach there also, for that is why I came out." And he was preaching in their synagogues throughout Galilee and casting out devils.*

One of the features of the ministry is the way Jesus keeps moving about from place to place, varying the multitude that hear him and that he can heal. There is a warning to us here for our personal life. It is a mistake to go on laboring at the same defect all the while. Not only does it ignore many other faults that need change, but it also makes us obsessed with improving one aspect of our character. For example, lust might affect us. If we concentrate on that alone, it may begin to obsess us so that all our thought is unnaturally stressed. But very often we cannot dig deeply into that one aspect until a more general improvement has come over many other matters. Jesus begins this new move "while it is still night," a reminder that there is still much darkness in our life that needs change. We need the effort to look more widely, to study and change the selfishness that affects our work, our home life, our leisure, and strengthen our whole mind to see more clearly the other problem. It will give us the chance to change it without being obsessed by it. We must try to consider the broad spread of our life and activity. Improvement in each aspect will make it easier to see and change others.

> *40–42. And a leper came to him, imploring him, kneeling down to him and saying, "If you will, you can cleanse me." And Jesus, moved with compassion, stretched out his hand and touched him, saying to him, "I will, be clean." And as soon as he spoke, the leprosy was gone from him, and he was cleansed.*

Leprosy is a condition in which the skin and eventually the flesh is attacked and destroyed. Very early on, the nerves to the skin fail, so that one can be burnt or scalded without realizing it is happening. The condition is contagious (though not so highly as was then believed), so lepers were driven out of the community to live in wretched conditions on what charity might be offered.

After the casting out of the evil spirit of selfishness in us and the healing of the long-lasting effects of such self-love in our diseased behavior comes the healing of a leper. It must mean something very specific and very important to us. If we are to translate this into the condition of our personal life, we have to look at its "skin," its outermost layer, where it contacts other people. Underneath that skin is the "flesh," the muscle, that can move for others and so can be of service to them; but if in our contacts with others we are insensitive and do not feel their needs, all our apparent efforts to help will be a mockery. The "skin" of our life will fail, and all our lauded activities in which we say we serve others will be mere hypocrisy. The one specific danger that is emphasized to us is that of thinking about and talking about truth and trying to feel sentimentally loving toward others, while never actually reacting to their needs and never actually doing anything to help others from love. It is important to see other people as human beings, and not as ciphers in our own spiritual development. Each person we talk to or help is a child of God, with his or her own battles of temptation, his or her own affections and love for others, his or her own need to be loved and needed by others. People are not there simply as so many opportunities for us to display our Christianity. Unless we see them as our brothers and sisters, we shall never really be touching their lives or truly feeling their needs. We shall be a leper, going through the motions of Christian love without feeling anything in the process.

It is surprisingly easy to become such a "leper." In church groups, so much talk is involved and so many situations imagined and solved that we can think this is Christian life. Even when we carry the ideas into action, our concentration may be more on the good effect it has on ourselves, or the image of the church it witnesses to others, than on the actual people we are helping who need love. Such a hypocritical approach really profanes the truth we know. We mix its vision and its planning with a total lack of love in the action. What is holy becomes debased and profaned because we never really feel another's need. All our thought and activity only desensitizes us to human beings and their need for love. We can never "touch them" and feel their human need of us. We need to examine ourselves and recognize this evil in the very stuff of our Christianity. Then we must come to Jesus, admitting his power to use our lives for others. Confessing our need of him welcomes his power of love into us to work his will. The term used for healing the leper is to "cleanse." This is because the truth is already present in ways that could be used, but we make it unclean by seeking our own advantage as we use it. The outward life needs to be cleansed by works of thoughtful love that truly touch the lives of others.

> *43–45. And immediately he sent him away, strongly commanding him, "See you say nothing to anyone, but go and show yourself to the priest and offer for your cleansing what Moses ordered as a testimony to them." But when the man went he talked freely, spreading the matter abroad, so that he was no longer able to enter a city openly but was outside in desert places. And they came to him from everywhere.*

There were specific commands in Leviticus 14 to be fulfilled by a healed leper. They consisted of making sacrifices, a word that means "making something holy" rather than merely offering gifts. There is a constant effort by Jesus to keep his work secret. Probably that made it a real contact with individuals, rather than a nine-days' wonder for crowds. The cured man's talk on this occasion brings pressure of crowds, so that Jesus leaves the cities to escape them.

We can see that a healed leper, in a spiritual sense, will be making his or her outward life holy by seeing that the true spirit of love is at work in all life's actions. This is what is meant by fulfilling the sacrificial obligations to the priest. But Jesus, speaking to the man, added to this a command of silence about the healing; the man did not obey. Because he advertised widely what had been done for him, extra pressure was brought to bear on Jesus, which made him retire from the cities to the desert places. We, too, when we accept Jesus' way, can be so personally delighted with the change made in some part of our life, that we exaggerate it out of all proportion to our whole life of service. To talk about the healing of our spiritual life is to concentrate on how it has changed us and what improvement it has made in us, rather than to rejoice in what we now do for others. Such an attitude opens up again the possibilities of pride and selfish claims. Such a reaction can make it difficult for the Lord to develop our new life further. It can tend to bring us back, in our pride and self-satisfaction, to the desert in which our own way was the most important factor in our life, and Jesus has to begin again to help us there.

Chapter Two

SINNERS AND FORGIVENESS

Sinners appear often in the Gospels. To a strict Jew, the slightest deviation from traditional practices was sin, though it might amount to no more than omitting observance of trifling restrictions on personal dress and manners. The Pharisees sought to multiply such practices, extending the commands of the Law into a complete system of behavior that was thought to ensure holiness. Their name probably derives from a word meaning "to separate," and their aim was to separate righteous persons by a strict rule. The Gospels show that some of their number still placed a high value on compassion and service; but by the time of Jesus, they had become, like most puritanical movements, restrictive and condemnatory. Those involved in worldly duties found their demands difficult to meet, and this made many ordinary folk sinners in the eyes of strict Pharisees. Breaking the great commandments of the Law was also rightly regarded as sin, of course, and at times it is difficult to know quite which interpretation to put on various accusations made in the Gospels.

Jesus dismissed the foolishness of the Pharisees and taught how forgiveness for real sins could be accepted. We must be clear that intention made the sin. A person might do what was evil and harmful to others in ignorance, and that was not sin. What was done from selfishness and evil was sin. The idea has grown up that sins need to be paid for before they can be forgiven, and the work of Jesus has then been seen as a punishment he bore for humankind. But the Gospel makes clear the truth that all sins are forgiven as soon as they are committed. God is love, and love does not condemn. The work of Jesus was to bring us power to resist evil and accept the love of God, not to lift a condemnation that does not exist. All our sins are forgiven, but forgiveness has to be accepted by the sinner if it is to be effective. That involves the offender examining him- or herself, recognizing the sin and that it came from self-love, and then living a new life that rejects such sin. Only if we accept forgiveness in a new way of life is it effective. To do this, we need the power that Jesus brought, the love of God able to work in us at our level.

1–5. And again after some days he entered into Capernaum, and it was heard that he was in the house. And immediately many were gathered together so that there was no longer any room, not even at the door, and he spoke the Word to them. And they came to him bringing a paralyzed man, carried by four. And not being able to come near to him because of the crowd, they uncovered the roof where he was; and when they had broken it up, they let down the mattress on which the paralyzed man was lying. And

Jesus, seeing their faith, said to him, "Son, your sins have been forgiven you."

A house in Palestine was usually flat-roofed, often with steps up outside the house, so that the roof could be used as we use a patio in the garden. The roof would be covered with wattle and daub, made of sticks infilled with clay and plaster, and it would be possible to break into it. Such a house is the scene of this story. The "mattress" is a simple pallet, easily carried about. The word used for it is from Latin, and may well have gained currency from the provision made for the occupying Roman soldiers in their local camps.

The scene at the house typifies the way our mind tends to approach the Lord. We gather to hear his teaching—so much so that there is no room for anything else to happen. Contact with the outside things of the world is through the door, but this is blocked. While we are completely set only on listening to truth, we cannot go out to do anything real for others. Such a state of mind really means that we are paralyzed in our life of love and service. This miracle tells us how to overcome such an imbalance when it occurs. It is not by ignoring truth. That is stressed by the faith of the four who carry the paralyzed man and persist until he is healed. Four people can carry him in a balanced way, and this is truth with a balanced view on life. But it is difficult for such a view to prevail against the fascination of just listening to truth. A mind in this state is lying down paralyzed on a bed. There are plenty of ideas, but they are used just to stuff a mattress for our mind to rest on.

Change only comes when the balanced view—the four carriers—start to break up the roof over the crowd's head. It seems strange at first to think that one must come to

Jesus from above; but it is this that changes our attitude toward our Christianity. Above our learning of truth there must be a motivation of love to come down into it and bring change in our lives. We cannot generate the love to work in us, but we can break up what prevents it. There are many accustomed attitudes that "roof in" our listening to truth: the idea that just knowing truth actually does something, concern for our own welfare and position, pride in our knowledge of truth, thinking of the rights it gives us rather than our responsibilities to others. Such attitudes prevent truth really healing us. We can break them up and reject them by our deliberate efforts. Every time we see some true idea, we must ask, "What in the way I live prevents this working in my life?" Never accept an idea about Jesus, or about responsibility to others, without making sure it is used in daily life. As we break up our accustomed, closed-in attitudes, we bring our Christian life to the Lord in a different way that enables him to heal us. We begin to live from the power of his love, and he is able to forgive our sins because we are working to receive his love and are showing a true faith. Jesus is always in the midst of our learning truth, but we need to act to break up our spiritual complacency and give him the opportunity to heal our lives.

6–12. But there were some of the scribes sitting there and reasoning in their hearts, "Why does he speak blasphemies? Who is able to forgive sins? Except God!" And immediately Jesus, knowing in his spirit that they were reasoning inwardly in this way, said to them, "Why do you reason these things in your hearts? Which is easier? To say to this paralyzed man, 'Your sins have been forgiven you,' or to say, 'Rise, take up your mattress and walk'? But that you may know that the Son of Man has authority to forgive sins on earth," turning to the paralyzed man he said, "Rise, I say, and pick up your mattress and go to your house!" And he rose up immediately and, taking up the mattress, went out before them all; so that they were all amazed and glorified God, saying, "We never saw anything like this."

The scribes have difficulty believing in Jesus' divine power, a difficulty that we sometimes share. Truth can seem to be mere knowledge, and it is difficult for us to remember that, in his work on earth, Jesus has brought his living power of love into it. That love is not just a forgiving love. It is an active power that can operate all our thinking and acting and send us out to take our place in the world as his servants. All the ideas we have stuffed into our "mattress" as a good mental position to rest on can be picked up and carried into action in our lives at the Lord's command. He has stored a power of love in these ideas of truth that enables us to carry them out into life. It is because of this that he can forgive our sins. Our sins are always forgiven, of course, as soon as we do them. Love can never fail to forgive. But forgiveness will do nothing unless it is accepted. We need a new way of life from love to accept forgiveness, and we get that from the power of love that Jesus brought into our natural lives. He calls himself "the Son of Man" here because he used the truth human beings must use in this world and powered it with divine love. Truth becomes saving because of the divine love Jesus brought into it. For us to use the truth from Jesus' love, to "carry our mattress" into life, is the same thing as forgiveness of our sins because, when we do use that truth, we are accepting the love that forgives us. The miracle was performed to help the scribes and others around to believe. Just so can a great miracle be wrought for us, if we break up our self-centered ways and come to Jesus to let his love work in our lives.

> *13–17. And he went out again by the sea, and the crowd came to him and he taught them. And passing on he saw Levi, the son of Alphaeus, sitting at the tax office, and said to him, "Follow me." And getting up he followed him. And it happened as Jesus reclined at table in his house that many tax collectors and sinners reclined with him and his disciples, for there were many who followed him. And the scribes and Pharisees, seeing him eating with tax collectors and sinners, said to his disciples, "Why is it that he eats and drinks with tax collectors and sinners?" And hearing it, Jesus said to them, "Those who are healthy do not need a doctor, but the sick do. I came to call not the righteous but sinners to repentance."*

If the call of fishermen as the first disciples seemed unusual, the call of Levi (identified apparently in Matthew 9:9 as Matthew) is even more remarkable. Tax collectors in the Gospels were of different kinds, collecting customs, head tax, sales tax, and so on. Since Capernaum was a border town, it is likely that Levi was some minor official concerned with customs. Such people were hated because, though usually Jews, they were collecting taxes for the occupying Roman power and were seen as traitors and often swindlers as well. The sinners despised with them were not necessarily evil people living in scandalous ways. It was a sin not to fulfill the Mosaic law; and that, as interpreted by the scribes and Pharisees, included many detailed daily observances of ritual that were often omitted in a hard laboring life.

To identify this tax collector in our own mind, we have to understand what in us exacts tribute from our life. Christian life is lived solely for the Lord Jesus, and there should be sufficient delight in living it; but we can "tax" it to get something for ourselves as well. We can take merit for what we do. As soon as that happens, the sheer joy of helping vanishes, and everything serves our pride and satisfaction in our own achievements. Such an attitude is bound to exist at some point, for we tend to judge the value of what we do by what praise it merits. This "judgment by merit" must be called as a disciple of Jesus, but then it will become a different kind of judgment. Any merit for what is done will be ascribed to the power that did it; and that power is the love the Lord is giving us in the truth. Once we realize that all merit belongs to God, then we shall judge things by the merit his love has in accomplishing them and cease to seek merit for ourselves. We shall be truly free in his love. The tax collector will have become a disciple.

We need to keep the sense of merit in proper perspective. There is merit in the love that serves and helps all others. If it were not so, vile and cruel actions would be valued as we value pure and loving ones. What we have to keep clear is that the merit belongs to the love that does the deed. We do not manufacture unselfish love in ourselves. We use the true way in life, and the love Jesus brought into it then works in our lives. However much we enjoy the sense of love and compassion in our hearts, it does not belong to us, but to the love from Jesus that does the works. All merit belongs to him. But now merit has changed its nature. In worldly terms, it usually means a sense of pride in what we achieve, a bonus given to the doer of good. God needs no pride in his love, no bonuses given to his love for us. Merit becomes only the quality of unselfish, giving love. One of the sure ways of finding out our state of mind is to see if we have any sense of personal merit because of our Christian life. If we have, we are taxing it for ourselves, and we have not called our sense of merit to be the Lord's disciple.

Jesus' rebuke to the scribes and Pharisees carries an important message for us. Only by recognizing that we are sinners (using our lives for ourselves) and tax collectors (taking merit for any good thing we do) can we see our need to change and accept the love that can use us and make us free. Recognizing our sickness is the first step toward spiritual healing. While, like the scribes and Pharisees, we think our spiritual life is perfectly healthy, the Lord cannot get near us to help us. He can only call those who know that, of themselves, they are sinners. Those who think themselves righteous cannot be helped. The Gospels seem to some to emphasize constantly that we are sinners, that the disciples fail Jesus, that we are proud, revengeful, and self-centered. It can seem harsh as the message from a loving God. But the emphasis is there to make us look at ourselves and repent. Our faults are not stressed to make us feel miserable about them, but to make us realize what needs changing in our lives, so that we come to welcome Jesus' love and sit at his table.

> *18–22. And John's disciples and those of the Pharisees used to fast, and they came to him and said, "Why do John's disciples and those of the Pharisees fast, but your disciples do not?" And Jesus said to them, "Can the sons of the bridechamber fast while*

the bridegroom is with them? As long as they have the bridegroom with them, they cannot fast. But days will come when the bridegroom will have been taken away from them, and then they will fast in those days. And no one sews a piece of unshrunk cloth on an old garment, otherwise the new patch tears away from the old cloth, and leaves a bigger hole. And no one puts new wine into old skins, otherwise the new wine bursts the skins, and the wine pours out and the skins are destroyed; but new wine is put into new skins."

The Mosaic law commanded the people to "afflict themselves" on the Day of Atonement by strict mourning (Leviticus 16). "Afflicting themselves" involved fasting. Other fasts were added, as is clear from Zechariah 8:19, to mark other national disasters. These fasts were associated with the idea of mourning for evil. By this time, the custom had been extended by the Pharisees to regular weekly fasts, as Luke 18:12 shows. The Pharisees observed these fasts strictly, and John's disciples apparently observed similar customs. The custom came into the Christian church, though the Gospels provide little warrant for it. Rather it suggests that such outward signs are better converted into changing the real behavior of life. Jesus insists that his teaching brings a new way of life that cannot be likened to mere fulfillment of religious customs, nor to the obedient repentance John the Baptist called for, but that is alive with a vibrant power of its own.

When fasting, the body is without food. If we transfer the idea to an individual's mind and life, then the spirit fasts when it has no good love to feed on. It is love that sustains the spirit as food sustains the body. John the Baptist's message, as we have seen, came in a time of repenting evil and seeking to obey, but the love that is Jesus had not yet been received. So John and his disciples fasted. One suspects that the Pharisees' fasting represents a deliberate refusal to accept love from Jesus. But neither of these two states applies to Christians working in Jesus' love. Such are said to be with the Lord Jesus as "the bridegroom" because he makes a bond like a marriage between his love and the truth they use. This bridegroom is only taken from us when evil attacks our Christian faith and, like the disciples in the garden of Gethsemane, we fail. In such a state, we cease to feed on Jesus' love and go back spiritually to fasting until he can be resurrected in our lives.

Such a "fast" is not really like that at the beginning before we received Jesus' love into our lives. The ideas that clothe our faith now are no longer just things learned; they are the way we live. They are strong "new cloth" in which we have seen the truth and used it, and this is too strong to be sewn to our old ideas. It would tear a great "hole" in the idea of just learning truth. The truth by which we have lived is a "new wine" with a zest that our old mere obedience never knew. You cannot put that new wine into the wineskin of our old blind acceptance. When we come to this new state of fasting, we shall see that it is quite different from the way we were at the beginning, for it will be part of the change that we are making in ourselves. As we go through Mark's gospel, we shall see that a step forward in Christian life often unveils deeper selfishness we could not see before. So we fail to feed on Jesus' love and times of "fasting" will recur. But we must not fall into the trap of thinking there has been no progress, and we are back where we started from. We have understood and accepted something of the new way of life, a good "strong cloth"; and we have some new wineskins, for we have known the zest of seeing by the truth. We may now have to fast as we see deeper selfishness, but we are not going back to the old self-centered way of life, nor are we starting to think from its evil.

> *23–28. And it happened that on the Sabbath day he went through the fields of grain, and his disciples began to make their way, plucking the ears of grain. And the Pharisees said to him, "Look! Why do they do what is not lawful on the Sabbath?" And he said to them, "Have you never read what David did when he was in need and hungry, he and those with him? How he entered the house of God when Abiathar was high priest, and ate the holy bread presented, which it is only lawful for the priests to eat, and also gave it to those with him?" And he said to them, "The Sabbath was made for man, not man for the Sabbath; so then the Son of Man is Lord also of the Sabbath."*

The commandment about the Sabbath is often seen simply as a negative command, denying certain activity. But if we look at the origin of the Sabbath, we are told it comes from the peace of the seventh day when the Lord had completed creation (Exodus 20:11). Its remembrance is meant to preserve that peace in the nature of humankind, a perfection in which love and truth work positively together to create good for all. But when Jesus came, the Sabbath day commandment was rigorously and negatively enforced by the Pharisees, and hence their complaint about the disciples' behavior. We must be clear about their criticism of the disciples. To our Western ideas, the offense might seem to lie in stealing the grain from the field, but the Mosaic law required that those in need should receive their due. The offense that enraged the Pharisees was doing work on the Sabbath in order to get food. Jesus points to David's action when he ate the holy bread displayed before the Lord and sacred to the priests (1 Samuel 21:1–6). Since David needed food to serve the Lord, there was no unholiness in his action. Similarly there was no unholiness in the disciples' action since they took the food to follow Jesus. He gives us a view of the Sabbath that makes it useful to people, not simply a restriction on their activity. We are to seek for that positive peace in our hearts that uses love to work in the truth and create good for all those around us. It is right to gather the love God provides so that we can help others. It makes any day a holy day, and then Jesus truly becomes the Lord of the Sabbath.

It is not really useful to apply the command externally to Sabbath day observance. Striving for a peace of love and truth in our lives will affect our behavior every day. Our worship will not be circumscribed to particular times on a particular day. How we serve our neighbor will become more important than telling him or her what not to do. Doubtless the Sabbath will focus our efforts, but nothing but contention will be achieved by a negative approach. The story seems a contentious way for us to learn about the real value of peace; but there is truth in this for, in our early Christian struggles, we can only see the Lord's peace in the midst of the mind's arguments and battles of the spirit. The time will come when we shall know true peace in ourselves.

Chapter Three
CROWDS AND CRITICS

We now begin to see the enormous disturbance that Jesus is making. Crowds seek him, some for healing, some perhaps to listen, and some, no doubt, because they want to stare at the latest sensation. The power he is showing arouses jealousy and opposition from those who already hold power in the community, and his family fear for his state of mind and seek to restrain him. It pictures for us what happens in our minds when we begin to follow Jesus and use his love and strength. We begin to realize the vast crowds of motives and ideas that need changing by his way of love. Our mind is in a turmoil, and all the selfishness in us rises up to prevent such a complete change in the whole nature of our life.

This selfishness will not necessarily appear as the evil that it is. Until now, even the respectable appearance of our life has been driven on by our selfishness. We may have appeared a model citizen, but our social behavior has been to gain acceptance in a group, where we can enjoy ourselves and further our own ends while living "within the rules." Our affection for our family has not been from real love, but from pride in them as our possession to boast of and use for ourselves. Even our religious behavior may have been to be accepted as one of a group useful to us and to be able to use the catch phrases of a faith. All of these appearances will attack our newfound faith and criticize its effort to change our motives and ideals. Very rarely do we admit that we have this "respectable" self-regard and greed that powers our life and resists any change. So the resistance to Jesus was spearheaded by the most respected members of the community, who claimed to be acting from the highest motives. This resistance to Jesus is not something to wonder at as a past phenomenon. It is something we shall experience in ourselves, a selfishness that seeks to prevent any change in our life. We need to look into our own motives, and ask ourselves why we live such respectable and religious lives. Is it so that God's love may fill the world, or is it so that we may fit into society for our own advantage?

> *1–6. And he entered into the synagogue again, and there was there a man with his hand withered; and they were watching whether he would heal him on the Sabbath, so that they could accuse him. And he said to the man with the withered hand, "Stand up and come into the middle." And he said to them, "Is it lawful on the Sabbath to do good or to do evil? To save life or to kill?" But they were silent. And looking round on them with anger, being grieved at the hardness of their hearts, he said to the man, "Stretch out your hand." And he stretched it out and his hand was restored as good as the other. And as soon*

as they went out the Pharisees plotted with the Herodians to destroy him.

The use of the Sabbath is still the subject, as it was in the last chapter. Now the issue is not seeking for love to feed the soul, but using love's power to heal. The Pharisees' attitude is one that will constantly trouble our mind, which is why it appears throughout this gospel. It sees truth as a bondage to be put upon the mind, as something that kills life. It can see all the things we are denied, but never sees the service from love in which we are to find our joy. Such an attitude in our mind is always critical of activity, because it might be against the truth. It never sees that the primary demand of the truth is for activity to serve others, so that they feel our love. The pharisaical attitude is really the way our selfishness sees the truth, as a restraint that must be accepted to gain the benefits of Christian society. This kills our life while declaring that it is trying to purify it.

Our power to help others is withered by our self-love, which seeks to serve only our own interests. The Pharisees' attitude will keep it that way. But Jesus calls this withered life into the very midst for us. When we are reading Mark's gospel, we are constantly aware of the way we do not use our religion to help others. Jesus can never let an idea of truth rest until we have begun to use it from love to others. The power to love others is Jesus' love, God's love brought to our level of activity; but we have to make the effort to receive it. Each of us can choose to accept the new way of life from Jesus. We choose it by using it and acting from it. To "stretch out our hand" at the Lord's command heals our power because it receives his love, which makes it work for others.

The combination of the Pharisees with the worldly

party of the Herodians is noteworthy. At first sight, it appears to be a combination of opposites. The Pharisees declared the purity of true religion, while the Herodians supported the worldly rulers from Herod's family and were interested only in earthly power. But there is a basic unity in them. Each wants control. At bottom, the pharisaical type of thought is not interested in what the truth can do for others, but how far the self can use it to control life. The Herodian type of thought sees all success in gaining worldly possession for oneself. The effort to control life for oneself is common to them both; only the method of activity is different. Thus, the opposition to Jesus is composed throughout the Gospels of the religious and the worldly powers combined. They both represent powers in us that seek to dominate our life for our own purposes, rather than to use it for others. The false religious attitude is the more dangerous to us inasmuch as it uses the truth intended to help others to restrict life selfishly. Then we could find ourselves with a withered religion without active love.

Jesus is said to look on the Pharisees' attitude with anger. The idea of divine love being angry is clearly impossible. God loves all his creatures; if he did not, they would not exist. Love forgives and is always seeking to help the evildoer. But love demands a loving way of life. We should never think of God as a placid, detached, superior being with no drive of passion. His love is so strongly opposed to selfishness that evil sees it as anger and condemnation from its point of view. In the Scriptures, God is often spoken of as angry, but the meaning is always the same. The anger is really the way our self-love sees the demands of the love of God. In the same way, a young boy will say his parents are angry when they oppose his will, although he is still aware that the opposition comes from love. Only when we can turn to use the power of love can we know its real attitude to us, as the child feels a parent's affection when he ceases to try to get his own selfish way.

7–12. And Jesus withdrew with his disciples to the sea, and a great multitude from Galilee and Judea and Jerusalem and Idumea and from beyond the Jordan followed him. And a great multitude from around Tyre and Sidon heard how much he was doing and came to him. And he asked his disciples for a small boat to help him because of the throng, that they might not crowd him. For, because he healed many, all who had scourges crowded round him to touch him. And the evil spirits when they saw him fell down before him, crying out, "You are the Son of God"; and he rebuked them strongly that they should not make him known.

As the story goes on, the numbers seeking healing become a multitude that comes from every direction. The places mentioned not only cover Galilee and Judea and the heart of Judaism at Jerusalem, but those from surrounding areas: Tyre and Sidon on the west coast and the lands east of Jordan, including Idumea (the ancient Edom) in the south. So great is the pressure of the crowds that Jesus asks for the use of one of the disciples' boats to keep them from engulfing him. Elsewhere in the Gospels he makes similar use of a boat in order to teach great crowds, putting off a little way from the shore. Here, he must remain at the shore presumably to do his work of healing.

In our own minds we have the same experience, for once we begin to follow Jesus in our lives, a multitude of ideas and thoughts in our minds begin to show themselves as self-seeking, contemptuous of others, planning only for our own advantage, and all needing spiritual healing. They come from all parts of our minds—the way we think about our everyday life, about our religion, about bad habits and worldly behavior, about money and possessions—and all need changing to the Lord's way. The situation would become impossible to handle; but the Lord brings some order by using "a boat." A boat enables one to fish or trade across great waters. We have already seen that water is truth, and what enables us to work on truth is the pattern of ideas we already have from the Bible. We have a basic pattern of truths we have learned—a "boat"—and from this we can consider new ideas and new challenges. Our learning by itself will do nothing more than the boat did, but the Lord can be alive and active in those ideas and begin to show us how to change our lives.

We also begin to discover that our motives have an unclean spirit of selfishness and our desires are evil and vengeful; we need to ask the Lord to cast out such motives. The contrast between our own nature and the love we can receive from Jesus makes us realize the divinely unselfish nature of his love, just as the evil spirits here cry out the true nature of Jesus. Yet that is a transient feeling and does not remain, for in our imperfection we cannot as yet live constantly with such a revelation. We shall all sense this sudden realization of the unique power of divine love. Our human spirit of self-love will realize how different is life lived from such unselfishness. Yet, even at the moment of recognition, the realization is silenced. With our imperfections, we cannot yet live with a sense of the whole joy of love. So it was that the evil spirits were not allowed to reveal Jesus' true nature, for in us the presence of God cannot be fully known until we are completely his.

13–19. And he went up a mountain and called those he wanted, and they went to him. And he appointed twelve to be with him, that he might send them out to preach and to have power to heal diseases and to cast out devils: Simon, to whose name he added Peter; and James the son of Zebedee and his brother John, to whose names he added Boanerges, which means "sons of thunder"; and Andrew; and Philip; and Bartholemew; and Matthew; and Thomas; and James the son of Alphaeus; and Thaddaeus; and Simon the Zealot; and Judas Iscariot, who also betrayed him.

To be "a disciple" of Jesus is to be taught by him, not in the academic sense, but in the way of life. The word contrasts with an "apostle," which is the word used in chapter 6 when the same twelve are sent out as ambassadors of the faith. "Apostle" has the basic meaning of one charged with a mission to others, not of one taught by a master. The word "disciple" is not dropped in the gospel after "apostle" is used. We are always learning and therefore are disciples. Specific occasions also cause us to be apostles. Some of the twelve are just names to us, and we know nothing of their call or their work, although tradition provides some information, largely vague and unreliable. Others play a major part in the gospel, and also in the early history of the Christian Church, as we know from the Acts of the Apostles.

In the Greek, the second Simon is said to be the "Canaanite," which by this time would be archaic. Luke 6:15 refers to him in Greek as "the Zealot." The word "Cananaean" (which transliterates a late Hebrew word from the root *qana*, "jealous," and not from "Canaan"), was used by those known as Zealots. They sought to overthrow the Roman occupation, beginning in Galilee as early as 6 A.D. and largely bringing about the revolt in 64 A.D. Presumably it is this word that is meant here. Whether Simon had been one of that party, or whether the nickname expressed his character, we cannot know.

Since the message of the Gospels is to each as an individual, there are many "disciples" in us. All the powers of our mind are disciples that are to be taught their proper use by the Lord. This is a conscious part of our effort to follow him. We have seen already that the disciples the Lord called to follow him stand in our mind for the various powers of thought and feeling that can serve him. The name "Peter," which means "a rock," is now added to Simon, who we have seen is our rock of faith. John and James, with their meaning of love and its work in us, receive the name "sons of thunder" because this is the power in our Christian life. The others will only take on a reality we can grasp in our minds when they begin to play their part in the story, as we have seen already with Matthew, the tax collector.

There are twelve disciples because this is the number the Word always uses for completeness when everything necessary exists. There are twelve tribes of Israel, twelve foundations to the holy city, and so on. It may seem strange that Judas Iscariot is called; but the Lord must call all the powers of our mind to serve him, and among them is a reliance on our own power to achieve things, which must eventually be seen to be destructive. But that will be shown as the story continues.

19–30. And they came to a house and again a crowd gathered, so that they could not even eat bread. And hearing about it those belonging to him came to lay hold of him, saying, "He is beside him-

self." And the scribes who came down from Jerusalem said, "He is possessed by Beelzebul, and by this prince of the devils he casts out devils." And calling them to him, he answered them in parable, saying, "How can Satan cast out Satan? If a kingdom is divided against itself it cannot stand, and a house divided against itself cannot stand, and if Satan has risen up against himself and been divided, he cannot stand but is finished. No one entering the house of a strong man to plunder his goods can do it unless he binds the strong man; then he can plunder. In truth I say to you, all sins shall be forgiven the sons of men, and all blasphemies they have blasphemed; but whoever blasphemes against the Holy Spirit has no forgiveness to eternity, but is liable to eternal judgment." This he said because they said, "He has an evil spirit."

We begin to grasp now the uproar caused by Jesus' teaching and healing. His ministry causes those from Nazareth, probably his family, to try to seize him and stop his activity because they think he is mad. Official scribes from Jerusalem arrive declaring he is possessed by Beelzebul. The word probably means "Lord of Dung," a derogatory reference to Beelzebub, "Lord of Flies," which was an evil heathen deity.

This episode pictures for us the turmoil that arises in our own mind when we really begin to listen to Jesus' teaching and try to let him heal our life. The disruption of what we have always accepted as a reasonable way of life rouses doubts about our new efforts with Jesus. The things relating to religion in our mind, which supported our having an apparently well-behaved, kindly life, lead us to think that this kind of dedication has gone quite over the top. It is madness to think that the whole of our life must be changed. We shall all know such a feeling as things become more dynamic from Jesus' love. Until then, any religion we may have had will have been no different from our other interests in pressure groups or political parties. Membership of the church will have seemed little different to membership of a club with particular aims. Now our eyes have been opened to see that the whole of our life is to be transformed by Jesus' love. The action of those connected with Jesus, which is described here, images our own bewilderment at what is happening to us.

More seriously, our desire to use our religious life to control others, symbolized by the scribes, can only make us feel that a religion that insists on loving others is totally false. They declare that the new power comes from possession by "Beelzebul," the selfish flaw in our nature. We shall know in ourselves this attack, which suggests that our new spirit is really an obsession from a false attitude destructive to our old comfortable religion. Jesus rejects such an accusation by pointing out that the new Christian life is "binding the strong man" of our old selfishness, and taking our time and possessions and powers to help others, thus plundering that old self-love. This is not our own self making changes. It is no "house divided against itself," as it would have to be if our egotism were transforming our life. It must be a new power that owes nothing to our old selfishness.

Jesus then gives a most serious warning. To accuse his new loving spirit in us of being evil and destructive can destroy us spiritually. All our faults and failures can be repented of and forgiven, and we can be renewed in Jesus' love. But to regard the love that calls us to unselfishness as an evil and destructive force leaves it with no power to help us at all. We shall have known the nature of his spirit and rejected it. This represents that fundamental choice for evil that, for all God's effort to forgive us, rejects all forgiveness and chooses selfishness as its way of life.

31–35. Then his brothers and his mother came and, standing outside, sent to him, calling him. And the crowd sitting around him said to him, "Behold, your mother and your brothers outside seek you." And he answered them, saying, "Who is my mother, or my brothers?" And looking around on those sitting round him, he said, "Behold my mother and my brothers, for whoever does the will of God is my brother and my sister and my mother."

We know of at least four sons of Mary, called James, Joses, Judas, and Simon; and there were at least two daughters. All, of course, were younger than Jesus, but since he was now about thirty, they were probably all adult. The fact that Joseph does not accompany the family has been thought to show that he had died by now, but there could be other reasons for his absence. Several times in Mark's gospel Jesus is shown separating himself from Mary and his family. Despite appearances, his attitude is not unloving, for Jesus on the cross sees that his mother will be provided for, and his brothers later became his followers. But he needed to show clearly that the life in him doing the works was the life of God, that he was replacing the evil heredity we all take from our parents and making a new humanity in himself that was divine. This was to be a source of love and power for all men and women for all time, and though it had been brought into our world by birth from Mary, it had been changed into a divine presence that owed nothing to our fallible human nature.

We have to realize this same uniqueness of Jesus' life in ourselves. When we begin to follow Jesus, despite the total newness of such unselfishness, it seems to arise in our mind in the same way that many other ideas do, and to be "born" out of something that belongs to us. It appears to have many "brothers" of a similar kind—belief in a political party, ideas of family loyalty, the drive to achieve ambitions. These call from outside as though they were no different to this new allegiance of being a Christian. But in effect there is no kinship at all. All these others arise from our self and serve our needs only. The new force at work in us is God's love in Jesus, which serves others. It will make a new "family" in our mind, loving others unselfishly and making quite different ambitions to love and serve them. All these new powers that do the will of God are of a completely different kind, and as they develop, they people our mind with new understanding and affection, which are "brotherly" and "sisterly" in a totally new way. Our life is no longer born out of our self-seeking, but there is a new center to our personal life that is the origin or "mother" of all our activity.

Chapter Four

PARABLES OF CHANGE

The use of parable is fundamental in the Gospel, and it is also basic to our ways of thinking, as we have seen in the introduction. What is said there must be borne in mind here. I shall recap only briefly, so that we have the ideas now when they arise directly in Mark's gospel. We shall gain no real understanding from parables, and we certainly shall not trust anything we learn from them unless we realize that they are part of the way the world is made and of the way our own minds work. Our minds, our bodies, and the outside world are made by God according to similar patterns. So the level of mind can be described by using the interplay of objects and happenings at the physical level. We have already been using the idea to understand incidents and healings. Now we find Jesus fashioning parables to teach those around. These are not some peculiar artificial method of conveying information, like an arbitrary cipher; his heavenly meaning clothes itself in the symbolism creation provides.

Jesus takes the subjects of his parables from the everyday world around, so they are familiar to the crowd listening to him. Each of them has a point, which conveys the general idea taught, but this is elaborated in the detail of the parable. In seeing this, we must not import meanings arbitrarily; the detailed meaning of Mark's gospel grows out of its immediate impact. As with all the Gospel, we shall not increase our vision on life just by learning a meaning for a parable as so much esoteric knowledge. The parable is a way of shedding light on our personal state, a light that grows as we see more, giving us a vision of what could be changed in our life and what we must do to be saved.

> *1–2. And again he began to teach by the sea. And a great crowd was attracted to him, so that he entered a boat on the sea and sat down and all the crowd was close to the sea on the land. And he taught them many things in parables.*

Here we move ahead in Mark 4 to consider also the following verses on parables, which are in between the parable of the sower and its explanation:

> *10–13. And when he was alone, those about him with the twelve asked him about the parable. And he said to them, "It has been given to you to know the mystery of the kingdom of God, but to those outside, all things are done in parables that 'seeing they may see and not perceive, and hearing they may hear and not understand, lest they should turn back and their sins be forgiven them.'" And he went on, "Do you not grasp this parable? Then how will you understand all other parables?"*

The idea that only some are to understand parables, while others cannot and so cannot find forgiveness for their sins, is totally opposed to God's effort to call and to save us all. The inability of some to understand and use the truth must be due to their own behavior. This becomes clear if we look more closely at what is meant by "seeing they may see and not perceive, and hearing they may hear and not understand." The passage is quoted from Isaiah 6:9–10. There it is clear that it is spoken to those who choose self-ishness and a false way of life.

Jesus' discussions with the scribes and Pharisees have shown a similar group around him. Those who are disciples, who want to understand Jesus, can do so, but those who choose to be selfish cannot. "To see and not perceive" is the state of someone who is capable of seeing the obvious meaning of a parable, but whose chosen selfishness prevents any real vision of how we can live for others. We need to re-alize that we can get no true vision unless we are willing to use what we see. "To hear" is to obey and to be receptive to the commands we hear. How many parents say, "Do you hear me?" when they mean "Are you going to obey me?" We "hear but do not understand" if we hear the truth but do not accept its commands for a loving life; then we do not really understand what we hear because we have no inten-tion of using it. Just to "know" a commandment does not mean we understand it. Only when we are willing to accept in our life the changes it demands do we really "understand" it. No barrier to salvation is meant by the Lord's words here. It is simply a reminder that we must choose to follow him, if the vision and life he offers are to mean anything to us.

2–8. And he said to them in his teaching, "Listen! Behold a sower went out to sow. And it happened as he sowed that some seed fell on the path, and birds came out of the sky and gobbled it up. And other seed fell among rocks where it had very little earth, and because it had no depth of earth, when the sun rose it was scorched, and because it had no root it withered away. And other seed fell among thorns, and the thorns grew up and choked it, and it yielded no crop. And other seed fell into good ground and yielded a crop, growing up and increasing, and yielding thirty, sixty or a hundred times the seed."

Later in Mark 4, Jesus gives the explanation of the parable.

14–20. "The sower sows the Word. And those on the path are such as hear the Word when it is sown, but Satan comes immediately and takes away the Word that was sown in their hearts. And similarly those among the rocks are such as hear the Word that is sown and immediately receive it with joy, but they have no root in themselves and so do not last; when trouble or persecution arises because of the Word, they take offense at it. And such as are sown among thorns hear the Word, but the worries of this life and the lure of riches and the desire for other possessions come in and choke the Word, so that it produces nothing. And such as are sown on good ground hear the Word and accept it and produce thirty, sixty or one hundred times its seed."

The parable makes its obvious point before we read the explanation. The Lord Jesus is trying to sow a new way of life in those who hear him, as a sower sows seed to grow into a crop. The bringing of new life to empty soil pictures the bringing of a new way of life into our empty lives. This time, Jesus enlarges on the meaning of the parable. Notice that he does not add to the original idea, but enlarges on the way its meaning works in us. It provides a key for our own effort to understand parables. Clearly, the various conditions of those who receive the seed can all exist in us, in varying degrees, at any time. The seed itself must obviously be what Jesus is teaching the people, the message of truth. The word used, *logos*, means "a word," but also much more than that. It is used of the rationality or vision that exists behind and before the words. John uses it in the opening of his gospel for the living wisdom from the love of God that saves us. We need to bear in mind that it is a real dynamic message that is meant, and not just the verses of the Bible.

The explanation provided with this parable illustrates how we are to see the real meaning of all parables. The parallelism between material and spiritual things can be seen in the way a seed of knowledge in the mind can grow into an idea for life, just as an earthly seed grows into a plant. Then the coming of harvest is like the actual deeds of service to others that the idea can produce in life. But, the parable emphasizes, the way a message of truth is received by an individual affects how it develops, just as the soil a seed falls into affects its growth. If it falls on the path that is beaten down hard by the passage of feet, it will never get into such ground. We need to look at our minds and realize that custom has beaten pathways through our thinking. We live so much of our life the way we always have. We may appear to listen to what the truth is saying, but in those areas it simply bounces off our routine of living. Then all the false thoughts about how to protect our own comfort will swoop down and snatch away the truth. One of the great uses of prayer and meditation is to go over the paths of our routine living and change them to receive the message of truth.

The seed on the rocks warns us of the danger of our deliberate hardheartedness, the false way we think only from our own desires. We cannot expect really to grasp and use the message of truth from our selfishness. Some truth will appear to root, but it is only so that we can use it to criticize others and get our own way with them. Once the truth starts to demand that we reject our selfishness, the truth is no longer acceptable and it withers away. Yet we can still have problems when we genuinely try to see what the truth is saying for our life. We may try growing the "thorns" of selfish behavior at the same time as the truth. In that case, the truth will never win, but will be choked out by our effort to protect ourselves and keep our prime interest in money and possessions. We cannot have a divided mind. We need the good ground of a loving heart to take the truth and make it work in our lives with increasing power. These are not just interesting ways of describing our reaction to truth; rather they give us ways of recognizing effects in our mind and acting to bring a good spiritual harvest.

> *21–25. And he said, "Is a lamp brought to be put under a basket or under the bed, and not on a lampstand? Nothing is concealed that is not to be made plain, and there are no secrets that will not come to light. If you have ears, use them!" And he said to them, "Take notice of what you hear. The measure with which you give will be the measure you get back, and more will be added to you who listen; for whoever has will be given more, but whoever has not will have taken away even what he has."*

Here is a clear warning to let Jesus shed light on the way we live. The wisdom he is bringing is not something we should refuse to listen to. Indeed, we cannot; for however we fight to prevent his message from reaching us, it will still illuminate our secret selfishness so that we must face it and make a choice. The image has changed to light. We have seen that truth is a growing structure that gives rise to the harvest of a good life but, in another sense, it is light shed into our minds that penetrates the darkness of our self-love and shows up the way we think. Our reaction is equally important here. Selfishness will try to blot out the light shed on our shortcomings, and in the process reveal its own nature. If we turn a basket upside down, or lie under a bed, we reverse their proper uses. Selfishness reverses the proper use of human abilities. They were given to help others, and self-love uses them to take from others. If we think from this upside-down attitude, we blot out the truth. Truth only sheds light in a mind trying to be unselfish, a mind that gives it its proper "lampstand." Selfishness will try to blot out the light shed on our shortcomings, but in the process it reveals its own nature. Nothing can actually be covered up, and none of the secrets of our way of life can really be concealed. The truth will shed light and leave us facing a decision. We can blot it out, or we can set the lamp of truth properly on a lampstand by using the truth.

The phrase "If you have ears, use them!" points out that we need to listen and obey, if we are to see what the truth is really saying to us. It is very easy to think that becoming a Christian is a process in which an individual understands the truth, and then automatically begins a process of salvation. Nothing could be further from the truth. Our reaction to truth must include our choosing to accept the love Jesus has brought into that truth, and this we do by denying our own selfish way of life. This is an essential part of the process. Listening, obeying, is the only way the truth can work in us. The moment we accept truth in this way, by "giving the measure" of loving service to others, we shall be given more light on our life. Truth has to be used if it is to enlighten and change more of our understanding and life. Only by giving in service can we receive more power in the truth. "The measure we give will be the measure we get." On the other hand, if we approach truth selfishly, we cannot bear to have it show up our faults. We deny its value, and we lose even the understanding of it that showed up our faults. Even what we had is taken away.

> *26–29. And he said, "The kingdom of God is like a man who throws seed on the earth, and sleeps and rises night and day, and the seed sprouts and grows up, and he does not know how. For the earth itself grows a crop, first a blade, then an ear, then full grain in the ear; and when the crop has been given, immediately the man reaps it with the sickle because the harvest has come."*

So far the parables have stressed the part we must play to receive the seed of truth and to use its light in our minds; but now the other side of our new life is stressed. For all our cooperation, we play no part in the new life that grows in us. The power that works and grows up in us is the love of God. It is that life brought to our level in Jesus Christ that really does the work. Nothing will happen unless we freely choose it, but what we choose grows in us without our knowing how. The love that Jesus brought to this earthly life provides the power that makes our new self grow, but we do not make any of that power. We are "asleep" as to that aspect. We shall be aware of it as our life changes, we shall enjoy the understanding and service it brings day by day, we shall reap the harvest; but we provide none of the power that makes it grow.

> *30–34. And he said, "To what shall we compare the kingdom of God? How shall we make a parable of it? It is like a grain of mustard seed sown upon the earth, which is smaller than all other seeds on earth, but when it has been sown it grows up and becomes larger than any other shrub, and grows great branches so that the birds in the sky roost in its shade." And he spoke the Word to them with many such parables that they could listen to, but he did not speak to them without a parable. And in private he explained everything to his disciples.*

The plant used in this parable is the black mustard, *brassica nigra*, which, though it is an annual, grows some ten feet, and branches considerably in its upper part. Its seed seems to have been proverbial for smallness because of the huge plant resulting, rather than from specific comparison with other seeds. The plant is common around the sea of Galilee and farther north.

We have seen how we must receive Jesus' message when it is sown in us; we have seen that its light will only shine in our minds if we are using it, and we have realized that we contribute nothing to the power of love that works in our lives. Now comes what might be interpreted as a cautionary parable. The "rule of God" that is to be our whole life is not at first a vast kingdom in our mind. It is the very smallest beginning one can conceive. It is the smallest seed our mind will ever know. Everything else has a larger beginning, because everything else can draw on our selfishness, can find things in our life that are already geared to getting things for ourselves. But the kingdom of God is to love and serve others, and it has the smallest beginning. It will have to be built from scratch. When first learned, the message seems just an observation about our life. We are not aware of the way it is going to grow and branch out in many different ways until it becomes the greatest thing in our mind.

For the message to grow in that way, we need to accept it. We tend to consider truth as a way of thinking. If it is only that, it remains like seed in the packet. When we take truth and use it in our lives, it begins to grow, to take over our way of thinking and acting. We shall not at first realize how it is going to "branch out," how much of our life it is going to transform, how much of our accustomed ways of thinking it is going to change. But when it has grown up in our life in this way, it begins to be inhabited from quite a different source.

Our view on our way of life ceases to be simply ideas growing by reasoning and obeying. What comes down into the branches begins to be a living vision, "birds of the air." Our thinking often seems completely self-contained, as though nothing can enter it unless we read it in a book, hear it said, or watch it happen. The truth is that our mind is subject to other influences. They will not convey information to us or manipulate our thinking (that would destroy our freedom to choose), but they make different connections between ideas and so show our life in a different light, revealing a new basis from which to choose. If we concentrate on growing our tree of truth, we shall draw in influences that will show us where it should change our life. Our vision of the Lord's way will never be detached from our learning and reasoning and obeying. The "birds of the air" must still come to roost in the branches. But our view of life will begin to see from love and have a true life within what we know, a life coming down from heaven. That can only happen if we are truly disciples, willing to be taught the way of life by the Lord Jesus and to obey him.

> *35–41. And on that day when evening came, he said to them, "Let us go across the lake." And they sent the crowd away, and took him with them as he was in the boat, and other small boats were with him. And a violent storm of wind came and the waves beat into the boat and filled it. And he was in the stern sleeping on the steering cushion, and they roused him and said to him, "Teacher, don't you care that we are perishing?" And when woken up, he rebuked the wind and said to the sea, "Hush, be quiet." And the wind fell and there was a great calm. And he said to them, "Why are you afraid like this? How is it you have no faith?" And they were greatly afraid and said one to another, "Who is this, then, that even the wind and the sea obey him?"*

The lake of Galilee is bordered on the east by a high dry plateau, and the rapid heating and cooling of large masses of air over it gives rise to sudden violent storms on the lake. Such storms were difficult for the small fishing boats to ride out, despite the skill of the local fishermen. They had only oars and a small sail, used mostly to run before the wind, and the boat was steered by an oar over the stern, not by a rudder. To ease the helmsman's long stints at this oar, he had a cushion to lean on.

From the quiet crowd, straining to listen as Jesus teaches them in parables, it seems an abrupt transformation to the storm on the lake. Its coming when they set out to cross the lake seems accidental but, remembering that we are reading a gospel, we may see in it a warning that at this point rough times are coming. Once we have grasped the message of truth and how to use it, as the parables expound, our whole way of life will have been called in question. We do not sail easily on into the Christian life we have come to understand. Instead, it grows dark and the storm arises. There will be a backlash. All our underlying self-love will be whipped up by a violent wind of argument and reasoning against such fundamental changes in us. We get involved in this great storm of selfish thinking and wanting, and so it seems highly dangerous to us. It could drown all our new life in our old selfishness. While we are involved in the storm in this way and afraid of its consequence, the Lord is "asleep" in our mind. That, of course, must be nonsense, for he "neither slumbers nor sleeps" in his effort for our salvation. It is our fear of all the selfish arguments and evil attractions that has made him seem asleep to us. We have forgotten the new power of love that is steering our life. The only way to be saved in this stress is to go back and acknowledge that power again, to wake Jesus on the steering cushion (where he has always been). We have been fighting the storm of arguments and temptations in our own strength. It is very easy to assume that the power in our mind is the truth we have learned. But that truth only has power from the love Jesus brought into it in the world. Arguments from truth are helpless if the love that uses truth is forgotten. We have to remember that Jesus' love is our power in life. We have to ask for his help, to acknowledge that only his power is going to save us from ourselves. As soon as we recall the power of love that God offers for our salvation, the storm of selfishness and false reasoning loses its strength, and we are confident and at peace in our new life again.

Such temptations are our only way forward. We always live from what we find delightful. We may have become aware of the new delights of loving others and living with God's love, but that does not mean we have chosen them. Our old delight in a selfish life is bound to rise up and seem attractive again. We can only get a permanent basis for life if we can choose between these opposing delights. While either of them dominates our mind, it seems irresistible: it just is us. We can only make a choice if the two kinds of delight clash in a time of temptation. Such storms build up as our state oscillates from selfish wanting to loving service. Each delight begins to destroy the other. We cannot want anything selfishly without our Christian faith intruding and spoiling our selfish pleasure, but we cannot serve in love without our selfishness intruding and destroying our joy. At the height of the storm of temptation, neither way of life is now delightful, and we make our choice in freedom, deciding to waken the Lord in our mind, or drowning in the waves of our own selfishness. Such temptations must come. We cannot simply learn and so be saved from our self-love. We must find a delight in using the truth, a joy in helping others. That requires us to make a choice in life when no accustomed delight is controlling us.

It is in such experiences that we learn the true meaning of our faith. Each time we try to move forward and make fundamental changes in the way we approach life, we shall feel the power of our selfishness and our false arguments again. Each time, we can confirm ourselves in the way we have chosen, and reject our self-love more firmly. It does not mean that we never know earthly fears and anxieties; but it means that we eventually learn to trust that the love of the Lord has power in our mind and that our old drive is helpless against it. Once the storm is calmed, the disciples are said again to be in fear, but this is holy fear. We shall always have this fear, which is really our recognition of the great power of the Lord's love and of our total dependence on it for our new life.

Chapter Five

HEALING

We have already seen that Jesus' ministry of healing reveals divine compassion and love in an immediate way, just as people's actions show their love and compassion. It was important that the divine life in Jesus should make known this truly human nature of God. We need to know how completely he loves us. Teaching about his nature needs also this direct manifestation of affection in helping the sick and diseased. We must realize that the Lord's miracles of healing are intended to reveal his nature and are not an attempt to solve the problem of the world's health.

We may ask why Jesus could not heal the whole world then and cannot heal us all today in body as well as in mind. He seeks to do so, but the causes of earthly diseases often make it impossible. The way we choose to use the world distorts the physical environment and the bodies within it, not just our own, but of others as well. We are given that world to choose to accept the love of God in freedom. God can only give us his kind of life in this freedom to choose to love others or to take life selfishly. To maintain that necessary freedom of choice with us all, the good cannot be rewarded with good health nor the evil punished with bad. The influx of physical disease has to be general, and it occurs where circumstances, not individual responsibilities, decide.

If God is to help all people in every age with physical healing, they must all accept his way into all their lives, not simply cry to him for help when they have already distorted their own and others' health. Meanwhile, he must exercise his love for us all by the skill and devotion he gives to surgeon, doctor, nurse, and caregiver. Only the more important and fundamental healing of souls and minds can eventually change our use of the world and so the world's physical health. Spiritual healing he can bring to those who will let him, but his love is restrained from healing us physically by the necessity to maintain our freedom to choose his way. The miracles of healing in the Gospel are there to show the full power and compassion of his love.

1–13. And they came to the other side of the lake, to the country of the Gadarenes. And immediately, when he left the ship, he was met by a man with an evil spirit, who came out of the tombs where he lived. And no one could bind him, not even with chains, for he had often been secured with fetters and chains, but he had torn apart the chains and smashed the fetters, and no one was able to subdue him. He was in the mountains and the tombs continually, day and night, screaming and cutting himself with stones. And seeing Jesus from a distance, he ran and knelt to him and screamed at the top of his voice, "What have you to do with me, Jesus, Son of the most high God? Swear by God not to torment me." For Jesus was saying to him, "Unclean spirit, come out of the man." And Jesus asked the spirit, "What is your name?" And the spirit answered, saying, "Legion is my name, because we are many." And the unclean spirit pleaded with him not to send them out of the region. Now there was a large herd of pigs feeding there on the mountain; and the devils pleaded with him, saying, "Send us into the pigs, that we may enter them." And immediately Jesus allowed them to, and the unclean spirits left and entered the pigs, and the herd rushed down the steep slope into the sea, some two thousand of them, and were drowned in the sea.

Having crossed the lake, Jesus is in Gentile territory, though it is not possible to identify exactly where on the east coast of the lake is meant. The herd of pigs, which appears in the story, would be kept in a Gentile area, not among Jews, to whom the animal was unclean. It is clear enough that this miracle of healing is told to assure us of the Lord's control over the most powerful evil. Recent history has shown us just what violent and disgusting evil can possess men and women and cause them to treat their fellows with almost unbelievable cruelty and hatred. The possessed man shows unrestrainable violence, and this not merely from one aspect of human evil but from so many that they are "legion." The word is really a Latin one used for a Roman military unit of some 6,000 men, but here carries its meaning to ordinary folk, to whom a legion seemed without number.

The selfishness in us powers every aspect of our lives—

things we want, power over others, hatred of restraint, pride that despises, desire for vile lusts, wanting to use others for personal gain or sexual satisfaction—there is no human power that the self cannot pervert to satisfy itself and harm others. If we live on such a "mountain" of selfishness, all truly human thoughts and feelings die, and we find ourselves living "among their tombs" with only our false arguments and excuses to scratch and cut at life. Community laws and social custom try to set bounds to such evil and to control its effects; but however strong these fetters and chains, we see them broken again and again, sometimes openly in whole nations as in Nazi Germany, and more recently by Iraq's regime and in the former Yugoslavia, but also under cover in every country and community. Such a force cannot be restrained merely by outward law. The advantages of fitting into the accepted pattern of social behavior may restrain it for a while with individuals, but selfishness sooner or later breaks these chains as well. Only a different power for life that removes the self-love can bring the true sanity of life lived from love for others and so make a change. The evil must be cast out by a new way of life freely chosen.

As this way of love from the Lord makes contact with our life, it throws up in contrast our selfish motive for living, and from its sheer opposition to the Lord's way, it recognizes his power. In the ensuing pain and distress, we can choose to accept his power by acknowledging the true nature of our self-centered life. The pig, which roots about in the soil and eats anything it finds, makes a good symbol for the natural lusts in our lives, which feed on any and every filthy desire. The wish of the evil spirits to enter the pigs shows how our self-love reveals its real nature when challenged by the Lord's way of love—and not only its nature but also how that vileness rushes human nature down into total destruction.

Unfortunate people, such as the man possessed by a legion of devils, provide a useful picture to show us the power of evil in us and its cure. Still, we cannot but wonder what was his real condition. Certainly, it was not the chosen condition we are responsible for when we let selfishness rule our lives; it only portrays that for us. It is customary to equate his condition with those who suffer from various forms of mania. When mental illness removes all restraints, behavior certainly mirrors that of violent evil in healthy persons. But we have also to remember that the reason our Lord came at that time was that evil had grown to a point where it would override all humanity's power for good. In this man perhaps we see such a condition arising, just at the time when Jesus gains the power to restrain the evil and heal him. Such thoughts can only strengthen our thankfulness to God for coming to accomplish the salvation of all of us.

> *14–20. And those who herded the pigs ran away and told about it in the city and the region around. And the people went to see what had been done, and came to Jesus and saw the man who had been possessed by a legion of devils sitting clothed and in his right mind, and they were afraid. And those who had seen what had happened to the man possessed by devils and what happened to the pigs described it all. And they began to plead with him to leave their territory. And when he got into the ship, the man who had been possessed by devils pleaded that he might go with him. But Jesus would not let him, and said to him, "Go to your own house, and tell how much the*

Lord has done for you and how he pitied you." And he went away and began to proclaim through the Decapolis how much Jesus had done for him, and everyone was amazed.

The Decapolis on the east of the lake was so called because (as the name means) it was a league of "ten cities," which had existed from the time of the Seleucids. It stretched east of the lake and down to Pella, some seventeen miles south of Galilee. The people of the region wanted Jesus to leave. Often in the Gospels we see this kind of reaction to Jesus when he helps people. The very power he shows seems to induce fear of his presence and a desire to be rid of him.

If we look honestly at our own spiritual development, we shall see that this reaction of the local people portrays our own reaction. We realize the power that the new way of love can bring into our lives, and there is a moment of joy and thankfulness; but the way of life it demands threatens to destroy all our accustomed comfortable ways of living, and so a wave of protest arises after each step forward. This is not a bad thing in itself, for when we realize the power of love, to try to hang on to that moment of joy would only be artificial. There is much hard daily work to be done to make our life conform to ways of love. So the man who was healed is not allowed to return with the Lord, despite his pleading, but is sent out into the region he knows to proclaim the nature of this new way of life. This is the way forward for us, to bring the new vision of living into our many daily duties and practices and change them for our Lord.

21–24. And when Jesus had gone over in the ship again to the other side of the lake, he was by the sea, and a great crowd gathered around him. And there came one of the rulers of the synagogue named Jairus, and when he saw Jesus he fell at his feet and pleaded desperately with him, saying, "My little daughter is at death's door. Come and lay your hands on her, so that she may be cured and live." And he went with him, and a great crowd followed and thronged around him.

Luke tells us they "returned" across the lake, so presumably we are in Capernaum. There was a great deal of opposition to Jesus among the scribes and Pharisees and those who controlled the synagogues; but here we find one of them who believes in him. The rulers of the synagogue were not scribes, but were leaders of the community who had the responsibility for running the synagogue and its worship. Jairus' plea is for his young daughter who is near to death, and Jesus shows his usual compassion in going with him in the midst of the vast crowd.

In this new young life that is threatened with death, we see the newness that can come into our life, which is threatened with spiritual death. In Jairus the story picks out the element of religion in the great crowd of our interests and activities, but that religion seems unlikely to have any new generation, for it cannot maintain its life. It is a situation we will all recognize, for religion can become just one aspect in a multitude of interests and preoccupations, and then it loses any quality of renewing our life. We shall all know the fear that Jairus knew. We want our life to grow in Christian love and service, but we are under so much pressure from the self-regard that crowds our worldly activity and from the constant desires to be selfish that throng our mind that we feel our new life may die before it can really begin to live.

> *25–34. And there was a certain woman who had had a hemorrhage for twelve years, suffering under many doctors and spending all she had, yet getting no better, but only worse. She had heard about Jesus, and she came in the crowd behind him and touched his cloak, for she said, "If I can only touch his clothes, I will be cured." And immediately the flow of blood stopped, and she felt in her body that she was healed of her trouble. And immediately Jesus, aware that power had gone out of him, turned in the crowd and said, "Who touched my clothes?" And his disciples said, "See the crowd around you, and yet you say, 'Who touched me'!" Still Jesus looked to see who had done this. But the woman, frightened and trembling, knowing what had been done to her, came and fell down before him, and told him the whole truth. And he said to her, "Daughter, your faith has cured you; go in peace and be healed of your trouble."*

Into the problem of reviving our Christian life, there comes another who also needs healing, and the gospel has a reason for weaving the two together. Jesus has set out to heal a young life that has only existed for twelve years, and there comes to him an old life that has been losing life blood for the same twelve years. The concentration has been on healing the new life that seems likely to die but, before that is done, an old life must be healed of its life-draining hemorrhage. There is a message here for us. We have our concentration fixed on a new Christian life that we want to be strong in us, but we are obliged first to do something about an old life that has been losing its vigor. We cannot forget our normal everyday life just to concentrate on a wonderful inner spirit we hope for. The new spirit can never be awakened in us unless we pay attention to our old way of life and do something about changing it in everyday behavior. We need to heal our outward life if the inner spirit is to live in us.

So it is that the woman brings her twelve-year-old sickness to Jesus to be healed. The image of a hemorrhage draining away the lifeblood is a perfect description of our outward life when it is lived for ourselves alone. All the strength of love, which might go out to serve others, drains away in a constant endeavor to care for ourselves and protect ourselves and gain things for ourselves. Such a sickness can only be cured by doing something about our everyday life. The woman knew she had only to touch Jesus' clothes to be healed. We may feel we want to experience Jesus' love in our hearts, but that love is clothed with his teaching about our way of earthly life. Commandments and instruction on our behavior to others may seem only an outward pattern showing Jesus' love, but that outward pattern is absolutely essential if his love is to live in our hearts. We can never have new life from him, unless we set about applying his outward commands to our daily life. The woman touched his outer garments and was healed. It seemed just an interlude on his way to heal a new young life, but spiritually it showed an essential step we must all take if he is to heal our inward life.

The disciples were amazed that Jesus should be aware in that vast crowd that one woman had touched his garments, but he was aware that his power had been called upon and had acted. It is a marvelous revelation of his relationship with us. So often we hear of Christians lumped together in denominations or churches or communities, and we can get the idea that we are just one in a more or less organized crowd. The truth is that whenever we use his commandments and so call on his love, Jesus is personally aware of us as an individual, as one of his children he is helping. This person-to-person relationship with the Lord is the way we should see our life. To the world, we seem to be just one of a large crowd, to be documented and controlled. Like church groups following the Lord, the disciples who struggled forward in the crowd found it startling that Jesus knew anything of one insignificant individual. Yet his life touches each one of us with his love and gives us power to change as a person. This is the only beginning of a better world, not in regimented communities, not in Church organizations, but in individuals who know and use the power of the Lord in their daily lives. He has no relationship with men and women in masses, but only as individuals whom he then weaves with his love into a true and spiritual community.

> *35–37. While he was still speaking, they came from the house of the ruler of the synagogue, saying, "Your daughter is dead. Why trouble the teacher anymore?" But immediately Jesus, hearing what was said, told the ruler of the synagogue, "Do not be afraid; only believe." And he let no one go with him except Peter and James and his brother John.*

The apparent death of the young girl comes as somewhat of a shock, especially as we have seen in the healing of the woman a real effort to change daily life to accord with Jesus' way of love. But it is just at the moment we set about changing our life that we realize how spiritually dead it is. We need then to hold fast to our faith that the love of Jesus can make a real renewal. At the moment Jairus is told his daughter is dead, the Lord urges him not to be afraid but to believe. The part our discipleship must play in trusting the Lord is emphasized by Jesus' taking with him specifically Peter, James, and John. We have seen that these represent our faith, the good works it commands, and our love to the Lord in what we do. We cannot heal ourselves, but the companionship of our faith, service, and love is necessary if the Lord is to help us.

38–43. And he came to the house of the ruler of the synagogue and saw a tumult, people weeping and wailing, and entering he said to them, "Why make such a fuss and weep? The child is not dead, but sleeps." And they laughed at him. But having put them all out, he took with him the father and mother of the child and his companions, and entered in where the child was lying. And having taken the child's hand, he said to her, "Talitha koumi," which means "Little girl, wake up!" And immediately the little girl, who was twelve years old, got up and walked. And they were greatly amazed. And he warned them no one should know about this. And he told them to give her something to eat.

Jesus arrived at the ruler's house to find everyone mourning in the fashion of the day. Jews even hired professional mourners to add to the lamentations at a death. They had no real knowledge of the nature of life after death, and so death seemed the greatest of calamities. Despite the inevitable grief at the loss of a loved one, the more grievous in the case of a child, we should try to keep such losses in context and remember that death is for us all simply a resurrection into a new life, a necessary part of God's plan for us. We should never think of death as a wall that terminates life, but as a door that opens into another room.

The story reminds us of the everyday language of the people. Jesus speaks to the young girl in Aramaic, the tongue she herself would use, and the gospel then translates the phrase into Greek. Aramaic was the general language of the whole area at that time and, though written in Hebrew characters, was not the language of the Old Testament. Like any people in a mixed language environment (compare the modern Swiss), Jews of that period used several languages, commonly speaking Aramaic, but learning to read Hebrew to understand the Scriptures, the common form of Greek to carry on commerce, and also probably a smattering of Latin to communicate with the Roman occupiers. No doubt Jesus used language in just this fashion.

When we set about reforming our outward life, we become conscious of the power of our self and realize that we ourselves cannot create a new inner life. This is the mourning and lamentation Jesus finds as he reaches the house to heal the girl. Our obedience can touch the Lord's teaching and commandments, as the woman touched his clothes, and prevent our life draining away in useless, selfish behavior; but we cannot believe that we can come alive, transformed into a new unselfish person. Jesus said she slept, and "they laughed at him." It is at the point when we realize how dead we are when left to ourselves that we need to hold to our faith that the Lord can raise a new spirit in us. When we use the truth he lived out in the world, we call on the power of love he brought into it. This, in the inner room of our spirit, can take hold of us and raise us up into a real life of loving and serving. The story emphasizes that we must never think of this as some kind of frigid, impassive salvation the Lord has brought into the world. The gentle words to the little girl, using the language in which she had known all her parents' affection, remind us of the immediate love the Lord has for each of us as one of his children. It is his love, stretched out to us all, that acts in us and becomes our new life, and Jesus' command to "give her something to eat" emphasizes that we must continue to feed on this love.

Chapter Six

MIRACLES AND APOSTLES

A miracle is a light thing for a person's faith, for only in the historical beginnings of Christianity does a miracle trigger faith, and then it is at once developed into a life of faith. Faith depends on a personal choice between seeing the world as a place we use only for self-satisfaction and seeing it as a God-given opportunity to love others. Faith is not something that is "proved" by miracles or anything else; it is something chosen from love and compassion for others. Nevertheless, we all need to be able to grasp the miracles in our faith.

In this chapter, we come to two miracles that depend obviously on the creative power of God: the multiplying of bread and fish and the power to walk on water. In reality, all the miracles depend on this divine creative power, for it is no less involved in creating again a leper's flesh or a withered limb, or making immediate and radical changes in the organisms causing fevers and sicknesses. But in those cases we know about slow processes of healing and are able to think of them speeded up, without realizing what a vastly different change we are glossing over. When Jesus begins to multiply food and control the powers of nature, the assumption of creative power is manifest. Therefore, it is at this point that arguments about miracles usually begin.

A real understanding of these miracles lies in the nature of Jesus Christ. We saw at the very beginning that in him the love of God was brought into the level of our minds, so that we can have its power in the truth he teaches. As the process came toward its end, the love of God had almost become the whole life of Jesus Christ. Only the last temptation of the passion and the cross remained. But the love of God is that which powers creation. It is small wonder that Jesus could direct that power in healing and in other ways. By continued harvests, this creative love multiplies food, and by continued generations it multiplies animals; it makes all the qualities of the physical world. In Jesus, when he was not in the stress of temptation, that same love could exercise the same power when he wished.

For us, with the witness of others to give us the chance to choose the life of faith, these miracles no longer act to trigger faith; but they still reveal to us the way the love of God works in our minds. And that is most truly a miracle.

1–6. And he went away from there and came to his own country, and his disciples followed him. And when the Sabbath came, he began to teach in the synagogue. And many who heard him were astonished, saying, "Where does he get these things from? And what is this wisdom he has been given, so that his hands do such marvelous things? Isn't this the carpenter, the son of Mary, brother to James and Joses and Judas and Simon; and his sisters live here with us?" And they were deeply offended at him. But Jesus said to them, "A prophet is not without honor, except in his own country and among his own family and in his own house." And he was not able to do any marvels there, except laying his hands on a few sick people and healing them. And he was astonished at their unbelief.

Jesus comes now to the district of Nazareth, where he had been brought up as a boy. Here he was not the unknown wonder worker, the Christ come to save people and teach them the way to a new life. Here he was the man they knew, who had run errands and shared in the family work with his brothers and sisters when he was a boy and toiled in the carpenter's shop as a man. They could not see him as this great new Savior and Teacher. We learn a little here of the family at Nazareth. Jesus had four brothers and at least two sisters, all younger than he. In a sense, they were stepbrothers and sisters since their father was Joseph, whereas Jesus was the Son of God. Growing up as a boy and maturing to a young man, he would have been the eldest in a large family, eventually supporting his father in the community and, since it is presumed Joseph died before the ministry, taking his place as head of the family. He was clearly a well-known figure in Nazareth. This very fact prevented him from showing his divine power, for any person he was to help or heal had to show some belief in his divine mission.

It is common today to speak of people being "inoculated against religion" by church attendance and the formalities of church learning, practices, and organization. The idea becomes set in the mind that religion is another subject you learn about and apply, like home economics, car maintenance, or biology. It becomes part of the "family" of our own learning and practice. In such a case, religion loses its power and true mystery, as Jesus lost his power to help when in his own country, family, and house. Certainly, we can see such effects around us today. The Scriptures given as divine revelation are treated as little different from any other historical record. Church hierarchies argue over who controls which people and presume to tell us who are saved and lost. In arguments over church practices, we see the same forms of destructive criticism and hurtful comment that the world uses in mundane struggles for power.

So there have been suggestions that children should not be accustomed to any routine of religious learning or worship and, indeed, that all church structures that help in such matters should be abandoned for a general anarchy of finding one's own faith as and when it happens. Then our mind will not assume that its childhood acquaintance with religion is its whole meaning and so prevent the living spirit changing our adult life. But Jesus' own teaching, while it dismisses human-made customs and superstitions, calls for a knowledge of divine revelation and accepts an orderly development. The real point of this sad little story is that we must never presume to regard God's presence with us as part of our own "family affairs." However we may learn about him and his ways, the reality behind is the very love that holds us in being and has taken the power to transform us by salvation. That should never be forgotten at any age by those who teach or those who learn. As soon as we lose that other dimension to our life, all the knowledge about it is classified with merely human behavior, part of our own country and family and house, without any power to heal and save our lives.

7–13. And he went round the villages teaching. And he called the twelve to him and began to send them out in twos, giving them power over evil spirits. And he ordered them to take nothing for the journey except a staff, no bag for food, no bread, no money in their belts. They could wear sandals, but not have two coats. And he said to them, "Wherever you go into a house, stay there until you leave that place. And those who will not receive you or hear you, when you leave them shake off the dust under your feet as a protest against them. Truly I tell you, it will be better for Sodom and Gomorrah in the day of judgment than for that city." And they went out and proclaimed that men should repent. And they cast out many devils, and healed many who were sick, anointing them with oil.

Now the disciples are sent out as apostles. They are given the exercise of Jesus' power to heal miraculously, but it never ceased to be *his* power. The apostles taught the nature of the Lord and his work, thus extending his power through their efforts. Clearly, the twelve are sent out so poorly equipped that they are dependent on God's providence, and not their own foresight, to cope with any problems they may meet. The parallel passage in Luke 9:3 denies them the staff also, and Matthew 10:9 the sandals as well, variations that probably come from the various types of journey envisaged, some of which might not be feasible without sandals and staff. The meaning is obvious for those who seek to convey the Lord's message to others: they must do it in his strength and not their own.

We have seen, however, that the gospel speaks to us individually and is fulfilled in each life. We realized earlier that many powers in our own mind are called to be disciples within us, and it is these that are sent out now into our own mind and life, to extend the life of faith into all our thinking and wanting. It is important that we do not depend on our own emotions and desires in this process. It is very easy to be carrying the baggage of what we want to do ourselves for our own pride, or to control others, or to earn the merit of being born again. The only love that should operate in our efforts is the love of God, which was brought into our mind in Jesus Christ. If we are careful to carry no resources of our own into our new life, we can do all things for the love of others and our Lord.

Once we set the story in this personal context, the harsh command to "shake off the dust" of those who will not receive the message becomes a necessary part of the effort of love. Those things in our own mind and life that reject the Lord's way are the evil dust of a self-centered life and must be shaken off "our feet," that is, off the outward life we live as we tread through the world. Sodom and Gomorrah marked the evil of a less enlightened age, and any evil that remained in our mind and life after knowing Jesus would be more culpable than that. On the other hand, if we truly repent of any evil we see in ourselves, we can make our thoughts and desires obey the Lord's commands, and the perversions can be healed and the devils of selfishness cast out. Throughout it all, our effort must be to bring the love of Jesus into all our activity to heal it. When we looked at the title "Christ," we saw it was the equivalent of "Messiah" or "the anointed one." In Jesus, the love of God came down to anoint our earthly life with love, and we must use this oil of love to anoint every distortion from truth in ourselves and to heal it.

14–20. And, because his name became well-known, King Herod heard of him; and he was saying, "John the Baptist has risen from the dead, and this is why he does such powerful works." Others said, "He is Elijah," and others said, "He is a prophet, or like one of the prophets." But hearing this Herod insisted, "It is John, whom I beheaded. He is risen from the dead." For Herod had sent and seized John and imprisoned him, because of Herodias, his brother Philip's wife. For Herod had married her, but John had said to him, "It is not lawful for you to have your brother's wife." Herodias held that against him and wanted to kill John, but she was not able to because Herod, knowing him to be a just and holy man, feared John and kept him safe, taking his advice on many matters and hearing him gladly.

Mark often tells a story within a story. Here, he divides the sending out of the disciples from their return by telling the story of John's death. The death of John the Baptist is woven with the vile and turbulent history of the family of Herod the Great. On Herod's death, his son Herod Antipas had been allowed by the Romans to become tetrarch of Galilee and contrived by sensible rule to keep his authority until now. But he seems to have fallen victim to the ambition of Herodias, wife of his brother Herod Boethus. (Mark wrongly refers to another brother, Philip, as her husband. The confusion may well have arisen because Philip married Salome, the daughter of Herodias.) Herodias left her husband, by whom she had this daughter Salome, and Herod Antipas married her, putting away his wife, an Arabian princess. That led to the Nabatean War, which hastened Herod Antipas' downfall; but the gospel concentrates on John the Baptist's condemnation of the liaison, Herod's fear, and Herodias' hatred of John.

The earthly rulers in the gospel represent the way worldly things are controlled in our minds and lives. Such things need proper organization, but the overall power must be with our Christian intentions in life. When the true spirit is in control within, it will ensure that mundane things are properly controlled and used for the good of our fellows and the service of the Lord. The particular ways in which we live and serve others externally will depend on what things are needed in our society and what outward organization exists in our nation. But the spirit from which our service is given comes from within, and this powers the way we live and work in worldly matters. If, however, self-love is powerful in our worldly living and false excuses and wrong methods rule our daily life, then there is an evil way ruling our outward life that opposes all true instruction about how we should use our abilities for the good of others.

The Herod family obviously portrays this evil ruling our outward life. It is really made up of two forces. Herod is the nominal ruler, standing for all the false reasoning and arguments we use to excuse a self-centered way of living. But the more dangerous part of worldly rule is the sheer selfishness that really powers it, the Herodias that eventually overpowers our Herod. Our Herod is made up of myriad arguments for our own advantage and ways to harm and use others in gaining our selfish way; but it also includes fearful reasonings, which cannot but see the arguments for a good society and the foolishness of a world of selfish anarchy, and so cannot bring itself to wipe the truth completely out of all its thinking. Instead, it tries to bind the true ideas to its own purposes, as Herod imprisons

John and listens to just enough to gloss over obvious and revolting evil. In this way our Herod keeps the voice of truth imprisoned to our desires without seeming to extinguish it totally. Such equivocation means nothing to the evil selfishness working in daily life. This wants to destroy all restraint of truth, even though that must eventually bring total disaster from someone else's evil. The truth that is our John the Baptist insists that this faulty self-love is no true wife to the ruler of our earthly life.

> *21–29. But an opportunity came when Herod on his birthday made a supper for his powerful courtiers and his chief captains and the leading men of Galilee. The daughter of Herodias came in and danced, pleasing Herod and those feasting with him, and the king said to the girl, "Ask what you will and I will give it to you." And he swore to her, "Whatever you ask I will give you, to the half of my kingdom." And she went out and said to her mother, "What shall I ask?" And she said, "The head of John the Baptist." And she immediately hurried to the king and requested, "I want you to give me at once the head of John the Baptist on a dish." And the king was grieved, but because of his oaths sworn before those feasting with him, he would not refuse her. And immediately the king sent a guardsman and ordered his head to be brought. And he went and beheaded him in the prison and brought his head on a dish and gave it to the girl, and the girl gave it to her mother. And when they heard of it, John's disciples came and took up his body and laid it in the tomb.*

Only the wanton and evil behavior of Herod's family makes this story seem possible, for no respectable woman would have been present with, let alone danced in oriental fashion for men at such a feast. But the story pictures exactly the sequence that undermines the careful hypocrisy of our worldly reasoning, causing it to abandon all restraint and destroy any semblance of respect for truth. Calculating use of truth to explain and excuse worldly behavior seems to ensure that our Herod of self-seeking life can keep the new life's demand for repentance on a leash, not really listening but maintaining an outward appearance of respect for the commandments. But if the reasoning Herod side of our life seems to have things well in hand, it reckons without the evil power of selfishness, which is married to all its self-seeking behavior. That "Herodias" has no respect at all for truth and simply hates its existence. The breakdown comes when selfishness breeds its persuasion of gross appetite and evil lust, its "Salome," and sends it to display the delight of sheer evil. All careful thinking breaks down and loses any respect for truth in the desire to enjoy the lust for evil. Its kingdom of apparently obeying truth is given to the delights of evil lust. Then John's call to repentance loses all control, even an external one, and is at last openly destroyed.

It is a sequence that can be seen in the sudden scandals that break through the apparently upright, controlled lives of men and women; and it can be seen in the behavior of absolute governments, as the power to do evil cuts loose from all outward restraints. But it can be repeated in the life of any man or woman whose outward pattern of living simply uses truth as a cloak for gaining personal satisfaction and delight. Such a state has no real permanence and will break down into sheer evil sooner or later. It is not enough for us to know the truth and apply it to the lives of others. We must be actively repenting day by day, examining our own lives, seeing the evil and selfishness that affect us and replacing such behavior with the life of love and service to others.

Mark tells this story within that of the apostles' being sent out to minister and their return. It is a style of "story within a story" that he favors; but this serves a purpose in the gospel, for the death of John the Baptist comes finally at the moment when Jesus is releasing his power to call to repentance. We need to remember that, though death symbolizes the killing nature of evil, for good souls death is the time of resurrection into a new life. John dies at this point because the nature of repentance is changing and being raised up. When we begin the battles of spiritual life, we hear the call to repentance as a voice calling in the wilderness and commanding us to change our selfish way of life. But mere external obedience is eventually shown as insufficient, and then the real call to repent and use the spirit of Jesus to change our life is heard. We shall all begin our new life at John the Baptist's call and find our first external obedience only reveals the death that comes from our selfishness. At that moment, the call we are hearing is resurrected into the demand of Jesus' love in our hearts, and a new way begins for true disciples. So it is that John's disciples take his body for burial, for spiritually "burial" means our resurrection into life. For us, at this point, the call for repentance has been resurrected from love.

> *30–34. And the apostles returned to Jesus and told him all they had done and what they had taught. And he said to them, "Come apart in a desert place by yourselves, and rest a little." For many were coming and going so that they had no time even to eat. And they went off in the boat to a desert place apart.*

And the crowds saw them going, and many recog-
nized Jesus, and they ran there on foot from all the
cities and got there before them and came to Jesus.
And when he got out of the boat, Jesus saw a great
crowd, and he was moved with compassion for them
because they were like sheep without a shepherd.
And he began to teach them many things.

When the twelve return, they are referred to as apostles. A disciple is one who learns from a teacher, as the twelve had learned from Jesus. An apostle is one who carries the truth to others and teaches them. The two functions are easily distinguished in our outward service in the world; but if we are to see the gospel in our own minds, the two functions must be there too. We have first to learn truth from Jesus, that is, truth that has love within it as its purpose. Then the disciple in us has to become an apostle and carry that understanding out into all our thinking and planning. Our knowledge of truth is not meant to be a separate compartment among our knowing. It is meant to be used in all the other areas of understanding and planning, ensuring that we use the true way in every activity of our lives.

Again we find ourselves in a desert place, deliberately entered because too much activity leaves no time to eat. The ministry of the apostles and the death of John the Baptist marks a new phase beginning; and whenever a new phase of our Christian life begins, we realize that, in all the busyness of our mind, we have not really absorbed what we need to follow the Christian way. We are in a desert because our life is uncultivated spiritually. Clearly Jesus' intention was to help his disciples and equip them for further things, but all the others anticipate his move and come to him for help. It typifies our own experience; for we would like to take our first principles and really think them through, but we can never get into an ivory tower to work truth out in the abstract. All the impact and activity of life raises thoughts and desires at ground level, and they arrive "running on foot" before the disciples of our Christian principles can be sorted out and fully grasped. Yet Jesus does not reject such a situation; rather, it highlights the reality of our progress. Our Christian life is not an intellectual process we can limit to certain arguments and conclusions. Rather it is a mass of "sheep without a shepherd." It is a mass of possible ways of loving and helping that has no proper direction. That is where Jesus teaches, in the actual living of life. Learning truth and working out ideas has its value, but Christian life is only lived where love goes into action to help others.

35–44. And when it was late in the day, his disciples came to him and said, "This is a desert place, and already the hour is late. Send them away that they may buy bread from the country and villages round about, for they have nothing to eat." But he answered them, "You give them something to eat." And they said to him, "Shall we go and buy bread worth two hundred denarii and give them it to eat?" And he said to them, "How many loaves have you? Go and see." And when they had found out, they said to him, "Five. And two fish." And he told them to make everyone sit down in groups on the green grass. And they sat down in groups, in hundreds and fifties. And he took the five loaves and the two fish, and looking up to heaven he blessed and broke the loaves and gave them to his disciples to set before everyone, and the two fish he divided among them all. And they all ate and were satisfied. And afterwards they took up twelve baskets full of pieces of bread and fish. And about five thousand men fed on the loaves.

There have been suggestions that the five thousand were fed by sharing their food with each other once Jesus had set the example; but Mark's gospel, both here and in its reference back to this incident, seems clear that Jesus now performs a miracle to feed the vast crowd around him. The food available is such as might be carried for a journey. John tells us that the loaves were of the usual barley bread. The fish would have been dried or pickled to preserve them. The disciples' estimate of the amount of food really required was considerable. Two hundred denarii was a laborer's wages for two hundred working days, or some eight months. There seems to be considerable emphasis on the orderly behavior of the crowd. They are described as sitting down in "groups," a word that describes the regular plots in a vegetable garden.

We too have a vast crowd of ideas and emotions that are hungry for a real way of life. Our first reaction, like the disciples, is to suggest that they go elsewhere since the problem seems too great. We can only realize the greatness of the task. We tend to give up on our Christianity as being able to satisfy everything, and we suggest we use other people's attitudes on life to feed our mind and organize everyday life, going out "to the villages and country around." Jesus directs us to find out what we actually do have, rather than simply relying on what others say or do. If we look into our mind, we shall find that we have some of the "bread of life" there. We have a little of the way that good love works in life, though it may be only the remnants of childhood loving and helping and the occasional innocent experience of genuinely loving others. If the number of loaves is small, it is enough. And we have two fish as well, for early on in the gospel we saw that disciples are fishermen who catch true ideas, though these ideas may seem far too few to feed our multitude of human problems and emotions.

We have to realize that we are dealing with human things in all these day-to-day problems and emotional stresses. Today every problem is summarized in economic and scientific terms, and these are assumed to define the action that will be taken. The human element, if it is admitted, must be bribed or coerced into such a solution. But the real question is that of human intention. The will to do anything helpful remains the decision of those involved. They must use the "bread and fish" of the love and wisdom they have from God to decide what must be done for others. Even where we cannot explain all the factors involved, the motivation for loving service must feed our life. Each of us has very real decisions to make on how we use our abilities and our time, how we react to other people and their needs, what purposes we use to direct our daily life. The crowd of problems may seem vast, but the only way to satisfy them is by personal action from love wherever we see the opportunity to help others.

The method of feeding the multitude has two parts. First, to make them sit down in order on the green grass. Green grass in that part of the world means it is newly grown, and we are required to sort out all our problems and desires on the basis of our new-grown faith. We have to bring them into order, seeing them against what is really a very simple pattern: the help our plans and attitudes are to others, not ourselves. While we set about this business of thinking out and judging our many plans and purposes, the second factor must also come into play. Jesus must bless the bread. We have to realize that the ideas of good we have from the past are not merely human judgments. The power behind our loving others comes from the saving love of God. If we accept that, there will be power in it to multiply into everything we try to think and do. Only when we think we manufacture our own power of love will it prove inadequate. And the ideas about what is right and true, "the fish," will begin to multiply too, because love is working in our understanding. Handling the multitude of our activities in the world is not a matter of finding out what others are accustomed to do and copying them. It is a matter of living from the love of Jesus and loving others in every situation. When we call on that love, there is always enough for every situation, and even more left over than we started with!

> *45–52. And immediately he compelled his disciples to board the boat and go before him to the other side of the lake to Bethsaida, while he dismissed the crowd. And taking leave of them, he went into the mountain to pray. And by the evening, the boat was in the midst of the sea and he was alone on the land. And he saw them toiling at their rowing, for the wind was against them, and about the fourth watch of the night he came to them walking on the sea. And he would have gone by them, but they saw him walking on the sea and cried out, thinking it was a phantom, for they all saw him and were badly shaken. And immediately he spoke to them and said, "Take courage, it is I, myself. Don't be afraid." And*

*he went up to them into the boat, and the wind
fell. And they were amazed and astounded beyond
all measure. For the incident of the loaves had not
made them understand, because their hearts were
hardened.*

The desert place was presumably somewhere in the region of Capernaum. Bethsaida was on the north of the
lake, near to the entrance of the Jordan river into it. There
is a tendency for Mark to make the story move in a confused way about the Galilean area. That may well be because he received stories from Peter or others that were
grouped in subjects for preaching, thus not chronologically.
Later we shall find that, "having passed over," they arrive at
Gennesaret, which was on the same side of the lake as Capernaum, but further south. Perhaps the contrary wind
blew them there. But divine providence will have used the
writer's method of gathering the stories so as to get the succession of places that convey the spiritual ideas in the
gospel.

The miracle that can feed all our life with love would
seem to settle everything; but it is no sooner done than the
disciples find themselves again toiling over difficult waters.
Our experience of Christian life is the same, for though we
may have grasped the source of loving power in our lives,
our efforts to make our minds and emotions obey only stirs
up a contrary force of false arguments from our selfishness.
The power of Jesus' love seems high up and withdrawn,
"praying on the mountain," as we wrestle with practical life
on a sea of selfishness and evil. But if we work away trying
to hold our Christian course through life, we shall come
towards the dawn (which is the "fourth watch of the
night"), and it will dawn on us how complete is Jesus'

power over this sea of evil and false ideas. He walks on it, and it cannot drown his love. The realization comes slowly. At first it would seem to pass us by; and then we think of it as not quite real in its power, a phantom. But eventually we take courage from his power, and we receive him fully into our lives. When that happens, the opposing wind drops away and evil forces have no power to oppose us with selfishness.

Whenever we hold on in such a temptation, there is a great sense of joy and wonder when the power of love works in our lives; and yet that very reaction reveals that there are still elements of self-love and hardheartedness to be changed in us. The presence of Jesus' love to feed the whole of our life is not yet completely received, and we shall have other temptations to endure.

> *53–56. And crossing the lake they came to the land of Gennesaret and landed. And as soon as they left the boat, people recognized him, and running all over the country they began to carry the sick around on their beds to where he was. Wherever he entered villages or cities or country places, they laid those who were sick right in his way, and they pleaded to touch just the hem of his garment. And as many as touched him were healed.*

They had set out for Bethsaida at the north of the lake. Now they cross to Gennesaret, which was a fertile and well-populated area beside the lake south of Capernaum. Again we have the scene of the healing of the sick, which presumably took place wherever Jesus went. Concentrating on the isolated incidents recorded, we sometimes lose sight of the turmoil in Galilee that his ministry caused. Knowledge of his powers had swept through the land, and everyone was crazy to get to him to be healed and to listen.

The way these people scurry about, to bring those who are sick to Jesus, is a reminder to us to be on the lookout for anything in our life that is selfish or evil, any thought that is false or part of planning for ourselves, and take steps to bring it to the power of Jesus' love in our hearts, so that it can be healed. Such are to be placed right in Jesus' way. They must not be hidden away in corners as we frequently want to do with shortcomings and failings we do not really want to change. Again we get the emphasis that just to touch Jesus' clothes, even if it is only the hem, will heal. It is a reminder to us that the teachings and commands of Jesus that clothe his love have power when that love is in them. The things we know will have that power, but only if we remember that they are the way his love acts and so keep the love acting in them.

Chapter Seven

JEWS AND GENTILES

This chapter sharply contrasts Jews and Gentiles. It is easy to misunderstand the attitude of the gospel to those within Judaism and those outside. Since the disciples themselves were Jews, and many other Jews are picked out for commendation, it is somewhat difficult to understand the antisemitism of the medieval period and after. Jesus reproves the Jews, not for their nationality or their faith, but for their misuse of their religion so as to make themselves a special people and despise others. Religion is meant to enable men and women to love God and one another. Its use to exalt a nation or individual destroys true religion in any age.

The difference the gospel is highlighting is between those who have knowledge about God and do not use it from love and those who do not have such knowledge but try to love others. The Jews did have the means to understand the purposes of God and could have welcomed Jesus as the Messiah their Scriptures promised. The Gentiles did not have that kind of knowledge. Like the Jews, they were good and bad, but they all lacked knowledge about the purposes of God in Jesus. They could accept his love in their ignorance but, to make any real and powerful use of its promised salvation, they had to learn about its nature.

The coming of God in Jesus Christ effected salvation for all men and women. They all understand some basic truths about not stealing, murdering, lying, or coveting. They can all be aware of God in some way and of their duty to love their neighbor. Since the incarnation brought God's love into all truth, it can act in such simple truths to save men and women from selfishness. The Gentiles were to be saved as much as the Jews. The only distinction was in the kind of truth that was available to them. The same division exists today between those who know about Jesus, whose great danger is that they may misuse their knowledge, and those who do not know but who may seek to love others and need to learn. Upbringing and environment may well make it difficult for some of them to accept new ideas in this world; but ideas can be learned in the life after death, decisions about loving others are made here and now. Salvation is universal. Every man or woman has the ability to choose to love others by the truths they know, and so receive the redeeming love of Jesus Christ, whether they know his name or not.

1–8. And the Pharisees and some of the scribes who had come from Jerusalem approached Jesus. They had seen some of his disciples eating bread with hands not ceremonially washed and that were therefore "defiled," and they found fault with them. For the Pharisees and all the Jews will not eat unless they ceremonially wash their hands, following the tradi-

tion of the elders; and they will not eat when they come from the market unless they have washed; and there are many other things that they accept as binding, such as the washing of cups and pots and copper vessels and couches. So the Pharisees and the scribes asked him, "Why do not your disciples follow the tradition of the elders, but eat bread with their hands unwashed?" But he answered them, "Isaiah prophesied well concerning you hypocrites, where it is written, 'This people honor me with their lips, but their heart is far away from me. But they worship me in vain, teaching as doctrine the commands of men.' For leaving on one side the commandment of God, you follow the tradition of men by washing pots and cups and many similar practices."

When Jesus came on earth, religion with many of the Jews had become largely a matter of performing certain external actions. Things and actions became holy if you went through a certain ritual. If you did not, you were sinning. The temple worship demanded the washing of priests, vestments, and vessels, so that they would be seen to be ceremonially clean for the service of the Lord. These commands were extended by the Pharisees to individuals and things for everyday life, and so an intricate system of customs was devised and made obligatory for those who wanted to be holy. The primitive Israelites had needed to grasp that God was holy and his will was to be respected, and in a simple way the practices of temple worship achieved this. At the same time, those methods of worship could act as a parable for the genuine cleansing of life from selfishness and its real dedication to the Lord. But the Pharisees had perpetuated these temple customs in everyday life, where the real responsibilities of religion had to do with personal service to the neighbor and so to the Lord, hence their obsession with outward observances and their failure to see their real duty.

The passage quoted from Isaiah 29:13 is not directly from the Hebrew text, but from the Greek translation used by many Jews, the Septuagint. The Hebrew has "their fear of me is a commandment of men learned by rote," where the Septuagint has translated "in vain do they worship me, teaching the commandments and doctrines of men." The ideas are similar, but the latter certainly applies better here. Jews accustomed to hear the Hebrew read in the synagogue, but used to reading the Greek of the Septuagint, were liable to quote from one or the other; and sometimes a quotation is recalled, presumably from memory, with changes in the order of words and phrases. All this can be woven together providentially by God to give a text with the inner sense we need.

We can recognize easily enough that some Jewish observances had become merely an outward sham that had nothing to do with the love in the heart that really makes religion. Yet it is surprising how often we seek to use our own religion in such ways. We argue over what should not be done on a Sunday, rather than working out what should be done to help others. And it is not so long since a certain kind of clothes or an unusual haircut were regarded as not fit for worship in church. As soon as one custom passes away, another one seems to be invented to judge the behavior of others and give us a cozy sense of conforming to our religion. The kind of church music people do or do not like, the kind of words they want to use in worship, the structure of their human organizations—all these become important religious issues, yet they have nothing to do with a genuine religion of life. We must realize how powerful is such behavior in our own individual life. It is comfortable to have a yardstick by which to judge our Christianity, and so we seek shelter behind certain outward deeds and words as though they were some assurance that we are being a Christian. We are only truly Christian when we are trying to use the love Jesus brought to us to judge and speak in all our life. We cannot set up a ritual to take the place of life itself.

We have seen already that water in the gospel symbolizes the water of life, the truth from God that slakes our thirst for his ways; the Jewish customs condemned here show us using that essential truth to prepare our own exemption from sin. Our hands, which should be powerful in the world, are ritually cleansed by going through the motions when others can see us, rather than directed with the power of love in every situation we meet. Every human-made container of correct behavior is carefully washed in the ideas about truth. The truth then ceases to have its real power in our lives but is reckoned to be fulfilled in following the human-made moral behavior. Truth is the living embodiment of God's love, the pattern by which it works in the world. If we separate the pattern from the love that gives it meaning, we have made it ineffectual, a ritual of a religion.

> *9–13. And he said to them, "You set aside completely the commandment of God, so that you can follow your traditions. For Moses said, 'Honor your father and your mother' and 'He who speaks evil of his father or mother, let him die the death.' But you say if a man says to his father or mother, 'Whatever you might have gained from me is corban, that is, a*

gift,' you no longer oblige him to do anything for his father or mother. Thus you make void the Word of God by the tradition that you preserve. And you do many similar things."

It is not possible now to know in detail what custom is indicated here. "Corban" is only known elsewhere as being a Jewish oath. But it is clear from Jesus' statement that, by this oath, what was necessary to maintain a man's parents could be vowed as a gift for religious purposes, probably in the temple. Such a promise might have been for the future and not an immediate gift, and thus a present responsibility to parents could be transformed into a future payment to religion. Thus, one of the commandments could be broken by following what was merely a religious tradition.

The command to honor father and mother goes beyond our earthly parents and applies to our heavenly Father and to the true mother church formed out of lives lived by men and women from his love. Our prime duty in life is to honor these spiritual powers. Outward practices of religious life can be substituted for this, and the individual may dedicate all he has to a "religiosity," a set of outward customs that do not arise from the genuine active love of a Christian. When stated blatantly like this, it seems obviously wrong, but it is very easy for us to fall into such an error. We prefer to use a system as our religion. It will keep all the love of Jesus at arm's length and prevent its activity in our lives. The need to bring redeeming love into every human relationship can be forgotten, and we can believe that all we need to do is to go through the usual motions. They soon become such that we think we can have exactly what we want, while declaring that we are serving God. So our lives neither sustain our love for our heavenly Father nor increase that true power of love that is the real mother church. Spiritually we are dead, which is why the command Jesus quoted says that one who offends father and mother so deeply shall die the death.

> *14–23. And calling to him all the crowd, he said to them, "Listen all of you, and understand. There is nothing from outside a man that can defile him by entering into him. But the things that come out of him are those that defile him. If you have ears, use them!" And when he went into a house away from the crowd, his disciples asked him about the parable. And he said to them, "So are you also without understanding? Do you not see that everything that comes from outside and enters a man cannot defile him, because it does not enter his heart, but his stomach, and then passes out of the body." So all food is made clean. And he said, "What comes out of a man defiles him, for from the heart of man go forth evil thoughts: adultery, lust, murder, theft, greed, wickedness, deceit, vice, envy, slander, pride, folly. All these evil things from inside him come out and defile man."*

Strictures about what foods may be eaten are a feature of many religions. In the Old Testament, the Israelites were given many such commands. They serve a purpose with primitive men and women, for when there can be no grasp of the real purpose of God's love, people need some external laws to obey and so show their willingness to submit to God's will. Such laws about food were fashioned as parables to enshrine our spiritual needs, but the outward laws do not achieve anything in themselves. Jesus taught the people to abandon all external rituals and instead to use the real service that his love could do in their lives if they would accept him. So he urges them to take care about what comes from their hearts into their lives, and not about what they are putting into their mouths.

When we read Mark's gospel personally, we can see a clear message for us in all this. We have a great tendency to judge life by what comes to us, and not by what we put into life. This leads us to concentrate on setting up a fence around our life to keep contrary things from intruding, rather than trying to put love into life by what we do. From medieval monasteries to the closed social circles of Victorian life, people have tried to prevent the intrusion of the unacceptable. But we shall not be contaminated by whatever wrong behavior may come into our orbit. If our love is to serve the Lord, it will come through from our heart and reject what is vile and evil. Our real danger lies within ourselves. The selfishness within us can produce every greed, lust, and abomination, if we let it. We are not controlled by outward circumstances, which simply come into our lives. They can be handled by our Christian will, which can cast out whatever is wrong. We are controlled by the things we let come out of ourselves. The real danger is expressed in that long list of evil powers that can come out of our hearts, if we do not live from the love of Jesus.

Inevitably, this subject brings to mind questions of censorship and efforts to restrict the lives of others for (it is asserted) their own good. While children are growing up and learning about life, there are clear grounds for some such influence, but still it has to be recognized that children have to be prepared for the actual world, with all its imperfections. There is no point in isolating them in a way that prevents awareness of such things. The value of censorship and restriction is limited. By adult years, only words and behavior that deliberately seek maliciously to pervert and mislead require such a fence. For the rest, "truth is great, and greatly will prevail"; or, to put it in the gospel terms, individuals can cast out whatever enters that is wrong and will only be harmed spiritually by that which they choose to let loose from their own evil within.

> *24–30. And leaving there, he went away into the neighborhood of Tyre and Sidon. And he went into a house and wanted no one to know where he was, but he could not be hidden. For hearing of him, a woman whose little daughter had an evil spirit came and fell at his feet. Now the woman was a Greek, Syrophoenician by birth, and she asked him to cast the devil out of her daughter; but Jesus said, "Let the children have all they want first, for it is not good to take the children's bread and throw it to the little dogs." But she answered, "Yes, Lord, but even the little dogs under the table eat what the children leave." And he said to her, "For that reply, go home; the devil has left your daughter." And going back to her house, she found the devil had left her daughter who was lying on the bed.*

Jesus has been talking with the leaders of Judaism. Now he goes out of their territory into Gentile country on the coast by Tyre and Sidon. Even though this area does not acknowledge Jewish teaching, his reputation as a healer is known, and it is still impossible for him to escape from the people. A local woman of Greek stock comes to him for help. Jesus' reply to the woman's request seems, at first sight, to follow the ideas of the very people he has been reproving, who believed they were a special people and all others lesser breeds without privileges. The epithet "dogs" was used for outsiders, likening them to the pariah dogs that ran around the streets, mere scavengers. The dog was not a valued pet in those days but scrounged a living from the food people discarded. At this distance, we cannot know quite why Jesus couched his response so sharply in the terms used by those who felt themselves superior to others, though it is intriguing that he softens the derogatory "dogs" by using the half-affectionate diminutive "little dogs." There are enough occasions in the gospel when Jesus declares that he loves the "sheep who are not of this fold" to make clear that he would not accept any despising of those not born into a faith. Perhaps his reply was teasing, deliberately intended to challenge the woman to respond as she did and find a truer faith in him.

We need to look for the personal message this incident has in our own individual lives. A certain amount of our living is done within what we know of the Christian faith. That can truly be said to be one of the "children of God" in us, and to feed at the Lord's table on his love and truth about life. But a great deal of our life does not feed directly on Jesus' teaching of love and has not yet been considered or planned by Christian truth. Such areas of thought and decision are on the outskirts of our Christianity, "in Gentile country" as it were. Most Christians have large parts of their lives and activity still not thought through from the vision of love. Much of our work is done in the economic structure and work practices that surround us. Contacts with others follow the social customs used by them. A vast amount of learning about scientific matters is not related at all to the love of God, which creates and maintains the universe science is examining. Yet much of the way our life affects others is decided in these areas, where we have no clear view of our responsibilities from faith.

Jesus' challenge here is to make us think about this fringe area of our life. It is characterized as being "a dog's life." Left to themselves, dogs tend to run round in circles and bark without much purpose. They provide a symbol for much of our outward life, which is full of purposeless activity. Clearly, we need help to remove any devil of selfishness from this worldly behavior, but how can it come to the Lord's power for healing? How can we relate it to divine teaching? You cannot take "the children's bread" and apply it directly to such areas of life. Yet, like the woman, we must recognize that our outward life needs the crumbs of true direction that fall from the table of a true faith. Many of the decisions we make in life seem so practical and earthly that it is difficult to work them out from exalted Christian principles. When we are discussing obvious matters of religious principles and moral decisions, we feed easily enough on the ideas and motives that are fed to us by the Lord from his table. Then we are in "religious country." When we go out into the surrounding worldly rat race and wrestle with its problems, we seem to be in an area that can hardly feed on such high principles. Nevertheless, the crumbs of loving others and serving them must fall down into these very mundane decisions, or the devil of our selfishness will gain power there. If we cannot reshape the world of business completely to love and serve others, still we can be honest and helpful and loving in the particular job we do in that world.

Such simple obedience to our faith in the turmoil of modern life will seem merely "crumbs," coming from all we love and want to do with our lives and falling into a very foreign environment. But only this will ever heal the world. Although the structure of society, economics, and business practice may seem to be driven on solely by

self-interest, lacking any thought of loving service, our behavior in it can still be thoughtful of others. We can concentrate on the service we give, rather than the money we
make; we can maintain truly human relationships with colleagues and customers. Such things will not change the
overall structure of society, for that will always reflect the
attitudes and efforts of the majority, but it will change its
impact on those we deal with and help. Like the woman,
we need to recognize our need for Christian love to affect
even the humdrum daily round, which can seem far away
from the heart of our faith. We need to see the world as
God's world, both when we learn about it and when we
live in it. Only so can the devil of selfishness be removed
from our earthly life.

> *31–37. And again, leaving the neighborhood of Tyre
> and Sidon, he came to the Sea of Galilee across the
> country of the Decapolis. And they brought him a
> deaf man who could only speak with difficulty, and
> asked him to lay his hand on him. And he took him
> apart from the crowd, and put his fingers in his ears,
> and spat and touched his tongue. And he looked up
> to heaven and sighed deeply, and said to him, "Eph-
> phatha," that is, "Open!" And immediately his ears
> were opened and his tongue freed, and he spoke
> clearly. And he commanded them not to tell anyone;
> but the more he told them not to do so, the more they
> talked about it. And people were greatly astonished
> and said, "How well he does everything! He even
> makes the deaf hear and the dumb speak."*

The ten cities of the Decapolis were east of the Sea of
Galilee, and a journey to the lake by that route would have
meant a considerable circuit from Tyre and Sidon; but

since the gospels are based on recollections of past happenings, they may not be in chronological order. Here we seem to have a series of incidents originally coupled together for teaching about Jews and Gentiles, and Mark does not relocate them so as to fit the geography of the area. We simply enter another Gentile area on the east of the Sea of Galilee; and again Jesus helps someone in trouble, a deaf man who can only speak with difficulty. This might mean a deaf-mute. The rare Greek word used for "speak with difficulty" is used as the equivalent of the Hebrew for "dumb" in translating the Old Testament. On the other hand, someone totally deaf was probably also practically dumb before modern speech therapy. Not being able to hear speech, he could not imitate it. The end of the passage makes it clear that one deaf and dumb, from whatever cause, was healed. The Aramaic word used in the healing is given and translated, as was that in Mark 5:38–43.

We have just considered the help that is needed in worldly life, where it may seem to be very detached from our Christian faith. This second healing in Gentile country really reveals how that help is gained. The problem is that, in everyday affairs, we may not be able to hear what the truth is saying. So the healing is of a deaf man. Now Jesus always makes a very strong link between hearing him and obeying. We have seen him call to the crowd to listen, and say, "If you have ears, use them!" And he is not calling just for them to hear his words, but to obey them. We have noted before that parents often ask a child, "Are you deaf?" when they mean "Why are you not obeying me?" To hear is to obey. For us, this miracle means that we are brought to obey Jesus in those Gentile areas of our life, which seem so detached from our faith. His power is a love for others, and it is this we obey in mundane situations. We may not be able to see the overall solution of all the world's problems, we may not at times see fully how our actions will affect all those involved; nothing is so cut and dried as in our theological discussions. But we can still try to find a way to love others in the situation we can see at the moment. Looking for a way to love others and to help them transforms our worldly life.

This healing is not done by vague emotion. Jesus uses the water of spittle from his mouth, as a sign that the water of truth from him is healing. We still need truth in practical everyday affairs, but now it prompts what individual action we should take in the situation we see, rather than providing a complete rational understanding of all the factors at work. Often an issue is clouded by arguments that, because a system is faulty or because others use a system dishonestly, we are also entitled to use it to our own advantage. The weakness of a system or its abuse may provide a reason to change it, but until that change comes about, we are required to act honestly in it and try to help our fellows by our endeavors. We must honor the water of truth that Jesus uses to heal our life. The attitude of the modern rat race of life insists that if we do not "keep up with the Joneses," we may let down our spouse, our children, and our friends. It is very easy to be driven on toward such goals set by a mercenary world. Let the truth wash over our minds and we can see immediately the falsity of the argument. The responsibility we have for our family is to try to provide the opportunity to love and serve the way of Jesus. To set an example to our children of ruthless acquisitiveness may provide them with an expensive education, but it will have taught them already that loving the neighbor as ourselves is not a sensible option. The decisions we have to make in practical "Gentile" life are constantly confused by the world's assertion that the economic stress of business working life makes self-preservation the only rule. Such an attitude will make us permanently deaf to the demands of the Gospel to love others and seek to share God's world with them; and yet in any system the opportunities to do just that are there.

Once we really hear Jesus and obey him, our mouths are freed to praise him, for every help to others is a way of praising the Lord. Praise in worship is only a way of acknowledging the love of the Lord and the changes it can bring about in our lives. When we obey him in daily life, we acknowledge that love and let it change our lives. We live the praise that our lips only say. In this spiritual way, there is a link between deafness and being mute. Until we hear, that is, obey in the way we live our lives, they are not able to praise. Once we do obey, every day of our lives speaks praise to the Lord.

Here, again, we see the Lord trying to silence those he has helped. This "conspiracy of silence" is almost a theme in Mark. It has its origin in the fact that too great rejoicing after a spiritual improvement can divert the mind from the work that still needs to be done and actually weaken what has been achieved. We are all aware that moments of spiritual development and insight can begin to fade and change as soon as we congratulate ourselves on what has been achieved. It is better to go on striving than to indulge in noisy spiritual stocktaking.

Chapter Eight

BLIND DISCIPLES

This chapter shows a growing intensity. So far the ministry of teaching and healing has shown his disciples that Jesus has power, but now this begins to involve them personally in stress and the prospect of pain. The very way God is doing his work means that his life in Jesus is to oppose and cast out all the egotism and evil men and women have brought into human nature. We can only realize the nature of divine love if we realize what it will endure to save us. And we can only use the power he brings if we too face up to the nature of that evil. Now we begin to see the battle lines drawn, and we personally may be as appalled as the disciples were when they realized the road they were treading. The gospel is not a description of events that we can read and enjoy. It portrays a divine love in combat with human evil. And it draws us into the same desperate battle in our own lives.

It may seem strange to us that the disciples seem to gain some understanding of Jesus' work and then often fail to use it. We might feel that they are stupid and slow to learn; but the change that had come over their lives was not easy to absorb, and they were unaccustomed to think as Jesus did. However, the disciples' constant backsliding illustrates a problem we all have in our Christian development. We learn ideas about God's purpose for us and other people, and we think this is adequate for Christian life; but we have deep-seated selfish desires that oppose those ideas. To start to live from the truth brings that selfishness into immediate opposition. While we are thinking about truth, it all seems acceptable and desirable, but when it begins to want to change our life, strongly opposing desires seek to destroy its action. This is why the disciples are often shown learning some idea from Jesus and apparently accepting it strongly and joyfully, only to be blind to its real meaning shortly after.

The repetition of similar stories in the gospel often causes scholars to suspect a second telling of one event; but in a three-year ministry, largely in one area, circumstances and problems must have recurred. Whatever their origin, they are in the gospel to portray our own lives. We find it strange that, in similar circumstances in a similar place, the disciples show the same lack of understanding and ask the same questions as they have already done; but this is our own experience. How often we find ourselves learning the same lesson all over again, simply because in our lives we have not applied what we learned the first time. Our spiritual development is not a logical development of ideas; it is a constant battle with recurring self-centered preoccupations.

The process of our development is, therefore, a succession of joyful visions, followed by disastrous backsliding. When we are involved in thought or worship with a religious group, we will for the moment share their confidence and their vision. When we pray to the Lord and talk out a problem with him, we think we see our way clear to repent and change our life to his way. But once we go back into ordinary life, our self-love (which so far has been untouched) rises up and opposes our new vision, often to such an extent that we cannot recall the certainty and joy of the moment when we realized our true way. This is a necessary part of our process of change. Our selfish nature must be subdued if the Lord's love is to control our life. So we endure fluctuations from a moment of truth down to our blind selfishness and eventually up to a genuine repentance and a regaining of the true vision. This is the only way our evil desires can be drawn into the battle and overcome. This process is the real reason for the religious grouping of people. They can lift one another by worship, teaching, discussion, and example into a vision of the real demand of truth. This is why we all need each other. We cannot save each other, but the Lord can use us to clarify the call of truth to each other. Then each must fight his or her own selfishness in the Lord's strength. It is tragic that religious groupings have often been seen not in this light, but as ways of controlling and disciplining people into particular patterns of worship and behavior. We should rejoice that such attitudes are now being questioned and broken down.

There is no way of short-circuiting this process of rise and fall by cleverer or more detailed learning. What blinds us is our selfish desires in life, and we have to recognize their opposition and conquer it. Only when what we want is in line with the truth shall we see what it can do to us. Until then, our selfishness will always blind us.

1–9. At that time, because the crowd was very great and had nothing to eat, Jesus called his disciples and said to them, "I am moved with compassion for this crowd, because they have stayed with me three days already without anything to eat; and if I send them away to their homes hungry they will collapse on the way, for some of them have come a great distance." And the disciples answered him, "Where can anyone get bread to satisfy them in a desert?" And he asked them, "How many loaves have you?" And they said, "Seven." And he told the crowd to sit down on the ground, and taking the seven loaves he gave thanks and broke them, and gave them to the disciples to distribute to them. And they set it before the crowd. And they had a few small fish, and having blessed these he asked them to give these to the people as well. And they ate and were satisfied, and they gathered up more than seven baskets of pieces left over. And about four thousand had eaten. And he sent them away.

The feeding of the five thousand in Mark 6:35–44 is very like this passage. It would seem that, in similar circumstances, Jesus acted to use his power in a similar way and expressed again the message that he was the power of God brought upon earth. Are we to assume, then, that for us personally, this adds nothing to the message of the feeding of the five thousand? The general meaning must be much the same. To be in a desert is to realize one's own lack of any true life. The small amounts of bread and fish show that we have only the beginnings of love and truth, and the feeding of so many shows that, if we obey Jesus' command, this can be multiplied to fill all our life and still leave power to fill yet more. The obvious differences are in the numbers of loaves, fish, people, and baskets of fragments.

Numbers appear to play an important part in the Word and are stressed beyond any casual use. Perhaps here the figure "seven" can add a little more to our personal understanding. The seventh day marked the culmination of creation, when rest and peace followed struggle. It marked what was holy, as the command for the Sabbath day stresses, and holiness comes from love and the good it accomplishes. It would seem that here the seven loaves used in the feeding express an increase in holy love, which is now available to feed the thoughts of the mind. Before there were five loaves, a handful as it were, showing little love available but enough to set the mind working from it. The seven baskets of fragments taken up point to the same idea as the seven loaves. What is still available for further development has the quality of love and its holiness, and this will be the prime mover in the future. Although we are fighting very similar battles against our selfish nature, some love will have been strengthened in us from our earlier efforts.

On the other hand the fish (which we have seen are the truths that disciples catch on to) were before clearly known to be two. Here the fish are vaguely a "few small fish," as though the fish were very much an afterthought to the loaves. It all suggests that things are progressing so that the heart with its love is much more the region from which the Lord is helping us and that the knowledge of truth is dropping into its correct level of importance as only the means to bring about such love.

The number fed shows the same emphasis. We saw that five indicates a little, but enough power to set things working. Five loaves feeding five thousand indicates a little working with a great many needs in our lives, which still only realize a little of their need. Seven loaves feeding four thousand indicates a holier power in love working with the great needs of a more balanced mind, a "foursquare" mind, in which any truth feels the need of love to make it work. The story as a whole, then, is showing a development that makes the love we show to our fellows the center of our lives, rather than what we know and understand of truth.

> *10–12. And immediately boarding the boat with his disciples, he came to the region of Dalmanutha. And the Pharisees went out and began an argument with him, asking him for a sign from heaven to try him. And having sighed deeply in his spirit, he said, "Why does this generation seek a sign? In truth, I tell you this generation will be given no sign."*

It is difficult to determine where the incidents in this chapter took place. Dalmanutha is unknown. At the end of chapter 7, Jesus was in the Decapolis, east of the Sea of Galilee. Later we find they set out to go to "the other side" of the lake and arrive at Bethsaida. If the feeding of the four thousand took place in the Decapolis, this boat trip may only have taken them along the coast. On the other hand, Mark is probably doing no more than stringing together incidents, possibly told in Peter's preaching, which have no real sequence of movement. Providence has ensured that they have a spiritual sequence of value to us in the way they are told here, whereas they have no discernible sequence topographically.

It seems at first remarkable that the Pharisees should challenge Jesus for a sign, when their whole confrontation had arisen from the many miracles he had done; but the request illustrates for us a considerable personal problem of our own. When we do not want to do something, we often insist that others must "prove" that we should. In effect, no amount of rational proof is going to prove anything to us because we do not want to do it. It is somewhat startling to realize how much our will controls what we see. We only see what we want to see. This is why the gospel begins with a demand for repentance, a choice to live life in a new way. We have enough understanding of what hurts our fellows and what can help them, and could make a decision about our way of life. What is required is an act of our will. Once that move is made, our love for others wants to see the truth, and so we accept the Lord's teaching and his action in our life as a true sign of his power. But without the desire to love others and follow his way, no amount of argument will change our hearts. They can only be changed by a choice about the way we live.

The Pharisees here show the attitude taken up by spurious religion in us. Since it has no wish to give up its selfish power and be obliged to love others, it only challenges the demands of truth in order to disprove them. The Pharisees have no intention of believing. No sign will ever be adequate to convince them; therefore, they cannot be given a sign. If our minds become defensive of our selfish ways, we shall never see the sign for change that the truth witnesses to us constantly.

13–21. And he left them, and boarding the boat again he went away to the other side of the lake. The disciples had forgotten to take any bread, and had only one loaf with them in the boat. And he warned them, "Watch out for the leaven of the Pharisees and the leaven of Herod." And they worked this out between them to mean that they had no bread. And knowing this Jesus said to them, "Why do you argue that it is because you have no bread? Do you still not see or understand? Have you still hardened your heart? Having eyes, can you not see, and having ears can you not hear, and do you not remember? When I divided five loaves among the five thousand, how many baskets full of pieces left over did you pick up?" They said to him, "Twelve." "And when I divided seven among the four thousand, how many baskets of pieces did you pick up?" And they said, "Seven." And he said to them, "Why do you not understand?"

On two occasions, by using the bread available, Jesus has taught his disciples to rely on his power to feed them, and in that we have seen represented his power to feed our minds with love. Now he introduces another factor, concerned in the making of bread. If the flour mixture is left by itself and baked, it does not rise into the kind of loaves we know, but produces a flat biscuitlike bread. Only if yeast is added to the dough and allowed to work in it will it rise from the gases produced and, when baked, produce the bread we are accustomed to. The Jewish custom was not to use new yeast for each batch of bread, but to preserve a little of the old dough in which the yeast was still working, "the leaven," and then add this to a new batch of dough. There were occasions, as at the feast of unleavened bread following the Passover, when the Jews were commanded to eat only unleavened bread; but at the feast of weeks that marked the end of the corn harvest, leavened bread was to be offered (Leviticus 23:15–17).

Jesus clearly uses the leaven to stand for some factor in our receiving "the bread of life." In Matthew 16:5–12, where the same incident is told, it is clear that eventually the disciples realized that the "leaven" of the Pharisees and others was their false teaching. When we are using the truth of Jesus' teachings in order to receive his love in our hearts, it is as though he is baking the bread of eternal life on which we are to feed. But if any wrong and false ideas from our self-love get into our mix of understanding and loving, then it will set up a ferment that will change the nature of the good we feed on in our lives. At all the pure and holy moments of our lives, there will be no leaven of falsity and the truth will produce genuine good in our lives. (The feast of unleavened bread at Passover represents such a time.) If any "leaven" of false ideas is present, then the good we use will be different.

If the false ideas come from our own evil and selfishness, they will pervert and destroy any real notion of what is good. This is the "leaven of the Pharisees and of Herod" that Jesus bids us beware. It is totally destructive of the genuine "bread of life" that loves and helps others. However, there will be mistaken ideas in our mind, which come from the way we have to learn and which we have not yet got rid of. They also will change our vision of the good we can see and accept in our lives. This "leaven" is not destructive; rather it is part of our growing up as a Christian, for it is steadily worked out and eventually recognized for what it is.

This kind of false idea cannot be avoided by any of us, however honest our endeavors. And this is why in Matthew 13:33 the kingdom of heaven with us is likened to a woman's hiding leaven in flour until the whole was leavened. Jesus knows that we cannot escape false ideas, which often come from oversimplifying truth in early days of learning. Part of the kingdom of heaven he establishes in each one of us must be by working out these ideas. In our efforts to live a good life, we come to realize that they are wrong. So we have leavened bread offered at the Jewish feast of weeks, which comes in the middle of the cycle of feasts; but at the end comes the feast of unleavened bread when all has become holy and no leaven exists.

The disciples were so concerned over the bread they had or had not got that they failed to understand Jesus' warning. We can be as blind if we concentrate simply on doing good and pay no attention to the kinds of ideas that exist in our minds. We must be on the watch for any ideas that our old self is using in us. These we can detect from their origin, and it is essential that we reject them, for as Jesus says they are the "leaven of the Pharisees and of Herod." They are the false ways of thinking that our selfishness manufactures in our inner desires and our worldly life, which will destroy us as a Christian. If we are holding on to any idea because it enables us to keep some selfish habit, or because it preserves our pride in our religion, or enables us to keep some men or women at arm's length from our compassion, then we are keeping some of "the leaven of the Pharisees and of Herod" in our thinking, and that will destroy our power to love others.

On the other hand, we shall all have made mistakes in our grasp of truth, and have blind and contrary ideas mixed in with our understanding of it. This is the leaven that the woman mixed with the flour in the image of the kingdom of heaven, and these wrong notions will eventually be seen for what they are. There is a warning here not to be adamant that the first way we see the gospel ideas is perfect. The more we read, the more we shall come to see what its message really means, and this will often mean changes of emphasis and understanding in our belief. All this will be worked out as we concentrate on receiving Jesus' love in a life of service to others. Only a hidden motive of selfishness behind any wrong idea makes it dangerous to our Christian life, and we need to examine our motives constantly to root out such evil leaven.

> *22–26. And he came to Bethsaida, and they brought a blind man to him, pleading that he would touch him. And he took the hand of the blind man and led him out of the village. And when he had spat upon his eyes and laid his hands upon him, he asked him if he saw anything. And looking up he said, "I can see men; but as trees walking." Then again he laid his hands on his eyes and made him look up, and he recovered and saw everyone clearly. And he sent him to his house, saying, "You must not enter the village, nor speak about it to anyone in the village."*

This appears to be another detached incident of Jesus' compassion in giving a blind man sight. But in the preceding section we have seen the blindness of the disciples over the warning about leaven. This healing enlarges our understanding of the remedy for that situation in our personal lives. We are blind when we cannot understand something of the Lord's way. The first step in the cure is bringing the blind man to be touched and healed. Obvious as it may seem, this is often forgotten. We try to work out truth by arguing with one another about what is meant. Our blindness can only be healed if we come to Jesus with his way of love and compassion. We must be seeking a way of loving life if we are to understand. While we argue in our own strength, we only increase our blindness.

If we come to Jesus, he first leads us out of our present attitude, "out of the village," for we are to seek now a way of loving and serving. Then Jesus spits water from his mouth on the blind eyes. He is the source of "the water of everlasting life," the truth of his Word. Our blindness needs washing in such truth; we must try to think from his ideas.

Then, in the power of Jesus' hands, we begin to see. At first, it is restricted vision. The blind man saw men as trees walking about. The basic difference between plant life and animal life is that plants only grow in structure, whereas animals also have lives active from their desires and purposes. While we are restricted to thinking about the truth, it grows into a pattern for human living, and our view of other men and women is restricted to this pattern. We see them as called to play their parts in the pattern of divine truth. We do not see beyond the way truth grows, and people appear only as "trees" grown out of ideas.

It is the general attitude of the world today to regard men and women in this way, as "thinking machines." A true vision would be of the affection and love in human beings, which makes them truly human. So, in this healing, Jesus increases his power and bids the man—and us—to look up, to grasp his high purpose—seeing from compassionate love for every man and woman, and so seeing them as living creatures of love. They are not just ciphers in a pattern of truth they can obey. Each of them is a child of God, wonderfully loved and so able to love others.

Once we have this vision of life, we must not go back to the old way of thinking, "back into the village," or have anything to do with it. With our eyes open to the real meaning of our lives, we must live them from the spirit of Jesus.

27–30. And Jesus and his disciples went away into the villages of Caesarea Philippi. And on the way he asked his disciples, "Who do men say that I am?" And they answered, "John the Baptist, or some say Elijah, and others one of the prophets." And he said to them, "But you, who do you say I am?" And Peter answering said to him, "You are the Christ." And he strictly commanded them to tell no one about him.

They go away northwards now, to the region where the Jordan has its source, perhaps to gain some privacy, perhaps to avoid for a while the increasing pressure in Galilee. Here Mark's gospel reaches a first climax. The disciples still have much to learn and to endure, but now comes the first assertion of belief in Jesus as the Messiah, the Christ. They begin to realize that they are not just following a teacher and miracle worker. They are caught up in something far greater. God is coming to them in his anointed one.

For us, personally, the gospel is teaching of a great change that comes in our Christian life. So far we have followed to learn about a new way of life. We have seen how it can cure so many of the world's ills. We have realized that it could change our lives fundamentally. But eventually it is borne in on us that we are not just following a new teaching, of which many abound in the world. We are entering upon a new relationship with God who sustains our life and everything around us. In answer to Jesus' first question, many attitudes to him are summarized. He can be thought of as John the Baptist risen from the dead, that is, as a call to repentance in life and a change in our behavior. He can be imagined as Elijah, the truth that comes before great change. Or he can be imagined as a prophet, a teacher of truth. How often do we see him this way, simply as a source of ideas about life?

However, when Jesus questions a second time, he is answered with a Christian's real understanding. He is the Christ, the Messiah, the anointed one of God. This lifts us into quite another dimension. We are not concerned merely with teaching about a way of life. We are to live for others with the power of love God has sent into our lives. The Messiah is anointed with the love of God. If we follow our new Christian life, we are living with God. From love he will illuminate our thinking and empower our activity in life. This does not mean that we have become perfect. We have seen that Peter stands for our faith, and this faith declares a belief in the Christ. It has accepted the relationship we have with God in Jesus, but, as the gospel shows, there are still many misunderstandings and weaknesses that will have to be realized and changed. It is just that we have realized the nature of what we are doing in following Jesus.

Jesus commands the disciples to tell no one about him; and the word used is very strong, as if he were rebuking them as he commands them. Much of the criticism directed at those who are "born again" comes because they can appear to claim a correct and infallible life from this point on. It is not so, and we are strictly commanded not to assume it. We must not assert that this new attitude is an accepted power, which is going to work in our lives with no further hindrance. We have still to realize how it will devastate much of our old life and in what danger we stand of failing in our faith. We have accepted the true attitude to Jesus. Now we have to work it out, not simply declare that we are saved.

31–33. And he began to teach them that it was nec-
essary for the Son of Man to suffer many things, and
to be rejected by the elders and chief priests and
scribes, and to be killed and after three days to rise
again. And he spoke about this quite clearly. And
Peter took him and began to rebuke him. But he,
turning and looking at his disciples, rebuked Peter,
saying, "Get behind me, Satan, for you are not
thinking of God's ways, but of the ways of men."

Jesus calls himself "the Son of Man" when he speaks of
the suffering and stress he must endure in his battles against
evil for our salvation. The term is used in Hebrew poetry
for "man" in general; but in Ezekiel it refers to the prophet
who is teaching truth and battling against evil in the people.
In the Aramaic of Daniel 7:13–14, it is used in a vision of
one who, after great conflict, is given dominion over all
peoples in a kingdom that will not be destroyed. Jesus is the
origin of the term for himself, and it does not seem at that
time to have been used of the Messiah. Presumably, without
asserting yet his claim to be the Messiah, it enables him to
refer to his use of truth in his desperate battles against evil
in the human mind by which he saved us all.

Now the heart of Jesus' teaching begins to be revealed.
He is the Messiah, or Christ, but not in the way the Jews
looked for him to come. They anticipated a conqueror,
who would free their nation and make them rulers of the
world. They remembered the assertions of his power in
Scripture, but they conveniently forgot the prophecies of a
suffering servant, who by his attitude of love and service
would accomplish the great change in the world. The
power of God is a power of love at work in humankind,
not a dominating despotism that satisfies us with what we

want. Jesus makes clear that his way of truth is to be a way of suffering and rejection by the world, so that he can show the power of love in the midst of hatred and evil. This love must be accepted in the hearts of men and women to bring about any change; God is not going to force a change upon humanity. Peter summarily rejects the idea of bringing change in this way. Whether from Jewish ideas about the Messiah or just from a rejection of so much suffering for Jesus and so much disaster for their hopes, Peter cannot accept such a way. The faith that had just declared belief in Christ cannot accept how he will work, and so becomes an adversary, "a Satan," to his purpose.

We must receive as severe a jolt from the gospel at this point as Peter did. We may have accepted that Jesus has brought God's love into us to change us; but we cannot accept that the only way it is going to work is by using truth, which will then be rejected by false and evil ways in us, suffering in opposition to our worldly ways. Yet those accepted ways in us kill God's love and make it powerless. Only then, if we will choose to reject them, can he rise up in us as our very life.

The Christian needs this warning, and it is repeated twice more in the gospel. There is no easy way for God in Jesus to power our mind. We shall not really let the power of his love rise up in our lives until we have realized how much in our religion is selfish and only wants peace and happiness and truth for us, and not so that we can love and help others. It is difficult to realize that our faith, which looks to Jesus, wants things for us and so is an adversary, "a Satan," to Jesus. Only by revealing this fundamental self-seeking in us can he help us. Only when we see that it kills the working of his love can we reject it, and then his love can rise up in the whole of our life.

34–38. And calling the crowd to him with his disciples he said to them, "Whoever wants to follow me must deny himself, and must take up his cross and follow me. For whoever wants to save his life will lose it, and whoever loses his life for me and the good news will save it. For what good is it for a man to gain the whole world and lose his soul? Or what can a man give in exchange for his soul? For whoever is ashamed of me and my words in this adulterous and sinful generation, the Son of Man will also be ashamed of him when he comes in his Father's glory with the holy angels."

The introduction of the cross here suggests the use of a well-known symbol for suffering, which it may well have been during the Roman occupation, when exposure on a cross was the common form of death for offenders. Nevertheless, for us it must also associate with the crucifixion of Jesus and indeed occurs here after his prophecy of his own death. The cross was not merely an instrument of torture made of wood, but it was the symbol of all the selfish love of power in the chief priests, and all the love of the things of the world by them and the Roman authority, which were the real agents of Jesus' death. So the cross symbolizes all the selfish evil in human beings, which Jesus had to challenge and expose, even to death.

In our case, Jesus openly challenges us personally to see this force at work in ourselves. Each of us has this selfishness deep down in our heart. It motivates much of our life, at work or at play. It contaminates our homes, our places of work, the whole of our social scene. If we accept Jesus' challenge, it becomes a cross of suffering, because we must oppose it as it tries to control our thoughts and our behavior. We cannot follow Jesus, unless we take up this cross in our lives. He brought divine love to us where we can receive it. But unless we receive it into all our thinking and working and playing, it cannot save us.

We face the fearful paradox that, if we try to cling to our own self-centered life, we shall lose all chance of real life. Only if we steadfastly deny our own selfishness—the only kind of life we have known so far—can we let into ourselves real life, the life of love Jesus has brought into our level of living in this world. We cannot avoid the challenge. We were created to choose the kind of person we will be, selfish or loving. If we choose to let selfishness go on working, we may gain all that our old way of life wants; but if we have the whole of that world, we shall have ceased to be alive, for we shall not be loving others. There can be nothing worth gaining at such a cost. Often this carrying of our cross is depicted as a total denial of any joy or happiness in life, and Christianity is seen as a gray desert of denial. The truth is that a new kind of joy in being able to help others, a new kind of happiness in giving instead of taking, will eventually fill the place of the old self-satisfaction. However, the denial of our customarily self-centered way of living is a very real denial, a time of stress and pain, a real "carrying of a cross." There is a night of denial and the horror of seeing our self as a killer of others' happiness, before the new life rises again.

Chapter Nine

TRANSFIGURATION AND FAILURE

A t this point in his ministry, Jesus finds it possible to go beyond teaching and to show to the chosen few disciples his real nature. It is a kind of climax; but, as we read on, we discover to our dismay that it is the prelude to a series of failures by the disciples that cascade down into their abandonment of Jesus at the betrayal. It is almost as though the very revelation at the transfiguration throws up in stark contrast the disciples' faults and failures. They fail to heal; they want to be the greatest; they cannot bear others to have a part in the kingdom. This will be our experience also. We shall reach a stage when we become aware of the real nature of the divine love that came in Jesus. We shall begin to look at others with the compassion and desire to help that come from that love. It sheds a new light on living, and we have a vision of how we might live and see from the love of Jesus. But as the nature of divine love begins to be revealed, we shall realize all the weaknesses in our selfish nature. We shall find ourselves without the power or constancy that has momentarily been revealed, and our self-love will send us tumbling down into failure and inadequacy. It is the only way we can grasp our need and make the fundamental change in our approach to life that will bring the love of Jesus fully into our lives. Eventually we shall realize that we have no power except the love of Jesus in our hearts to raise us up anew.

1. And he said to them, "Truly I say to you, there are some standing here who shall not taste of death until they see the kingdom of God come in power."

This verse is part of Jesus' words at the end of Mark 8, after he has spoken of the Son of Man's coming in his Father's glory; but it is worth taking it separately here because it introduces a new idea that recurs in the gospel—that the kingdom of God will come at some future point and some will not know death until it occurs. It was a coming that was taken literally by many and expected very soon before they died, but that interpretation needed to be contradicted. The ending of John's gospel says of John the beloved disciple that he would tarry until this coming; but then goes on to point out that this does not say he will not die but "what is it to you if he tarry till I come." In this chapter it is said some "shall not taste of death." The expectation of a second coming of the Lord very soon had to be combated by the early Christian church, for it tended to lead to wild unruly anticipation and complete neglect of a rational Christian life of love towards the neighbor.

We can see that, in a personal sense, the message is that a life following Jesus will not taste the death of evil and will lead to a fullness of love and joy, when God's truth is operating in us with all his power. Mark 13 contains a detailed description of the second coming, and we will consider then the question of any historical fulfillment of the idea and also develop more fully what it means for us personally.

> *2–10. And after six days, Jesus took with him Peter and James and John, and brought them up into a high mountain by themselves. And he was changed in appearance in front of them, and his garments became shining white like snow, whiter than any bleacher on earth could whiten them. And Elijah and Moses appeared to them, talking with Jesus. And Peter exclaimed to Jesus, "Master, it is good for us to be here; and let us make three shelters, one for you, one for Moses and one for Elijah." For he really did not know what to say, so greatly were they frightened. And a cloud came, overshadowing them, and a voice came out of the cloud saying, "This is my beloved son. Listen to him." And suddenly looking around they saw no one but Jesus alone with them. And as they were coming down from the mountain, he commanded them to tell no one what they had seen until the Son of Man was risen from the dead. And they kept that saying to themselves, questioning what was meant by rising from the dead.*

Now that the disciples have acknowledged Jesus as the Christ and begun to realize something of the awe-inspiring future they are committed to, Jesus shows his real nature to three of them in a vision. The disciples began to follow Jesus because he was a miracle worker. They were drawn to him by his power to heal and by the message of peace and love that he taught. Only slowly does it seem to have dawned on them that they had become involved in something so vast as God's work among men and women to redeem them, to give them the opportunity of a new life of salvation. There is always a tendency for us, with hindsight, to regard the disciples as slow and unperceptive because of the time it took them to wake up to their involvement in something so immense. But that is a very rash judgment. Would we have done any better?

The Gospel is revealing God's love acting to save humanity from its selfishness, but in a personal way it is also talking to us of our own individual salvation. We are no quicker in seeing what is happening to us than the disciples were in grasping the nature of Jesus' presence with them. At first, we are keen to understand a message of change that will heal our lives. We accept a command to repent and follow the teaching, but it is quite a while before it dawns on us that God is coming alive in us. We are dealing with a Christ, a Messiah, a "Coming One," anointed with the love of God to make that life our life. Eventually the change in us will be immense. We shall have to go with him through the agony of realizing the cruel selfishness of our own life. We must see how it kills his life, before he can truly rise up, a new life in us.

On the way, we do see something of the real nature of Jesus with us, as the disciples were granted a vision of him totally changed in his appearance, "transfigured." The word used is a very strong word, conveying the idea of a magical change. To the disciples it must indeed have seemed to be that. Jesus' clothes shone with whiteness. Matthew and Luke tell us that his face shone. He became a being of light, the living Word, God's love working through the truth. In him, divine love was rebuilding human life unselfishly by using the way of truth revealed in the Word of God.

This was made obvious by his companions in the vision, Moses and Elijah. The whole of the Law was attributed to Moses. Elijah, as one of the first prophets and the one who was to be forerunner to the Messiah, stands for all the prophets. To a Jew, the Word of God was the Law and the Prophets. They represented the truth of life, and this was coming alive from the love of God in Jesus. Yet the disciples did not grasp what this meant. We, like them, begin to understand that a totally new force is at work in us, but we do not grasp its real nature. We tend to think of it as a new set of ideas. Peter's witless remark about making three booths for Moses, Elijah, and Jesus portrays our inability to realize that Jesus is not just a way to transmit truth to humanity, like the Old Testament, or the New Testament for that matter. He is the truth alive from the whole love of God. The admonition from the cloud shows that, even in our clouded understanding, we are driven to understand at last that the love of God has come alive at our level. It has been born into our natural life in its own truth from God, "a beloved son." We, and all men and women for all time, have God's love alive in us as our redeemer.

It is at this point that Jesus again emphasizes to the disciples that he is to be killed and will rise again. The only way for Jesus to fill human life with divine love was to face all the evil and selfishness of which human beings are capable. He had to maintain love in the torment of the passion and the agony of his rejection on the cross. The disciples were unlikely to find this an obvious way for the Messiah to save them. The idea that he would rise again, a complete force of love in the minds of men and women, was baffling to them. They could not see beyond what he was doing at the moment. We are similarly baffled as the Lord leads us towards salvation. We think of the teaching and the discipline of Christian life as being the great change in us; but this is only the preliminary to a horrifying revelation of how selfish we are, and the rising up of new life from Jesus to be the nature of our whole life. As yet we do not understand this "rising from the dead."

> *11–13. And they asked him, "Why do the scribes say that Elijah must come first?" And he answered, "Elijah does indeed come first and restores everything. And just as it has been written of the Son of Man that he should suffer many things and be regarded as nothing, so also Elijah has come, and they did to him what they liked, as it has been written of him."*

The disciples ask about the teaching that Elijah must come first, which is in Malachi 4:4–6. Those verses couple together remembering the law of Moses and the coming of Elijah to change people's hearts, so that when the Lord comes he will not "smite the earth with a curse." Clearly, this passage was recalled by the appearance of Moses and Elijah with Jesus. Jesus identifies John the Baptist with this work of Elijah, for John's call to repentance began to change the people so that Jesus could work among them. But there had been no more real acceptance of John as Elijah than there was of Jesus as the Son of Man. Both were ignored and eventually killed.

We, too, need an Elijah to come to us before the Lord can come. We need a personal call to repent and change our lives. Without that initial step, the Lord could not enter our lives without bringing a real curse of good mixed with evil. Only that first "Elijah" change brings us to a point when we can understand and react to the Lord's message. Yet there is no more stability in our changed life of repentance than our first resolution. It is mixed with a good deal of self-concern. We have seen in Herod's killing of

John the power of this selfishness. We still have to read in the gospel the same sad tale of our denial of Jesus himself. It is part of our wholehearted change that we should come to know our own weakness and the power of evil from our self. From our first repentance to our final acceptance, we must come to know—and so be able to reject—the power of our own selfishness. Only so can the Lord rise up and truly control our lives.

> *14–22. And when he came to the disciples, he saw a great crowd around them and scribes arguing with them. And immediately when the crowd saw him they were greatly surprised and ran to greet him. And he asked the scribes, "What are you discussing with them?" And one of the crowd answered, "Teacher, I brought to you my son who has a dumb spirit. And wherever it seizes him it throws him down, and he foams and gnashes his teeth, and he is continually growing weaker. And I spoke to your disciples to cast the spirit out, but they had no power to do so." But he answered him, "O unbelieving generation, how long must I be with you? How long must I bear with you? Bring him to me." And they brought him, and seeing Jesus immediately the spirit threw him into convulsions, and he fell on the ground and rolled about foaming. And he asked his father, "How long has he been like this?" And he said, "From childhood; and often it has thrown him into the fire or into water to destroy him. But if you can help us, take pity on us."*

The disciples had performed miracles of healing when they were sent out by Jesus, but here they find themselves powerless to help. Jesus ascribes this inability to lack of faith. It is important to remember that powers are not transferred to men and women. They only exist with them because of the creative power of God. Once there is insufficient faith in God, the power no longer exists. We can understand the tumult of the crowd at the disciples' failure, but it only serves to emphasize that the source of power is in Jesus. It is customary to describe the boy as an epileptic; but the violent reaction, when Jesus commands his healing, shows that forces deriving their power from evil are responsible for the symptoms. We see again the intrusion of such forces into our world, and the need for divine action to give humans back their freedom to choose. Such epileptic effects still exist in a disorderly world, but now they act in a controlled state in which humanity is free to choose, and so are symptoms of physical disease, not symptoms of a breakdown in our hope of salvation.

When we look here for the message about our personal salvation, we see the contrast between the vision on the mountain and the boy thrown about by evil forces down in the valley. Our realization of Jesus' power with us only throws up in ghastly contrast the mad disorder of our earthly life. Our spirit of self-love casts us into the fire of hating others when they cross us; it drowns us in a flood of false ideas about life's purpose and value. Our approach to life is to "show our teeth" to any and everybody who gets in our way, grimacing with hate and "foaming" with our own selfish plans at every problem. If we are to change, we need to realize this has always been our nature. There is a great feeling in us that we are "not so bad really" and just need a few changes. We need this revelation that our life has been dominated by selfishness, which throws us about in violent opposition to the good of others. And as the father says, we have been like this since we were a child. There is nothing of our adult life that Jesus can use. It must all be changed.

23–29. And Jesus said to him, "If you can believe, all things are possible to him who believes." And immediately the father of the little child cried out with tears, "I believe, Lord, help my unbelief." And Jesus, seeing that a crowd was gathering, rebuked the evil spirit, saying to it, "Dumb and deaf spirit, I command you to come out of him and never enter him again." And crying out and throwing him into great convulsions, it came out, and he seemed dead, so that many said he was dead. But Jesus, taking him by the hand, lifted him, and he got up. After Jesus had entered a house, his disciples asked him privately, "Why couldn't we cast it out?" And he said to them, "This kind will not go out except by prayer and fasting."

The crux of the situation is belief in the Lord. It is often imagined to be belief in ideas about the Lord, but that is not belief in the Lord as the source of power in one's life. One can believe in ideas as a matter of thought, just part of a plan for one's own life. What is needed is belief in Jesus' being alive in one's life, being the power for good in every affection and action. All things that make up a life of good are then possible. When we hold to that belief, we live from his life. How do you achieve such belief? The father in this episode makes it clear in his cry, "I believe, Lord, help my unbelief." It is a realization that one's belief does not accept the Lord's love as one's only real life. Anyone believing at all must be living in Jesus' way. What the man cries out for is the life of Jesus as his only life. To recognize Jesus as our life is more than our effort to live his way in our daily life. It is an acceptance that the life alive in us is not ours but his redeeming presence. Even while believing in a life of faith to help others, we can still have an "unbelief" that any good thing we do is actually done by Jesus working in us. Our life of faith is unbelief without the confidence that Jesus is our new life. Once that belief is with us, the spirit of selfishness can be cast out of our earthly life.

Jesus calls the evil spirit "dumb and deaf." As we have seen, to be deaf spiritually is not to be able to hear the Lord's commands because we are not obeying them; this prevents our life from speaking any praise to God and leaves us dumb. Removing this accustomed life of selfishness makes us seem dead, as the boy was thought to be. It is difficult to imagine that we can be alive if our selfishness is not allowed to operate on our behalf. Yet we, like the boy, can be raised into life by the hand of Jesus. If we accept the power of his life to act in all we want and do, we are still truly alive, making our own choices to help others but transformed from the selfish being we were.

The transformation wrought in this healing is too vast to be accomplished in us in a moment. The disciples' failure to accomplish it has them questioning their effectiveness, but Jesus tells them how they can make such a change. It requires prayer and fasting. The way Jesus taught us to pray is to talk with him, asking for his help, admitting our sins, trying to see our life in his way. Spiritual fasting involves denying ourselves those things that our selfishness wants. There can be no change unless we really talk to Jesus, and then deliberately deny our selfish impulses and judgments and make ourselves live in his way. While Jesus has shown his power to change life by healing the boy in a moment, we disciples cannot receive such power without a longer process. Genuine personal prayer has to become a way of life. We will consider that fully at Mark 11:25. There must also be a spiritual fasting that tries to reject all the impulses and thoughts that are selfish. Only by talking over with him the actions and motives of our lives and striving for hourly obedience can we give the love of Jesus the opportunity to heal our mind and life.

30–32. And leaving there, they went through Galilee, and he wanted no one to know. For he was teaching his disciples and saying, "The Son of Man will be delivered into the hands of men, and they will kill him, and on the third day he will rise up." But they did not understand what he was saying, and were afraid to ask him.

Jesus takes time alone with his disciples in an effort to make them understand his coming passion and death. When he first made such a statement at Caesarea Philippi, Peter had reproved him and called down a severe rebuke on himself. Now the disciples do not contradict what he says, but still they do not understand it. We have the same problem. At first, we rejected the warning of the enormous change that must come in us. Our own self-absorbed nature reacted violently against such a revelation of its evil intent, denying any confrontation that would make so complete a change in our life. Now we oppose our selfish nature and refuse its attitude toward life; this prevents a total rejection of Jesus' way, but still our selfishness has enough strength to stop our understanding of what must happen for our salvation. We cannot realize that we are the life even in our effort to be a Christian. And we shall not, until we see our inherent self-love killing Jesus' life in us. Because we still want control of our own life for ourselves, we are afraid as yet to dig any deeper. Like the disciples, we are "afraid to ask him."

> *33–37. And he came to Capernaum, and once they were in the house he asked them, "On the way, what were you talking about among yourselves?" But they were silent, for on the way they had been discussing with each other who was greatest. And sitting down, he called the twelve and said to them, "If anyone wants to be first, he must be last of all and servant of all." And taking a little child, he put him in the midst of them and put his arms round him and said to them, "Whoever receives one such little child in my name receives me, and whoever receives me does not receive me but him who sent me."*

How little the disciples understood now becomes clear. They had not understood Jesus expressing his purpose in terms of the "suffering servant" of Isaiah. They could not grasp that the strength of love is in its complete unselfishness, its giving without counting the cost, whatever the situation. They had been spending their time arguing over who would be greatest in this new kingdom. Jesus shows them the true nature of unselfish love. While that love is the greatest virtue, it achieves that by being the last thing thought of, by seeking ways of serving all others. He drives home the nature of a Christian by lovingly embracing a child and demanding love and care for the innocent and helpless.

What is revealed here speaks home to each of us. The desire to be first creeps into our life in so many ways. It is the whole ambition of so many in business, in sports of all kinds, in politics and government. There are voices that speak against such overweening ambition, but in the world around us there seems to be limitless admiration for "the greatest." This regard penetrates, too, our Christian life. When we help others, we want things to be done our way and people to appreciate us. When we see the impact of some truth, we are pleased we understood it. We make it our own, instead of simply using it to help others. When such attitudes show themselves in church and charity organizations, we are quick to condemn them; it is harder to realize that such an attitude underlies much of our personal effort to be a Christian. Love, as the driving force of our life, should never think of itself, but only of those we can help. In a strange way, it is very easy for religion to be all obedience and to lose all love. The Lord with his arms around that tiny child must be for us the real picture of our faith. Such innocent love and care must not be from any earthly motive. It must be done in the quality of his own unselfish love, so that we receive him into our hearts; and that brings into us the love of God that lives in Jesus.

38–42. And John said to him, "We saw someone who isn't one of us casting out devils in your name, and we told him not to because he does not follow us." But Jesus said, "Do not stop him, for there is no one who can do a mighty work in my name and be able easily to speak evil of me. For anyone who is not against you is for you. For whoever gives you a cup of water to drink in my name because you belong to Christ, in truth I tell you, he shall not lose his reward. And whoever makes one of these little ones who believe in me turn away, it would be better for him if a great millstone were put around his neck and he were thrown into the sea."

The height of insularity is expressed in the old Lancastrian joke, "Everyone is queer except thee and me; and even thee's a bit queer." John shows here this spirit of separation that has cursed the Christian churches. No one else must have a part in the kingdom, lest it deprives us of the honor of it. That such separatism could arise shows how selfishness blinds people to the obvious teaching of the Gospel. Jesus asks rather that the quality of anyone's service should be the judge of his or her religion.

Personally the message digs deeper than just our attitude toward church organizations. The "name" of Jesus is his quality, that by which you call him and can recognize him. We shall often find that there are thoughts and actions that we cannot yet weave into the "disciple pattern" of our accepted faith; but they still have the quality of love and service, and they strive to get rid of some devil of selfishness in our lives. The fact that we cannot weave such ideas into the fabric of our present reasoning about God is no reason to deny them. So long as they genuinely are in "the name" or quality of Jesus' life, they must help if they cast out our devils of selfishness.

There is always a danger that we shall despise anything that we have not already seen as part of our faith. It is not just in ways of working against selfishness that it can restrict us. It can prevent us drinking in ideas because we feel they are not exalted enough for our faith, or because they open up again ways of thought that we have sealed off as being completely understood. Any concept of truth that slakes our thirst for eternal life, even if it is not a great concept but only "a cup of water," a simple practical idea, brings something of the reward of true service. We have much to learn, and every idea is valuable, so long as it has the quality of Jesus' name.

In all the changes that try to affect us, it is our own basic self-love that stands in the way. The small beginnings of affection and compassion in life, "the little ones," can all too easily be turned aside and contaminated by our self-centered thoughts driven by our desires, and a selfish desire can turn it like a millstone (and here it is the great millstone turned by an ass) and make it grind out any argument that leaves us still able to get our own way. Such a process, using truth we have learned to restrict love in our lives, is dangerous. We need to recognize the origin of any such tendency in ourselves and throw it out into the sea of falsity that it generates, with its own false reasoning hung round its neck.

> *43–48. "And if your hand should cause you to offend, cut it off. It is better for you to enter life maimed, rather than with two hands to have to go away into Gehenna, into unquenchable fire, where their worm does not die and the fire is not quenched. And if your foot should cause you to offend, cut it off. It is better for you to enter into life lame, rather than with two feet to be thrown into Gehenna, into unquenchable fire, where their worm does not die and the fire is not quenched. And if your eye should cause you to offend, pluck it out. It is better for you with one eye to enter the kingdom of God, rather than with two eyes to be cast into the Gehenna of fire where their worm does not die and the fire is not quenched."*

Now Jesus drives home the danger of selfishness in a human being. Attractive as evil may sometimes seem, it creates a hell inside us in place of the heaven Jesus offers. To give up selfish ways may seem like cutting off part of ourselves, but that is preferable to letting them destroy us. The strength of language here was misunderstood by some early Christians, who actually mutilated themselves in an effort to achieve salvation. A moment's thought will show that it is never the hand or foot or eye that offends, but the mind that is using it. It is there that the source of pollution must be cut off.

The triple exhortation here covers the three dominating aspects of our life. The hand is the means by which we accomplish things, our source of power. We need to watch what we are doing, to ensure that selfishness does not control our actions. Where we detect it, we must cut it out of our doings among our fellows. The feet enable us to walk in a certain direction. We plan our life to go along a certain way, and we must ensure that it is the Christian way of love and service. If we find we are walking into ways of selfish ambition, we must immediately cut it out. It cannot exist alongside following Jesus. With the eye of the mind we see by understanding what Jesus is telling us. But we control the way we see things. If we want our own way, we shall deliberately not see what will help others. Allowing our mind to think from such a distorted vision of life will lead us into evil. We must "pluck out" any such attitude, so that we see clearly the true way.

Many find the description of the result of failure too horrifying to accept. Nevertheless, the images used express in a parable the terrible consequences of remaining in evil. Gehenna is an image from the Old Testament. It refers to the valley of "the son of Hinnom" alongside Jerusalem, where human sacrifices were made by fire to Moloch (see 2 Kings 16:3 and 21:6, as expanded in 2 Chronicles 28:3 and 33:6). For the Jews, it came to mean every evil that opposed the way of God's love. While we stay in our evil, we are burnt up by the fire of our selfish love, which never stops but only feeds on its conceited gains. People often speak of the fires of hell as though they were a punishment meted out to sinners. How could a God of love punish anyone? The torment arises from the burning hatred inside a person, which cannot be allowed to destroy others as it wants, but must be restrained and kept in bounds—this is the "Gehenna of fire" that is not quenched.

The state of corruption that goes with it is expressed by the "worm that does not die." In selfishness, there is a desire for the things of this world that corrupts the whole of a human life, eating away at all compassion, honesty, and care for others. While men and women remain in evil, that corruption does not die but by its selfishness eats away at all their humanity. It is horrible to think of human life so mutilated and destroyed in men and women, but it is a picture we need to be shown. It can make us abhor our old way of life and be open to receive a new life from Jesus.

49–50. "For everyone will be salted with fire, and every sacrifice will be salted with salt. Salt is good, but if it loses its saltiness how can you make it salty again? Have salt in yourselves and be at peace with one another."

To understand this series of sayings on salt, we need to grasp what is the "salt" of our Christian life. Salt lends flavor to food and makes it appetizing. On the other hand, in too great quantity it can make food unpalatable and, indeed, destroy the fertility of land to grow food. We need to feed on the love of God. We are drawn to that love by the truth we understand about him. Our affection for that truth "salts" our appetite to use his way of love. But this will only happen if there is a fire of love within our knowing God's truth. We have to be "salted with fire," so that there is a longing in what we know that makes us want to be loving.

Such a longing for God's love to work in us "salts" every holy thing in our lives, every "sacrifice." All our truth should have this longing to feel his love at work. But if truth becomes important to us just as knowledge, something we can show off to our fellows and be proud of, then it loses its "saltiness." The whole point of knowing what is right is so that we can show love to our fellows by means of that truth. To have truth and not use it to work with God's love is like having useless salt that cannot arouse the appetite for God's food. If we regard our Christian truth in such a useless fashion, we shall be unable to show any love or compassion and be destroyed, as salt destroys life in the ground. All of us need to "have salt in ourselves," that is, we need everything we know about the Christian way to be longing to work with love in our lives. This brings a true peace into the hearts and lives of men and women.

Chapter Ten

TO JERUSALEM

The story now moves away from Galilee towards Jerusalem. John shows Jesus going three times to Jerusalem, and is careful to distinguish the journeys. The other gospels telescope the journeys together into one movement towards Jerusalem. The movement is important for our understanding of spiritual things. We have seen that Galilee, far from the temple in Jerusalem, is the sphere of daily life and learning. It is concerned with outward understanding and obedience. However, when we make a beginning here, we begin to be disturbed at a deeper level, and to question our more fundamental attitudes to life and its meaning. This brings us to our basic belief in God, to the purpose of our life and the way it worships God. So we travel towards Jerusalem. It is not that we are no longer active in the ordinary affairs of life, but the deeper reason for all our activity is beginning to be stirred. The challenge is no longer whether what we are doing is right and in accord with the Lord's command. We begin to question the reason for our life and whether the motives from which we live are in the love of God or our own self-seeking use of life for personal satisfaction. Is our religion a God-driven way of life or a hypocrisy? It is because this fundamental decision is being fought out that the thread of the story becomes argument about interpretation of the Scriptures and an examination of the disciples' motives.

> *1–12. And then he arose and came into the borders of Judea by the other side of the Jordan, and crowds gathered around him again; and as he had been accustomed to, he taught them again. And the Pharisees came testing him, and asked him if it was lawful for a husband to put away his wife. But he answered them, "What did Moses command you to do?" And they said, "Moses allowed one to write a notice of divorce and then to put her away." And Jesus answered, "He wrote this commandment for you because of your hard hearts. But from the beginning of creation, God made them male and female. 'Therefore a man shall leave his father and mother and be joined to his wife and the two shall be one flesh.' So they are no longer two but one flesh; therefore what God joined together do not let man divide." And when they were private in the house, his disciples asked him about the same matter, and he said to them, "Whoever puts away his wife and marries another commits adultery against her. And if a woman puts away her husband and marries another, she commits adultery."*

In the last chapter, Jesus and the disciples came to Capernaum and had been traveling south from Caesarea Philippi. Aiming for Jerusalem, it was possible to go down west of Jordan through Samaria (a route that John 4 shows Jesus using in one of his journeys), or to go east of Jordan through Perea, and then cross back over the Jordan to go up through Jericho to Jerusalem. This was presumably the route Jesus chooses here, coming into Judea from beyond Jordan. The presence of multitudes to be taught might well be because his reputation had gone before him, but, once again, it must be remembered that Mark is not careful of places or chronology in his writing. John makes it clear that Jesus went three times to Jerusalem for Passover, the last of which was this visit, which brought about his death. By now, therefore, he would be well known in Judea as well as Galilee.

The Pharisees did not come to learn, but to prove their own point. Jesus' attitude toward marriage was probably well known, and they hoped to trap him into denying the law of Moses. There are two ways of approaching any matter: either to try to work it out honestly or to make your reasoning justify what you want regardless of others. If people are trying to work things out honestly, we need only to tell them the truth of the situation. If they are trying to get their own way selfishly, we must limit them by obvious laws that prevent them doing too much harm. Jesus points out here that both attitudes are addressed in Scripture. The question of marriage turns upon the reason for the creation of man and woman. He directs attention to the idea in Genesis 2:24, which he quotes, that the man and his wife were made to live together in love. The whole intention was to make them "one flesh." This is the truth about the relationship of men and women in marriage. The Jews had inherited many ideas destructive of this. Their great men of earlier times had practiced polygamy. Wives had been at first virtually in the position of slaves. The laws in the books of Moses reflected this, while still providing some protection for women. The Pharisees were relying, presumably, on Deuteronomy 24:1–4, which specifies the steps to be taken if a marriage is terminated because of immodest behavior. They do not use the Scripture to consider the positive use of marriage but to find ways of breaking it. Such an attitude ignored much in the prophets. Malachi 2:14–16, for example, bitterly attacks the breakup of marriage by divorce. There was plenty of teaching on the real purpose of marriage in the Scriptures, but the Pharisees preferred to quote the restraints placed on offenders as though they encouraged the offense and expressed the purpose God intended in marriage.

We can approach marriage from the same false angle. Indeed, most modern discussion of marriage does so. Concentration is on when a marriage can be broken up, rather than what can be done to keep it intact. So passages such as this in the gospel are quoted to control marriage legally and applied to legal divorce. Their real message is far different. Jesus is stressing what a disaster is the breakup of a marriage, what it does to those involved. He is urging the effort to maintain true marriage, neither condemning without compassion those who fail (as his words are often made to imply) nor supporting a view of marriage that seeks to permit its termination because it is never really regarded as anything one should strive to perpetuate.

We should concentrate on the point Jesus makes. Marriage is not like friendship, though it will include friendship; nor is it a contract, although it can be expressed in one. Marriage is a way by which a man and a woman become one. Such unity is not possible if either wants to maintain a self-centered life. Unity means the two must have a common way of regarding opportunities and prob-

lems in life. And since that cannot be for the selfish purposes of either of them, it must be for purposes in which
both join together. This means that marriage involves personal change and development so as to live unselfishly. The
rebirth of the partners is part of the possibility of their
marriage. That will not happen in a moment. The entire
process of rejecting selfishness and accepting Jesus' love will
go on with man and wife as part of the building of their
marriage, and they will do it together. They will still discuss things, disagree about things, have their own particular duties and interests in life; but in all this they will be
seeking to work together. All the joys of physical lovemak-
ing and the delight of living together will be part of the
way they achieve this. They will be drawn closer together
until they become one in what they want to do in life, and
the way they see and plan it. If marriage is seen in this way,
both partners enter it realizing they must change themselves and find their joy in helping each other. If difficulties
arise, they will see them as things to be understood and
worked out together, not as reasons for doubting their purpose and destroying each other's joy.

Their lives become an effort to marry up the truth they
learn with the love from God that can make it work. Here
is a deeper meaning for us in these verses, which applies to
everyone, whether they have had the opportunity to enter
into a marriage or not. Life is an effort to make a marriage
between what we learn from God and the love he will give
us to use it. Each individual is striving to accomplish this,
though married partners involve each other in the work. To
"divorce" this spiritual marriage is to use the truth without
the love, to use it to judge and criticize others but
not to change one's life from love and service. Only the
"hardhearted" do this. God's intention is always that love

and knowledge shall be married together in service to others.

> *13–16. And they were bringing to him little children that he might touch them, and the disciples reproved those who brought them. But seeing it Jesus was indignant and said to them, "Let the little children come to me and do not stop them, for the kingdom of God is made of such as these. In truth, I tell you, whoever does not receive the kingdom of God like a little child will never enter it." And taking each of the children in his arms, and laying his hands on each of them, he blessed them.*

The reaction of Jesus to his disciples' behavior suggests more than that they sought to protect him because he was tired. They probably thought the children not important enough to have a part in the kingdom. Jesus reacted by pointing out that the children typified the only attitude that could receive the kingdom of God. The divine love in Jesus, which healed and taught great crowds, shows now its personal depth for each one of us, as he takes each individual child in his arms and lovingly blesses each one.

The innocence and dependence shown by children are exactly the qualities that make it possible for us to accept the Lord. With children, these qualities arise from their ignorance and inability to care for themselves. Disciples require innocence in their experience and knowledge. A child is innocent of any thought of him- or herself because that child is not aware that he or she can be the controller of the situation. An adult must have the same complete innocence of any thought of self, but adult innocence will have come from a hard-gained rejection of self. A child accepts dependence because it cannot provide for itself. An adult must be dependent on the Lord because all personal pride and planning has made way for an acceptance of what the Lord can give. Without innocence and a willingness to trust the Lord's way, nothing of the love of God can be received in our hearts.

> *17–22. And as he started again along the way, someone came running up to him and kneeling to him asked him, "Good Teacher, what shall I do that I may obtain eternal life?" But Jesus said to him, "Why do you call me good? No one is good save God alone. You know the commandments. You should not commit adultery, you should not murder, you should not steal, you should not bear false witness, you should not cheat, and you should honor your father and mother." And answering, he said to him, "Teacher, all these have I obeyed since my youth." And looking at him, Jesus loved him, and said to him, "One thing you lack. Go, sell everything you have and give it to the poor, and you shall have treasure in heaven; and come take up the cross and follow me." But he was sad at this and went away grieved, for he had many possessions.*

A strictly orthodox Jew would have regarded keeping the commandments as sufficient. This man appears to be seeking for more than that, without realizing what it entails. Jesus rejects the epithet "good," possibly because it seemed flattering in this man's mouth, but probably also with the emphasis we meet with elsewhere that "the Father who dwells in me does the works."

We often hear of the conflict between the letter and the spirit of the law. In answering this man, Jesus sets them both into their correct relationship. He commends the keeping of the commandments. This is the pattern that should control all human life, denying all behavior that would harm our fellows and so creating a good life of service. It is this that Jesus seeks and loves in each of us; but, by itself, it does not bring the joy of eternal life. The selfishness in us can still possess our lives, even when we obey the commandments. Here it showed in the great possessions of the man, which he could not give up. Obedience, yes! Giving his whole life, never! We can fail in the same way, even though we may possess no worldly goods. We still possess our knowledge and ideas and the active life we plan from them. While we regard these as our own possessions, we are doing even what is good to gain self-satisfaction and praise. The spirit of our life is not a love for others, even though we might serve them. The only love in what we do is still reserved for ourselves.

To seek eternal life is not to seek to live forever. All of us do that in the afterlife anyway. Eternal life is the kind of life that draws its love and joy from the love of God. That can never cease because it comes from the eternal life of God. All his love is unselfish, seeking only to give itself and its joy away to us, for that is the whole purpose behind creation. We can only receive the quality of such love and joy when we too have no thought of ourselves, but only of how we might help others. To give up possessing one's own life for oneself is the only way to gain the joy of God in our living and so gain the "eternal" kind of life.

> *23–31. And looking around, Jesus said to his disciples, "How difficult it is for those who have riches to enter the kingdom of God." And the disciples were astonished at his words. And again Jesus said to them, "Children, how difficult it is for those who*

trust in riches to enter into the kingdom of God. It is easier for a camel to pass through the eye of a needle, than for a rich man to enter the kingdom of God." And they were shocked, saying among themselves, "Then who can be saved?" But looking intently at them Jesus said, "With men it is impossible; but not with God, for all things are possible with God." And Peter began to say to him, "Look, we left everything and followed you." But Jesus answered, "In truth, I tell you there is no one who has left home or brothers or sisters or father or mother or wife or children or fields because of me and the good news who will not receive a hundredfold now at this fit time homes and brothers and sisters and mothers and children and fields, with persecutions, and life eternal in the age that is coming. But many who are first shall be last, and the last shall be first."

The possession of riches has presented the church with problems from earliest times, and this passage has been in the forefront of its ideas. The early church attempted to hold its possessions in common, with deacons as administrators—a kind of Christian communism—so as to avoid possessing anything. What the Christians overlooked was that, even if they had things in common, they still owned possessions. These might be used for the poor, but in such a situation everyone has become poor. It is not systems to remove possessions that are wanted but the lack of the desire to possess even what we have, so that we can use it to serve others. There is no harm in possessions, either worldly riches or knowledge and ideas. Jesus often tells parables in which people are given great riches to use for him. But as soon as we regard them as our own, rather than given to us to use and help others, they destroy our apparent Christianity.

All of us who possess any Christian truth are rich, and the more we understand, the richer we are. We need to consider this deeper level of possession. So ludicrous is Jesus' analogy of the camel going through the eye of a needle that it must have raised a smile among his hearers, but its purpose is not just simply exaggeration. When we become rich in knowing how to help and serve our fellows, we may simply pile up that knowledge, as a merchant piled his goods on a camel's back. But that knowledge is really given us so that we can embroider our lives with love and service to others. You cannot get a camel through the eye of an embroidery needle. If we regard our knowledge of Christianity as so much goods on our camel's back, it cannot be threaded into any intention to love and serve others. The comparison shows the two attitudes are incompatible, and to feel personally rich in our Christian ideas ensures that we can never enter the heaven of true love and service.

To abandon the sense of possessing either ideas or worldly riches is quite impossible for our selfhood, as the disciples pointed out when they despaired of anyone being saved. But it is possible with God. In Jesus Christ, he has brought his love into our mind, able to work at our level and replace our selfishness. Choosing to let him use every possession and every idea we have to serve others means that our old selfhood no longer possesses them, and we are saved from our selfishness and free to use them for the good of others. At first sight, Peter's reminder of what the disciples had given up seems a request for a reward in place of them. Jesus' promise that all that has been given up will be replaced, though with persecutions, is not a promise of such a reward. Rather it is an assurance that we shall gain the same powers in life, but powered with Jesus' spirit and so unselfish. Such a change will not be gained without persecution from our selfishness as we fight to receive his life, but eventually we shall use his love and know his heavenly joy.

Those who give up what they have to follow Jesus are promised a reward that hardly seems possible. In literal terms, no one can be given a hundredfold children or mothers or homes. The emphasis is simply on the greatly increased quality of life when all is given up for Jesus. But these things that are given up, and then renewed a hundredfold, sum up all we are. The "house" is our settled way of life; "brothers" and "sisters" are the thoughts and affections in our mind; "father" is the origin of our activity and "mother" the attitude that nourishes it; "wife" is the love we are married to and "children" the plans it breeds; and "fields" are the ideas about life that feed us. In the beginning, all these will serve our selfish ends; but, if we give them up to work for Jesus, then he blesses us with the same powers from his love. Powered by unselfish love, they become vastly stronger in every way. Self-love is always blinded by its own ambitions and weakened by fear for itself. Unselfishness sees all others clearly and follows its purpose without fear.

32–34. And they were on the way up to Jerusalem, and Jesus went on in front, and they followed, astonished and afraid. And gathering the twelve around him again, he began to tell them the things that were about to happen to him. "Look, we are going up to Jerusalem, and the Son of Man will be handed over to the chief priests and the scribes, and they will condemn him to death, and hand him over to the

Gentiles, and they will mock him and scourge him
and spit on him and kill him. And on the third day
he will rise again."

For the third time, Jesus warns the disciples of what is to come. There is to be no acceptance of him. His way of love will destroy the power of the religious leaders, who only seek to dominate others. Therefore they will despise his way, beat, deride, and kill him. But there is still the promise that this is not the end, for he will rise again on the third day. The disciples' reaction is not given this time, but it is clear from all that follows that they did not understand. Once again, we must not regard them as weak and foolish because of that. We all endure the same failure. We find it difficult to believe that the only way we come to know the love of God is by seeing our egotistical nature try to destroy it. There is no other way for us to realize what we are, what his love is. Yet the promise is always there: If we endure all this, he will rise in us as our true life.

35–45. And James and John, the sons of Zebedee,
came up to him, saying, "We want you to do for us
whatever we ask." And he said, "What do you want
me to do for you?" And they said to him, "Give us to
sit in your glory, one at your right hand and one at
your left hand." But Jesus said to them, "You do not
know what you ask. Can you drink the cup that I
drink, and be baptized with the baptism I am bap-
tized with?" And they said to him, "We can." But
Jesus said to them, "You shall indeed drink the cup
that I drink, and be baptized with the baptism I am
baptized with; but to sit at my right hand and at my
left hand is not mine to give, but is for those for
whom it has been prepared." And hearing about this,

the other ten disciples began to be angry with James and John. But Jesus calling them to him said to them, "You know that those who are regarded as rulers over nations lord it over them, and their great men dominate them. But it shall not be like this among you. Whoever wants to be great among you must be your servant, and whoever wants to be first must be the slave of you all. For the Son of Man himself did not come to be served, but to serve, and to give his life as a ransom for many."

How little the disciples understood becomes obvious now with the request of James and John, who seek to become the greatest in the kingdom of heaven. There would seem to have been a genuine desire to be part of Jesus' kingdom, for he does not totally condemn what they say. Rather he challenges them to think about what such an ambition means. To be fitted for what they ask, they must endure his temptations, "drink the cup that I drink." They must be baptized as he is baptized, for in those same temptations, the water of truth must wash away all evil. They can never, of course, fight against those temptations as Jesus does, for he is the love of God at work, but their willingness to endure it all is possible from the love he is bringing into their world. In a sense, all of us must drink the same bitter cup of temptation and be washed clean by the truth, but we shall all do it only in his strength and not our own. Still, to sit on his right and left hand is not a gift to be given. Our place has to be prepared by long endurance and striving, for this phrase does not mean to sit in some outward position of power in heaven, but to reach a state when only divine love and wisdom will control our lives.

The world's view of power and position is commonly

that it gives the right to control others and make them do what suits the leader, providing the opportunity for wealth and ease. Jesus points out that this is not the way God uses his power and position. He seeks only to give the joy and power of his life away to others. When he came into the world, he sought only to help humanity and bring his love again into people's lives. Anyone who thinks of dominating others by using Christian truth or earning admiration by living a Christian life has missed the point of life. We can only use life God's way when we use it to help others.

> *46–52. And they came to Jericho. And as he was leaving Jericho with his disciples and a great crowd, Bartimaeus, the son of Timaeus, a blind man, was sitting by the road begging. And hearing that this was Jesus of Nazareth, he began to shout, "Son of David, Jesus, pity me." And many scolded him, telling him to be silent; but he yelled even more, "Son of David, pity me." And Jesus stopped and asked for him to be called. And they called the blind one, saying, "Be of good courage, stand up, he is calling you." And throwing away his coat he stood up and came to Jesus. And Jesus said to him, "What do you want me to do to you?" And the blind man said to him, "Master, that I might see!" And Jesus said to him, "Go, your faith has healed you." And immediately he had his sight and followed Jesus along the road.*

Jesus and his disciples have been following the route down the east side of Jordan and now cross over to the west bank to go up by Jericho to Jerusalem. The name "Bartimaeus" is translated into Greek: "son of Timaeus." It is not possible to say whether it was used as his Aramaic name or whether it only names his father.

This healing comes aptly, almost as a summation of what has just gone before. We have discussed the problems of those who possess things, and here is a beggar with nothing. We have considered those who would be great, and here is one of the lowest of the low, sitting in the gutter. The realization that there are no possessions for our greed, no domination for our self, leaves us knowing we are a beggar. And we are blind because we begin to realize that we do not see what the Lord is working for. Knowing now that our selfishness blinds us, we cry out for help, and no crowd of opposing thoughts is going to silence us. Our self-sufficiency is destroyed once we realize our true state. It is when we understand our state and cry for help that the Lord can help us. When we put our selfishness away, he can let us see things from his way of love. Every situation is transformed, if we can look at it the way Jesus does. Once we look with his love, we see the needs of others, instead of how to get our own way. A faith that can realize its need can have its eyes opened and be healed and follow Jesus along the road of life.

Chapter Eleven
ENTRY INTO JERUSALEM

Now we come to Jerusalem, and the real nature of our redemption begins to show. Jesus makes his claim to be the Messiah. The high priests and the Jewish Sanhedrin seek to preserve their selfish domination in the name of religion and take action to oppose the rule of love witnessed by Jesus. Against this opposition, Jesus reveals the true nature of his love in mercy, forgiveness, and care for others. One doubts if the Jewish leaders appreciated the depths of self-love and evil that their actions portrayed. But in his own experience, Jesus poured his love into those depths and fought with the evil of humanity until he brought the love of God in its stead and made that love forever available to us all.

The gospel record of Jesus' passion acts, too, as a parable of our battle for salvation. We have to use the strength he brought to fight the same evil. We must recognize and reject the self-love that strives to control us. At this point, we realize we are faced, not just with a lack of understanding in our discipleship, but with powerful opposition from the selfish evil in our own personality. What began as a quiet following of an idea in Galilee, an effort to change our outward life, now in Jerusalem opens up our very self. We begin to feel how great a change must be made if we are to accept this kingship of divine love. Even though the contest is not so dire in us as when God opposed selfishness in Jesus Christ, yet it must still shake our souls. If the power of Jesus is to prevail, we must fight in the inmost depths we can realize and know in ourselves. Nor should we think this means retiring from our active worldly life to fight some abstract battle of ideas. We come to know our real self in our reactions to others in the world. Each mundane demand by others upon ourselves opens up the abyss of selfishness, in which the love of Jesus dies as he seeks to save us with a new life. We see the death of his love in our day-to-day decisions for our own ease and our own satisfaction. Only when we acknowledge how our inherent self-love kills all the love in our daily life and how in our lives we abandon Jesus' way of love can his new life come alive in us.

> *1–6. And when they drew near to Jerusalem, to Bethany and Bethphage, and to the Mount of Olives, he sent two of his disciples, saying to them, "Go into the village before you; and immediately on entering it you will find a colt tied up on which no one has ever sat. Loose it and lead it away. And if anyone says to you, 'Why are you doing this?' say, 'The Lord has need of it,' and immediately they will send it here." And they went, and found the colt in the open street tied up outside a door. And they untied it. And some of those standing there said to them, "What are*

you doing, untying the colt?" And they replied as Jesus had told them to, and they let them go.

Jesus comes to Jerusalem from the east, past the villages of Bethany and Bethphage and so to the Mount of Olives that overlooks the city from that side. Until now, the authorities have gone to Jesus to question and attack him. Now Jesus has come to Jerusalem for the feast, and, in the very heart of Jewish authority, he begins openly to make his claim to be the Messiah; but it is a claim made as a bringer of peace, and the warlike expectations of a Messiah are not aroused. The entry into Jerusalem is clearly meant to be the fulfillment of the prophecy in Zechariah 9:9. It is a claim to be king, yet he is not riding on the horse for war but in peace on the colt of an ass.

The personal aspect of the story is of Jesus entering our lives as Savior, and the details explain something of the way that is done. Jesus is often seen asking questions, challenging those around him, so that they themselves will begin to think out the meaning of life. He urges us to understand our relation to him. If Jesus is to enter our life, we must find a faculty in ourselves that will enable him to do so, and he sends us to look for it. The ass is notorious for obstinacy and going its own way, and most of the debate and argument that goes on in the human mind is just as obstinately concerned with getting our own way and defending what we think we possess. But there is another ability born out of this power of thought, one that is truly rational and can think and plan from the Lord's purposes for us. This "colt" from the ass of reasoning would provide a way for him to ride into our minds, but it is tied up unused outside a door that could open up our lives. We tend to forget that there are influences in our thought and reasoning that enter from sources other than ourselves. Often they are selfish and cruel and destructive, and we are familiar enough with such things suddenly intruding into our mind; but there is also a door from heavenly thought and illumination that can affect our thinking in a true and loving way. It is outside this door that our Christian rationality is tied up. Yet our false ways of thinking of ourselves ensure that our ability to think of others is never released. It is never ridden by any true humanity in our lives; no one has ever sat on it. The Lord sends us to look into our living and to release this genuine Christian rationality so that he can use it.

Our accustomed way of life will question such a release, but this challenge has to be answered with the conviction that the Lord has need of this power. We must make the deliberate choice to think and reason about life for others and not ourselves. What is required is not some esoteric understanding of life, which would release unknown ideas. This colt is tied up outside in the open street. It is the power to think of others and understand their needs in everyday life. We are well aware it exists in us, but we have tied it up by a self-centered approach to living. What seems a simple exchange of question and answer in the story has much deeper implications for us. We are required to begin releasing the colt, to begin thinking of others and planning our life to help them rather than ourselves. As soon as we do that, our selfishness will begin to object. It is then that we must assert, "The Lord has need of it." The only way to break our selfish use of life is to accept that the Lord has need of our efforts to help others.

7–11. And they led the colt to Jesus, and threw their coats on it, and he mounted it. And many spread their coats on the road, and others cut down branches from the trees and spread them on the road. And those who went in front and those that followed cried out, "Hosanna! Blessed is he who comes in the name of the Lord. Blessed is the kingdom of our father David coming in the name of the Lord. Hosanna in the highest!" And Jesus entered Jerusalem, and went into the temple; and, when he had looked round at everything, because the hour was already late he went out to Bethany with the twelve.

Submitting our way of thinking to Jesus enables him to ride in triumph into our lives, for now his way of love will be at its heart. Yet it is not a process that goes on apart from our cooperation. The Lord must sit on our coats and ride over them and also the branches we provide from the trees. As disciples, we are clothed in many ideas of truth gained from the Scriptures. These provide the seat by which the Lord sits on our "colt." They also enable us to welcome the Lord's way of thinking into our minds. As we think of them, they become a pathway he treads into our lives. As well as things we have learned from Scripture, perceptions have grown up from them like trees, branching out into all aspects of life. These ideas of faith are the branches, which also pave the way by which the Lord can enter our lives.

The cry with which Jesus is greeted is drawn principally from Psalm 118:25–26, but introduces other ideas and recalls other phrases from Psalms. *Hosanna* in Hebrew means "save now," and the passage looks for salvation from him "who comes in the name of the Lord" and brings "the kingdom of our father David." Jesus is acknowledged as the "coming one," the Messiah, who is bringing the expected kingdom. No doubt, in the minds of those who welcomed him, there were mistaken ideas about that kingdom, but its meaning for us is simple and obvious. The only one who can save us from our selfishness is Jesus. We must welcome him as the new life coming into our lives and governing them for the purposes of his love.

12–14. And on the next day they returned from Bethany, and he was hungry. And he saw a fig tree a long way off that had leaves on it, and he went to it to see if he might find some fruit on it. And when he reached it, he found nothing except leaves, for it was not the season for figs. And Jesus said to it, "Let no one eat fruit from you ever again." And his disciples heard this.

This seems a strange incident. To blame a tree for failing to produce fruit is strange enough, but to do it when the fruit was out of season seems unreasonable. Yet it is not really out of character, for Jesus constantly seeks to startle his disciples, then and now, and to make them remember the challenge of his message. The incident is really an enacted parable and comes after Jesus' entry as a warning of the state of those who do not receive him. All who use the Bible are familiar with the idea that a man is like "a tree planted by rivers of water" (Psalm 1) and that we are meant to grow and yield fruit in our lives. Jesus is attracted to the fig tree by its leaves, which enabled it to breathe in the atmosphere and grow. We all have perceptions and thoughts that breathe in truth and enable us to grow as Christians. But thinking is never enough for us. We are required also to put our thoughts into practice in a good life of service and to do it now. For us, there is no season when we should not be yielding fruit. In Revelation, the tree of life yields its fruit every month. Jesus blames the fig tree because, as in a parable, it stands for us when we know what we should do, but do not carry it out in our lives. Such a state is a curse, and Jesus does no more than declare what such a state is like. While we concentrate only on thinking about truth, "growing leaves," we shall never yield a heavenly harvest. Mark's record of it shows how such an enacted parable sticks in the mind by its very strangeness and acts as a warning.

> *15–19. And they came to Jerusalem. And Jesus entered the temple and began to cast out those buying and selling in the temple, and he overturned the tables of the moneychangers and the seats of those who sold doves, and he would not let anyone carry anything through the temple courts. And he taught them saying, "Has it not been written, 'My house shall be called a house of prayer for all nations'? But you have made it a den of robbers." And the scribes and the chief priests heard it and they tried to work out how to destroy him, for they were afraid of him because all the crowd were marveling at his teaching. And in the evening he went away out of the city.*

When Jesus first rode into Jerusalem, he entered the temple and saw all that was going on there. Now he takes steps to change it. People had obligations to fulfill at the temple. They must pay the half-shekel temple tax, which meant that visitors needed to change their native money. They needed to perform sacrifices, and many could no longer bring the animals required over long distances and must buy them before going in to sacrifice. Such needs were now catered to in the very courts of the temple by moneychangers and those selling doves for sacrifice. Worship had now become a superstitious fulfillment of commands, and the sense of union with God and its holiness had been swallowed up in a temple market, so much so that the temple courts were used as a thoroughfare like any street, and anything and everything carried through.

It is a degradation that our own lives can suffer. We often speak admiringly of the silver of truth from the Word of God, but we can spend our time changing ideas from the world into obligations toward God. Each generation, though it can see the false coin of past generations—the purchasing of salvation in medieval times, the harshness of Puritan condemnation, the hollow hypocrisy of much Victorian religion—will still exchange the genuine silver of truth, which understands human beings from love, for the false coin of the day's ambition, which seeks only applause and personal satisfaction. Jesus seeks to overturn such ways of thinking, so that we will use truth only to help others.

Sacrifices (as the word means) were intended to make something sacred, holy to God; but holiness comes from unselfishness, and we cannot buy that by merely copying others. Such a quality must come from the heart and involves our personal commitment. Jesus wants to overturn any religion bought by routine fulfillment of religious behavior and make it a genuine life of service from the heart. It is very easy to let our religion lose its real spirit and become absorbed into our own purposes in life. Jesus seeks to prevent it from becoming part of the selfish thoroughfare of our life, and to make it a new spirit that will bring holiness into all our earthly service. Jesus expresses his condemnation of the misuse of the temple in words from Isaiah 56:7 and Jeremiah 7:11. It was to be a house of prayer, a way of talking with God and finding his way, not a den of robbers taking religion for selfish use. That it was to be "for all nations" was a necessary reminder to the Jews of that time, who tended to think of God as their own private preserve and may have taken advantage of others in the temple market. We must also take the injunction to heart ourselves, for we all have a tendency to think of God as more interested in us than in other people, asking him to take particular care of us, thinking he has a different relationship with us from that he has with those who know less about him. A good parent loves a handicapped child as much as one fully gifted, and our heavenly Father is the same.

> *20–26. And coming by in the morning, they saw the fig tree withered from its root. And Peter, remembering, said to him, "Look, Master, the fig tree that you cursed has withered." And Jesus answered by saying to them, "Have faith in God. For in truth I tell you, whoever says to this mountain, 'Get up and throw yourself into the sea,' and has no doubt in his heart but believes what he says will happen, then indeed it will happen as he said. Therefore I tell you, whatever you pray for, believe that you receive it and you will get it. And when you stand praying, forgive whatever you have against anyone else, so that your Father who is in the heavens may forgive your sins also. But if you do not forgive, neither will your Father who is in the heavens forgive your sins."*

The warning about trees that have leaves but no fruit is completed here by the destruction of the tree, and it comes most aptly after the condemnation of the Jews for destroying their religion. A faith that is never used to love and serve others eventually withers away. The root of faith is the love it springs from, and in this case there is no real root. Faith that does not spring from love will wither away until it has no real effect on one's life at all. Jesus does not answer Peter in this negative image of a faith that has withered, but he turns his mind to the positive power of faith.

Again, the image he uses is intended to startle. Few of us feel the urge to command mountains to throw themselves about. Yet the image is chosen for more than its physical size. We all have mountains of selfishness in our minds, and it is these mountains that a real faith can handle. If love from Jesus is powering our faith, we can reject our selfish promptings. It is important to realize what a sea of arguments and excuses for ourselves is generated in our mind by our selfishness. We have to order the mountain of our self-love into the sea of excuses it has created. Only when we realize their relationship can we be freed from reasoning and thinking in ways that hold us in thrall to the self. But we must believe that the love of Jesus is in us to give our living and thinking a new nature. Only a true faith in God can achieve the miracle of removing our selfish life.

The ability to "receive whatever we ask" has misled many Christians, largely because the nature of praying to God has not been clearly understood. To pray is to talk with God, and if we have talked our life over with God, we shall only ask him for those things that he would want us to have. We shall be willing to submit ourselves to his providence and its care for all others, and we shall accept his effort to save us from selfishness. The things we shall ask for are the things we can truly believe we shall have, if we accept his life. Prayer has too often been thought of as a way of getting what we want, but what our self wants is neither for the good of others nor for our own eternal good. To pray is to talk with God and to draw out before his love all the selfish desires and false ideas that fill our life. Once we see them in the light of his love, we must reject them and what we want will change.

Prayer is part of the way God changes us; it is part of our being born again. It is not simply a series of requests for what our selfish desires would like to happen for our own good. Prayer involves a real change in the way we live. This is why prayer is coupled with forgiving others. Mark does not tell us how Jesus taught his disciples the Lord's Prayer, but this passage recalls the warning that is given after that prayer in Matthew 6:14–15. As a way of praying, the Lord's Prayer demands something quite different from the traditional passive prayer. It asks us to accept obedience to his kingdom of truth and to let his will be active in our lives. It asks for the day-to-day love for others that is the bread for our soul. It asks forgiveness for our selfish faults and accepts the change in us that must be there to receive such forgiveness, setting our lives right with others in love. It asks to be protected during the attacks of evil, but recognizes that they cannot be avoided if we are to be delivered from our selfishness. It ascribes all the love and wisdom and power that works in our lives to the love of God that works in us for our salvation. All of that active effort to receive God's love, which is detailed in the Lord's Prayer, is briefly summarized here in the warning to forgive others. It is a fundamental basis for prayer that we can only be forgiven as we forgive others. Forgiveness is always offered, but we can only accept it if we change our ways of thinking and living. We need to reject our selfish pride and our greed for our own way in life, and adopt an attitude that can look with love at anyone who offends us, seeking only to help them. Only with such an attitude can we truly pray.

> *27–33. And they came again to Jerusalem, and as he was walking in the temple, the chief priests and scribes and elders came to him and said, "By what authority do you do these things, and who gave you the authority to do them?" And Jesus answered them, "I will also ask you one question, and if you answer me I will tell you by what authority I do these things. Was the baptism of John from heaven or was it from men? Answer me that." And they consulted with one another saying, "If we say from heaven, he will say, 'Why then did you not believe him?' But if we say, 'From men . . .'" then they feared the people, for all held that John was indeed a prophet. So they answered Jesus, "We do not know." And Jesus answered them, "Then I will not tell you by what authority I do these things."*

We have already been told how the temple authorities feared the way the people listened to Jesus. His cleansing of the temple had been a direct challenge to their authority, which permitted such abuses. Now they openly challenge him by asking for the source of his authority. As he does so often, Jesus answers their question with another question.

At first sight, it seems just clever debating that he should trap them by demanding a clear judgment on John the Baptist's work; but far more than that is involved. John's call to repentance was the forerunner to God's kingdom. To repent of our evil and selfishness and to change our lives is the first step toward a Christian mind. No change is possible, and we cannot begin to accept Jesus' love and think and plan and work from it without the recognition of our selfish state. Men and women who want to remain in their natural evil are in a dilemma when they are challenged about the repentance call of John. If they say they believe everyone should live to help others, the question arises, "Why do you not do so?" On the other hand, few want to declare that they do not believe it, for all "the people" can see that mutual help provides the only basis for human society. So they take refuge in not giving an opinion, neither changing their lives nor abandoning John's call to live well but using it to batten on others. But anyone who does this is unable to understand the authority of Jesus' love. He cannot speak to those who will not accept that they must change their way of life. Each of us has the power to choose between good and evil as far as we see it. Unless we choose to reject our selfishness, there is nothing that can receive and understand the authority that love brings into life.

Chapter Twelve
JESUS REJECTED

T he rejection of Jesus is often seen as a rejection of his particular claim to be God's way of saving humanity. The implication is that a different claimant might be more acceptable. But Jesus shows here that what is rejected is a way of life demanding unselfish service to others and that people have been rejecting that option down the centuries. The parable he tells shows this rejection. Subsequently, his opponents argue from the Scriptures and show themselves as using God's teaching to maintain their own evil way. It is important to realize how fundamental is the opposition to Jesus. It is not an argument about a particular way of seeing things or niceties of interpretation. It is the basic argument between good and evil, between unselfish love and the fundamental selfishness that powers the lives of men and women. What rejects him comes not from the way we think, but from what we want to do with our lives. So much argument about details of faiths often obscures this real contest for our souls between good and evil.

Christians have tended to argue about the coming of Jesus Christ as though they were supporting one particular candidate for office. Faith or heresy has turned upon a particular human-made definition of Jesus. Yet what is really asserted in the incarnation is the love of God and its effort on our behalf. Men and women need divine love to power their lives. In Jesus, God brought it to them and showed what they must do to reject their selfishness and use the power of that love. This unifies people; it does not divide them. Anyone who rejects self-centeredness and strives to love others is living from the love made incarnate. He or she may know little or nothing of how Jesus brought God's power to them, yet each is saved by it as it replaces personal desire. Obviously, the more clearly we understand the nature of the love of God and how it is present with us, the more powerfully and surely we can use it. These are differences of degree. What unites all people is the love of God brought to all human minds by the work wrought in Jesus. And all men and women are united in their efforts to reject selfishness in their lives, so that the love of God works through them in the world. To "deny Jesus" is to accept evil and never use the love of God to help others. We can do that in complete knowledge of Jesus' work, or in complete ignorance of his life on earth. This chapter shows clearly that the rejection of Jesus is not a theological quibble or a dilemma of history. It is a decision for evil in the face of good; and it is a decision made in the way men and women live, not in what they say they believe.

1–12. Then he began to teach them in parables, and said, "A man planted a vineyard, and put a fence round it, and dug out a trough for the winepress, and built a watchtower, and let it out to farm work-

ers, and went away out of the country. And at the right time he sent to the workers a slave to receive the fruit of the vineyard from them. But they took him and beat him and sent him away with nothing. And he sent to them another slave, and they stoned him and hit him on the head, and they sent him away after they had reviled him. And again he sent another, and they killed him. And he sent many others, and some they beat and others they killed. But still having one left, his own greatly loved son, he sent him to them at the last, saying, 'They will respect my son.' But those workers said to each other, 'This is the heir. Come, let us kill him, and the inheritance will be ours.' And they took him and killed him, and threw him out of the vineyard. What therefore will the lord of the vineyard do? He will come and destroy those workers, and will give the vineyard to others. Did you never read this Scripture, 'The stone that the builders rejected has become the cornerstone; the Lord did this, and it is wonderful for us to see.'" And they tried to take him, for they knew he had told the parable against them, but they were afraid of the crowd. And they left him and went away.

This parable is clearly a sequel to the argument with the temple authorities in the last chapter. No Jew would have any difficulty in seeing Jesus' parable as an attack on the church authorities. They were familiar with the symbolism in Isaiah 5:1–7 of the vineyard that produced wild grapes after everything possible had been done for it, and the prophet specifically identified the vineyard with God's people. Jesus extends this in the parable. The prophets and leaders sent by God to call the people to his ways are seen as messengers to the vineyard, who have been rejected, reviled, and killed. The climax comes when the only son is sent, and he is slain in hopes that this will give all into the hands of the murderers. The parable, therefore, becomes a condemnation of the behavior of the Jewish leaders and their threats against the Son of God sent to save them. The only outcome must be the destruction of their church and the beginning of a new one.

This parable also speaks to us in the "I-Thou" situation in which we are trying to read the Word of God. Each of us is a vineyard intended to produce the fruit of a good life, and we have to do this in God's strength, acknowledging that all the good we may do comes from him. He has set up his vineyard in us. He fenced it around by teaching us what is evil and how we should reject it. He provided us with the winepress of understanding, by which we may squeeze out of his words the truth we need. He has given us a watchtower, for we have the power to look out over human activity and see the threats to our Christian life. Everything necessary he provides, but he does not oblige us to live from him. He leaves us to choose the way of life we will follow and gives us the impression that he has gone far away, leaving us with the responsibility for our decisions. Still, there is a constant stream of messengers from him, truths from his Word urging us to live in service to others from his love, and so render to him the fruit of our vineyard. Selfishness in us has no desire to use life for anyone else. It will revile such truth by arguing against it; it will try to beat it into subjection to self. It will prevent any life from such truth and so kill it in our mind.

The choice between using the life we have from God for him or living it for our own purposes becomes ever clearer, until we realize that it is not just the messengers of ideas about life that we are rejecting. We are rejecting the love God sends into our minds to work in this world, the love that should be using those ideas of truth. Eventually our evil rejects God's presence in us, and the Son is killed. The message then is clear. The self-absorption that does this in our mind must be rejected with God's strength and wiped out of our life, and our life must be given over to a new spirit. We need a new life from God that will truly give him the fruits of our service to others. In us, the vineyard has to be taken away from our selfishness and given to the new life from Jesus.

While we learn truths about our selfish nature and try to build up our own approach to life, there is always one stone of truth that we reject. Jesus continually emphasizes this most important truth of all: that we need the love he brought into the world to power the ideas of truth in us. This is "the head of the corner." Clever thoughts do not change our selfish nature. Only loving others can do that. This fundamental saving truth has to become the very keystone of all our Christian life. We cannot raise it in our own strength. Only accepting the heir to the vineyard, and letting his life work in us, can do that. It is the Lord's doing, and it is wonderful to see.

13–17. And they sent to him some of the Pharisees and the Herodians, that they might trap him in discussion. And when they came, they said to him, "Teacher, we know you are truthful, and you care for no one's opinion; for you do not regard a person's outward pretense, but honestly teach the way of God. Is it lawful to give tribute to Caesar or not? Should we give, or should we not give?" But he, knowing their hypocrisy, said to them, "Why do you test me? Bring me a denarius to look at." And they brought it, and he said to them, "Whose face and inscription is this?" And they replied, "Caesar's." And Jesus answered them, "Give to Caesar the things that are Caesar's, and to God the things that are God's." And they marveled at him.

Now those he has been challenging try to break Jesus' hold on the people by trick questions. Those who come first are an unholy combination, made up of the Pharisees who demanded obedience to Jewish law and tradition and the Herodians who supported Herod's family and curried favor with Rome. Possibly the Herodians were brought along to make official note of any denial by Jesus of Rome's authority. The question they asked had explosive possibilities. There was a great hatred of Rome among many Jews, who felt they should be free of all foreign rulers. To support paying tribute to Caesar would alienate the people. But to deny tribute to Rome would bring Jesus into conflict with the Roman authorities and might bring his work to a summary end. The tribute to Rome had been imposed when Judea was placed under Roman procurators after Archelaus was deposed. It had to be paid in imperial coin, the silver denarius, which carried the head of Tiberius Caesar. A denarius was the daily wage of a laborer.

Our first impression is of the hypocrisy of the Pharisees with their flattery of the one they hope to destroy and the cleverness of Jesus in sidestepping the trap they laid. Deeper thought shows how apt these are to our own Christianity. The promptings of the love of self rarely come out into the open in our own life. Much that serves and delights our self is tied up with remaining an acceptable member of the community, able to keep the friendship and help of other people. Therefore, we know in ourselves this abominable flattery of God, which emphasizes for our own purposes what a good thing upright moral values are in the community. Such an attitude is not really interested in those values but wants to be able to use them for selfish purposes. To do this, it is essential to destroy their connection with God's love and discredit any demand for genuine love for others.

The attack is two-pronged. Either there is no real difference in a religious life, and its moral values are there for worldly use and are not really different from other worldly motives that "pay tribute to Caesar." Or we must say that religious values have no connection at all with worldly things, and so bring them into complete opposition to any worldly life and make them mere abstractions. Jesus' answer, we can now see, is not an evasion of the difficulty, but is a true solution of it. We must recognize that there are two levels to our life, and both must correctly obey the appropriate authority. We have to "give to Caesar the things that are Caesar's" by sensible planning and working in this world; but at the same time we must "give to God the things that are God's" by accepting his motive of love in all we plan and do. Jesus' answer has often been misused by asserting that it gives independent authority to the "Caesar" of worldly government and behavior. But the answer gives no independence as to motive; that must always be given to God. Only practical restrictions and difficulties that affect the moral realm are recognized.

The pattern of civil life changes and poses different moral decisions. To park a car in a restricted space offends the civil law, though once anyone could park anywhere. The love of helping one's fellows demands that we cooperate in our community, and so obedience to this arbitrary regulation becomes a moral obligation. Caesar regulates where we can park the car. Love for our fellows motivates our obedience. Again, the state may decide to pay from taxation for charitable work that once was supported by the free gifts of individuals. Love to the neighbor demands that we willingly pay the taxes, while at the same time showing personal interest in helping those in the community. Only when "Caesar" demands that we harm our fellows—the Nazis' instruction to persecute Jews, for example—does government demand what we cannot give. And then it is because earthly government has trespassed on the things that are God's and asked us not to love our fellows. All moral values, though related to civil obligations, depend on the prior acceptance that we must love God and our fellows. This is most apt for today. There is a great deal of pressure in our time to equate moral standards with whatever is the most convenient behavior for the moment. To regard morality in this way is to cut the heart out of human behavior. If we have not given to God a willingness to love his way and serve our fellows, any moral standards we may declare will only be a more acceptable face for our selfishness.

> *18–27. And there came to him Sadducees, who say there is no resurrection, and they questioned him saying, "Teacher, Moses wrote instructing us that, if any man should die and leave no children, his brother should take his wife and have children by her to continue his line. There were seven brothers, and the first took a wife and died leaving no children. And the second took her and died, also leaving no children. And the third did the same. And the seven brothers took her and left no children. Last of*

all the woman also died. So, in the resurrection when all of them rise up, to which of them will she be wife? For all seven had her as wife." And Jesus answered them, "You are entirely wrong, because you know neither the Scriptures nor the power of God. For when they rise from the dead, they neither marry nor are given in marriage, but are as angels are in the heavens. But that the dead do rise, have you not read in the book of Moses in the passage about the bush, how God spoke to him, saying, 'I am the God of Abraham and the God of Isaac and the God of Jacob'? He is not the God of the dead, but of the living. So you are quite wrong."

This challenge shows clearly that it was known widely that Jesus taught there was a heaven all came into at death and, as we saw in Mark 10:1–12, that he regarded marriage between one man and one women as a holy thing. The Sadducees held that only the Law was binding on the people. They insisted that it did not speak of a real afterlife, but only of a place of shades called Sheol. The Pharisees, who accepted traditions as well, had adopted ideas of an afterlife that probably began in Persian thought, but that were confused and at times bizarre. Jesus considered heaven as an obvious and orderly sequel to this life; it was therefore on this point that the Sadducees tried to discredit him. At the same time they could reiterate teaching in the Law that seemed to debase marriage. In refuting them, Jesus quotes from Exodus 3:6, in the section about Moses' vision of the burning bush. At the beginning of Mark 10, we saw the Pharisees, in conflict with Jesus, misusing Scripture to make their argument. Now we shall see the Sadducees using the same method. If, from Scripture, you consider the way God's love makes men and women and his constant effort to fashion them to his way, then the concept of an afterlife in which he can continue to show such love and care seems an obvious extension, whether it is specifically described or not. Angels appear in the Bible and are mistaken for men, which certainly seems to imply a heaven in key with this world. But the Sadducees preferred to ridicule Jesus' teaching by using an argument from the laws Moses permitted them. They used the law on "levirate marriage" in Deuteronomy 25:5–10.

As in most primitive societies, the family in Israel had to be a self-sufficient caring unit. Children were necessary to the pride of a father and were expected to look after their parents. A woman left childless when her husband died would have no one to care for her, now or in her old age, and her husband's pride would be dead among the people. Levirate marriage was a device to cope with this situation. It became the duty of the dead man's brother to make his widow pregnant, and so provide her with a prop for her old age and a remembrance of her dead husband. The device was not really one of marriage, but a way of providing the widow with the protection of the brother's household while her children were young and a family to care for her in due time. In a polygamous society, such as early Israel, the method would work; but it really had nothing to do with true marriage, of the kind we saw Jesus define to the Pharisees in chapter 10. It is used in the Word as a parable of humanity's early efforts to change and bring to birth something spiritually alive, but it was not an instruction on real marriage. Nevertheless, the Sadducees used it to pose their bizarre problem and ridicule Jesus.

Jesus dismisses their nonsense, which shows no real understanding of what Scripture is about. He obliges them to think of all the implications of Scripture, which regard those gone from this world as still alive. If they had read it properly, they would have realized that God is a God interested in living men and women, not a dead source of permissive laws. No one is given to anyone in heaven in the sense in which they are using the word "marriage." From the permanence that Jesus gives to the true marriage of a man and a woman in Mark 10, that relationship would surely continue into heaven; but the two would already have become one flesh by their life together in this world. That would bind them together in heaven. No artificial giving of one to another, as in levirate marriage, could be part of heaven's reality.

The personal implication of this passage is important to us. The Gospels use the symbol of a marriage in parables concerned with the development of our Christian life. All our Christian effort is really to marry up our ideas of truth to the love from Jesus that should work in our life. This conversation reveals something to us about that process. If we have no belief in our resurrection from selfishness to live from the love of God, then we shall deride the idea that the truth we know can be married to such a love from Jesus. We shall have no belief in any power behind our thinking and living except what we want for ourselves. We shall be willing to marry up our plans for life to any desire that is alive in us at the moment, hoping that a permanent selfish solution will be born. But it never is, just as the seven brothers never produced a child. Such an attitude can see no lasting purpose in human life. It cannot understand Scripture's call to use the love of God in our lives. On the other hand, if we do marry up the truth we know to the love of Jesus in our lives, then we do more than the earthly service that results. We provide inwardly in our souls an angel. The root meaning of the word is "a messenger," and truth that is being used by love is a messenger of God in our souls, not just an idea in our earthly mind. We can only gain such inward strength by the discipline of our life here. It is no use waiting till death and then hoping that we can marry love to truth to empower it for good. We have to do the work here and now, to provide ourselves with the kind of character that can live in heaven.

> *28–34. And one of the scribes, coming up and hearing them discussing together, saw that he answered well, and asked him, "Which is the greatest of all the commandments?" And Jesus answered him, "The greatest of all the commandments is: Hear, O Israel, the Lord our God is one Lord; and you shall love the Lord your God with all your heart and with all your soul and with all your mind and with all your strength. This is the greatest commandment. And the second, which is like it, is this: You shall love your neighbor as yourself. There is no other commandment greater than these." And the scribe said, "You are right, teacher, and have truly said that God is one, and there is no other besides him. And to love him with all one's heart and understanding and soul and strength, and to love one's neighbor as oneself, is more than all burnt offerings and sacrifices." And Jesus, seeing that he answered wisely, said to him, "You are not far from the kingdom of God." And no one dared to question him anymore.*

The scribe's question now draws into the open the principle that has been at issue in Jesus' conflict with the various factions, namely, that the heart of our life is in our relationship of love to God and to those around us. In his answer, Jesus quotes Deuteronomy 6:4, adding in his answer "all your mind," which was simply a Greek retranslation of "all your heart," which alone appears in the Hebrew; to a Jew, the heart was the seat of the mind. He couples this with Leviticus 19:18. To Jews, the command in Deuteronomy to love the Lord was the greatest and most fundamental command of Scripture. Known from its first word as the "Shema," it was used in worship, and was written out and bound upon the forehead in the phylacteries which devout Jews wore. It would appear that the scribes had already realized its affinity with the command in Leviticus to love the neighbor, and that the two were coupled together in their teaching. In answering the scribe's question, Jesus was not asserting something new, for some Jewish teachers answered the scribe's question in the same way. (In Luke 10:27, a lawyer provides this answer from his study of Scripture).

We have already seen in Jesus' previous answers that it is fundamental for us to receive the love of God to work in our lives. It can only happen if we ourselves love God. While we desire self at the center of our lives, we cannot receive new life. We have to love God as a tiny child loves its father, seeing him as the loving, protecting power in our lives and the source of all wisdom for us. There can be no bargaining in this attitude, no loving to protect ourselves or to gain peace and satisfaction for ourselves. It has to be the driving "heart" in our thought, the "soul" that inspires it, our only source of "strength" in what we do. The love that makes and maintains us all, that binds the whole meaning of life into a unity for us all, is a love for "one Lord." The assertion is not just a choice of one in place of many gods. It is a declaration of the nature of life as having one power and one purpose, one unselfish love that wants to give itself away to all. More than one would bring in an idea of "selves," centers to be served in life. One Lord makes total giving the purpose and meaning of life. Such unselfish life is made known in Jesus Christ. In him, the one love that is God lived in our evil and infirmities to bring us a caring life in a way we can use in this world. The Father in him did the work, and in him God is made manifest to us and we can love him.

We cannot love God in this way by abstract thought and by generating emotions in ourselves. Reality only comes by the effort to do something. Real love shows itself by service to others. We are given the company of our fellows, so that we can exert this unselfish love as God gives it to us. God could not make one creature, for that would deprive him or her of the opportunity to be unselfish. We must form part of a world of people. So the command to love our neighbor is coupled with the command to love God. These loves are the very center of our existence, and in the challenges made to Jesus by various groups there has been shown again and again our need for them as the heart of our life.

After seeing so much antagonism and hypocrisy from various Jewish authorities, it is a delight to meet this scribe and know that he is "not far from the kingdom of heaven." It can be a comfort, too, to us personally. We have seen how our self-love brings about hypocrisy and antagonism to Jesus; but in this scribe we feel the assurance that our study of Scripture can give us ideas of truth, if we read with a love that is "not far from the kingdom of heaven." It is a warning never to read from our own narrow perspective, seeking what we want out of life, but always to summon up a love to God and our fellows and read Scripture only in its light.

35–37. While teaching in the temple, Jesus said, "How can the scribes say that the Christ is a son of David? For, speaking from the holy spirit, David himself said, 'The Lord said to my Lord, Sit at my right hand until I put your enemies as a footstool for your feet.' Therefore David himself calls him 'Lord,' and so how can he be his son?" And the great crowd listened to him gladly.

We have seen how strongly the Jews desired a Messiah who would make an earthly kingdom for them and make them great as a people. Such looked for a descendant of David to arise and lead his people. Here Jesus challenges the idea that the Messiah is a member of an earthly dynasty and puts the whole idea on a much higher plane. He does so by using Psalm 110:1, which was held to refer to the Messiah. Quoted in or translated from Greek, its implication may be obscured by the double use of the word "lord." In Hebrew it would read, "Jehovah said to my Lord." Jewish people never pronounced the divine name, but they would all be perfectly aware of the meaning of the verse. The Psalms were believed to have been written by David, so the effect of the passage was to have David calling the Messiah "my Lord." The result was to elevate the Messiah above David or any mere man descended from David. In such a style, Jesus seems to use the labored exegesis of the Jewish scribes; but, though it was suited to the Jews around him who were used to such arguments, it contained a far deeper meaning.

The four gospels declare clearly that Jesus was born of the line of David and provide genealogies to show it (Matthew 1:1–17, Luke 3:23–34), although no Jewish woman could trace her genealogy and it has to be done through Joseph, who is assumed to be of the same family as

Mary. Why has there been so much effort to show what Jesus here denies as applying to the Messiah? The problem is clarified if we remember that Jesus had to take on our fallen humanity; but his purpose was to use consciousness in this world to obey the truth from God, and so put off the evil he inherited by that birth from Mary. (And it is noteworthy that, in the genealogy in Matthew, there is an emphasis on the evil inherited through Mary. Four women are named, which is unusual in a Jewish genealogy, and all of them are associated with evil: Tamar, the daughter-in-law of Judah, whom he used as a prostitute and who conceived twins by him; Rahab, who appears to be the prostitute of Jericho who hid Joshua's spies; Ruth, who was a Moabitess; and Bathsheba, whose husband Uriah was killed by David, who lusted after her.) In temptation Jesus rejected the evil of this heredity and lived by the truth, so that he was never himself the son of Mary. The Messiah is not of any earthly line of David or anyone else. He emphasizes this during his ministry by never calling Mary "Mother," despite his kindness and consideration towards her. In Jesus, the life of God was coming down into this world and living out the purposes of his love. So he was the Son of God, and he made his humanity divine.

For us in our Christian life, this double emphasis is essential. We need to know that Jesus is the son of David's line born of Mary, for we need to be sure that he has faced and taken power over all the inherited evil and falsity that the human mind has generated. We cannot be attacked by any evil or selfishness that he has not fought and conquered. The power for love exists from him in any temptation we may endure, for he has brought divine love into that very battle. But if it is important to remember that he was born "the son of David" through Mary, it is even more important to remember that he is not David's son. He has left nothing of human evil or frailty in his presence. He is the Son of God, God's presence born into our level of life for us to use. What seems to be an academic argument pinpoints the two facets of our trust in him: that he came as man, but he saves us because he made his humanity divine.

38–40. And in his teaching he said to them, "Beware of the scribes, who like walking about in robes, and receiving greetings in the market place, and the most important seats in synagogues, and the chief places at suppers, who eat up widows' houses and cover it up with long prayers. Such will receive heavier judgment."

Now Jesus returns to the faults of the scribes, who because they understood the Scriptures demanded a position of authority among the people. Unlike the scribe he has just been talking to, most of them saw their office as an opportunity to gain position and respect among their fellows and to gain wealth from the poor while maintaining an elaborate appearance of piety. Such behavior has been seen from some clerics in most ages, but we are not to assume that this warning applies solely, or even chiefly, to them.

God speaks to us personally in his Word, and here he gives us a grave warning. We can easily assume that knowing the truth like a scribe is enough and that this knowledge automatically entitles us to respect and power. It is one of the greatest dangers to a Christian. Learning from Jesus' teachings is a joy, and if we are not careful, we may simply enjoy it and fail to remember its purpose. Our selfishness is just as powerful in this apparently religious work as in any other. It will wrap itself up in the gospel teaching as a cloak and then stride through our life as something to be respected because it is wearing the "long robe" of knowing truth. It will feed on the heart of all our life, so that we regard it as a sufficient way to live; but in reality it will have killed off the love that should be married to the truth. It will have made it a "widow," and so it will eat up all the life of good service that is our real Christianity, our true "house," while still talking about all the theory of a good Christian life. Our selfishness is more dangerous here than in obvious evil. There it can be challenged by the truth; but here it has taken over the truth to use for its own purposes and nothing is left to challenge it.

All this chapter has been a revelation of the way things apparently of the church challenge the love of Jesus. As the honest scribe showed, the way to prevent this is to remember that loving the Lord and our fellows is the principal part of religion. The heaviest judgment falls on those who know and do not love to do. Whenever we read the Scripture, we should not ask "What does it mean?" without at the same time asking "What does it want me to change in the way I live, so that I love others?"

> *41–44. And Jesus sat down opposite the Temple treasury, and saw how the crowd threw money into the treasury. And many rich people were throwing in a great deal. And one poor widow came and threw in two tiny copper coins (which make up a penny). And calling his disciples he said to them, "In truth, I tell you this poor widow threw into the treasury more than all the others. For the others threw in something from their plenty, but she from her poverty threw in all she had, her entire living."*

We are not told here anything about how freewill offerings for the temple were collected, but there appear to have been trumpet-shaped collecting boxes in the temple, and these must be meant by the general word "treasury." Jesus reminds his disciples that giving involves more than the act. The will to give is the important thing. The painless giving of some rich people, who were simply making a casual gesture with money they would not miss, is contrasted with the poor widow who gave all she had to live on. (The two tiny copper coins she gave are two lepta, the smallest coin that existed, two of which made a quadrans, or penny. All she had would have purchased very little.) The message for our own charitable giving is obvious enough. In the common phrase, we should give to others "till it hurts." It is no sign of generosity to give what we do not miss, whether of money, time, or labor.

As always, there is a deeper message for us, too, in which God speaks to our very soul. If we feel that our life is our own, to do what we like with, we feel we possess it all and we are rich. Nothing we can give from such an attitude is of real value. We are giving part of what we think belongs to us, part of our small, self-centered world. Instead, we should realize how poor we are in spiritual things, that we have no bond with real love in ourselves alone, and are just a "widow." Once we realize this, we can give our whole life to the Lord and accept his love to rule our life. Then we shall give greatly to others in love and care and compassion, our "entire living"; yet it will always be a tiny thing we ourselves give, for we shall acknowledge that the love of Jesus works in us. All we can give is to let it work by the way we choose to live. Once we can abandon our selfishness, we shall accept our poverty by using the power of Jesus' love and letting it work in all our planning and doing. Here is the new spirit from which we are born again into true life.

Chapter Thirteen

THINGS TO COME

The nature of Mark's gospel seems to change at this point and takes on the characteristics that we find in places in prophetic books of the Old Testament and in the Book of Revelation in the New. Jesus speaks now in a series of images that seem to have nothing to do with ordinary life, and the theme becomes one of total disaster, a sudden divine act of judgment and a new world. This style was termed an "apocalyptic," meaning "a revealing" since the apocalypse was a revealing by God of what would happen, and also "eschatological," that is, to do with the "last things." The idea familiar to the Jews was that when things got bad enough there would be a total disaster for the world and a new coming by God to change all things.

In Matthew and in Paul's epistles, the word *parousia* is used of this promised coming of the Lord. The word takes its meaning primarily from the idea of "presence," though the idea of "coming" is obviously there. Thus, it came to mean a coming of the Lord to bring his permanent presence with humanity. In John and in places in the other gospels, the idea comes, not as a historical event but as an assurance that the Lord's presence is always with us. Later Greek Fathers coined the term "Second Coming" for the historical idea of a *parousia*.

As Jesus approaches the passion and resurrection, the final stage of his work to bring God's love to humankind, it seems strange that he should describe a disastrous sequel in which all will appear to be lost. Yet he has already made it clear that the effect of his presence is to show up the evil in men and women, so that they are obliged to see themselves for what they really are and set about radical personal change. What is described in this chapter is the destruction of things as they have been, and through much pain and distress, an acceptance of the life he is bringing, which will create a total presence of his way. We cannot doubt that with knowledge of our Savior such a change may occur in human society at large; but that is beyond our judgment and understanding. If it happened, it would only be a historical event, with little illumination of our personal condition. So far, our effort has been the more useful attempt to understand what God is saying to us about our own state. If we can grasp something of that, we may be able later to understand a little of such change on the larger scale.

The passion and crucifixion are imminent, when Jesus will finally provide the love of God at our level for us to use in our lives. When from this love we begin to change the attitude and purpose of our lives, we have all the preceding mess to clear up. It would be simple enough if everything in the past was only false and evil, but we have known about the truth probably from our childhood. We have obeyed it in outward ways and yet used it to satisfy our own selfishness. We have performed our duties in life and have done the outward acts of goodwill that are part of a good life, and yet we have tied them on to our pride and used them to curry people's good opinion. All the truth we want to use for God now in a new life is tied to this selfish evil and so falsified. All the affections of love and service exist in us but are contaminated. Our old ways of using truth and loving others for our own sake must be disentangled from our new vision of the Word and the practice of a good life. Then we can use the same powers in holy ways. It will seem that nothing of value has ever existed with us until now, and that all past learning, service, and joy are destroyed. Such a change will devastate each mind and seem to tear it apart, while making way for a new coming of true life. This is the warning that is contained in this chapter.

> *1–8. And as he was going out of the temple, one of his disciples said to him, "Teacher, look, what stones and what buildings!" And Jesus answered him, "Do you see these great buildings? Not one stone will be left upon another that shall not be knocked down." And as he was sitting on the Mount of Olives opposite the temple, Peter and James and John and Andrew asked him privately, "Tell us, when will these things happen, and what sign will there be when they are about to happen?" And answering them, Jesus began to say, "Take care that no one deceives you. For many will come in my name saying, 'I am he,' and they will mislead many. But when you hear of wars and rumors of wars, do not be disturbed; for such things are bound to happen, but the end is not yet. For nation will rise against nation and kingdom against kingdom, and there will be earthquakes in*

various places, and there will be famines and distur-
bances. These are the beginning pains of a birth."

Jesus begins from his disciples' admiration of the temple, which had been built by Herod and which was the
heart of Jewish religion. It is worth noting that the new
temple had been vastly enlarged, so that the surrounding
courtyards and gates were never finished before it was destroyed. It was more a symbol of Herod's wealth and power
than a holy place. To the disciples, it seemed a wonderful
and permanent achievement. Jesus' response was to foretell
its total destruction. In 70 A.D. that earthly temple was destroyed, together with the Jewish state in its rebellion
against Rome. But, as Christians eventually came to realize,
this was no fulfillment of this prophecy, for no wonderful
new world came out of it. Jesus was talking of real change
in men and women, of the destruction of the temple of our
personal worship and the devastation of our own lives.

Such destruction and devastation is hard to take. Each
of us has erected from childhood some form of religion,
even if it has not been fashioned by some specific sect. This
basic attitude toward God and our fellows and the meaning of human life now form the apparently permanent core
of our adult life, our "temple." From these attitudes we
form our judgments and direct our influence on life. We
are now to learn that a real and living awareness of Jesus as
our Savior is not going to be added on to this imposing
system of knowledge and practice. The whole thing is to be
destroyed, so that nothing remains. Such a change is necessary because, all the while we were building up our life attitude, we were doing it from our inherent self-love. It is
something of which we are proud, something we have used
to judge others—all corrupted because we have been at the

center of all we wanted and worked for. Being born again means that all this has to be destroyed.

There are many things in our old attitudes that will assert that they are the way of Jesus' love. We have to be careful that no system of thought deceives us into thinking it is the Christ, anointed with the love of God. There has to be an actual presence of love motivating what we do. Understanding and reasoning about things must not deceive us; it is loving others in Jesus' way that must power our life. The realization of this will only come through great disturbance of mind. "Wars and rumors of wars" refers to the inner battles of the spirit that will happen. Ideas we had from truth, but which were powered by our selfishness, will conflict with one another, and the evil underneath will be drawn out into the fight as well, as "nation rises against nation and kingdom against kingdom." The old world we lived in will be broken up as with "an earthquake," as our old self is shown for what it is and is riven apart. All this is not going to give us a new paradise, for we shall know "a famine" as our old ideas of truth are shown to be inadequate, and our minds are troubled. But the sorrow all this brings into our mind is really the beginning of our new life. The word that is used for such sorrow is one that means the pains of a new birth. Our new self is not going to be born without this painful realization of how much of our old way must be broken up and destroyed.

> *9–11.* "*But look out for yourselves, for they will deliver you up to sanhedrins and to synagogues, you will be beaten, and brought before governors and kings for my sake to be witnesses to them; but first the good news must be proclaimed to all the peoples. But whenever they take you away to try you, do not*

worry beforehand what you are going to say or think
out your reply, but say whatever is given to you at
that moment, for it is not you who will speak but the
Holy Spirit."

Historical examples can be seen in the Acts of the Apostles and the early history of the Christian church of trials and tribulations like those mentioned here; but for us this is a personal history. All the destruction of our old self will bring great strains upon our newborn Christianity. It is the Sanhedrin, or Jewish Council, and the synagogue authorities that are seen as the persecutors. Our old ways of religious thinking and judging and acting, apparently correctly but really for ourselves, conflict with new unselfish efforts. All that ruled our life, "governors and kings," will need the witness of a new motive of love to change them. All the thought and activity that "peoples" our mind must know the good news, that the love of God has been brought by Jesus into all the truth to power all our living. In all this stress, we are not to go in for worldly reasoning to prove the changes that must come; we are not "to think out our reply." That would soon tie us up again in our selfish use of truth. It is the Holy Spirit of love within the truth that provides us with our attitude to life; and, if we hold fast to it, it will give us at any moment the true vision within the truth we know. One of the hardest lessons to learn is that wanting to love and help others is essential to any wise thinking. Reason and argument appear to direct thought, but it is really guided by what we want to do with our lives.

12–16. "And brother will betray brother to death,
and a father his child; and children will rebel
against parents and put them to death. And all will

*hate you because of my name, but whoever endures
to the end will be saved. But when you see 'the
abomination that desolates,' spoken of by the prophet
Daniel, standing where it should not be (let him
who reads understand), then let those in Judea flee to
the mountains; and let no one on the housetop come
down into the house nor go in to get anything from
his house; and do not let anyone in the field go back
to pick up his coat."*

All our thoughts and affections are related to each
other in our mind. There is enough in our new way of life
that is similar to our old religious ways of thinking and
wanting for them to seem to be related. New ideas of truth
at first will seem to be "brothers" of old ideas that served
ourselves. A new way of thinking will seem to have been
"fathered" by old false ways that really deny it; and what
was born apparently out of belief in God will be seen to be
selfish evil that really kills it. The stress into which we
come will show that the one wipes out the other. The hatred of our old selfishness for the new ways of love will become obvious to us. All this turmoil must be endured
because there is no other way to show up our nature and
enable us to choose a new birth. It will reveal the self-love
that has been at the root of what we thought was our religion, of all our beliefs about God and our use of commandments and truths in our lives. It is this basic evil in us
that is "the abomination that desolates" all our living, as all
the prophets have always been declaring. Daniel 11:31 and
12:11 are mentioned because these verses refer to such a
desecration being erected in the temple sanctuary by Anti-
ochus IV Epiphanes in the time of the Maccabees. To destroy the Jews' worship, he placed an image of himself as

god in their temple. There could be no more apt represen-tation of our selfhood's profaning all the worship of our lives.

Once this complete devastation of our old character has been accomplished, we must react in the right way if we are to be saved by new life. We must hold to the new higher motive of unselfish love from Jesus that we know. We cannot stay down in our old religion of life. We must get up higher into "the mountains" of a new love from Jesus. We must not go back into the old "house" we lived in, but keep above it with the new love from Jesus. If we are growing a new life in the "field" of the world, we must not go back to our "coat" of old ideas and clothe our life again with them. Once we can see what our old life was and how it corrupted even our use of God and his purposes in the world, we must be sure we never return to it.

> *17–20. "But woe to those who are pregnant and those suckling babies at that time! And pray that your flight may not be in winter! For in those days there will be distress, the like of which has not been seen from the beginning when God made creation until now, and never shall be seen again. And unless the Lord cut short the time, no flesh would be saved; but for the sake of the people he has chosen, he has cut short the time."*

The danger for us when new ways of love are being born and raised up is expressed as being a "flight in win-ter." There is always the danger that the warmth of love may cease to be the primary motive in our lives. As the stress increases we may think that proving ourselves right in what we do is important. We may think that just obeying will keep the new life coming. But we must never let the love grow cold, for that will bring a winter totally destructive of the new life that is being born and is growing up in us. This new birth is the greatest stress there can be. Nothing else requires such resolution. Being asked to choose a new way, against all we have ever used in life, is bound to bring the greatest distress.

The whole message of Jesus is that love for others is the only power in our lives. We must look at the world with those eyes of love, or all that we gain of new life will be profaned again by selfishness and evil, and now most disastrously. Only the Lord's presence with us keeps us steadfast and prevents our slipping back again. If we listen to him, he will have us active in helping others in the world, and he will "cut short the time" we spend on justifying ourselves and working out schemes for our lives. The idea that he protects those he has "chosen" has led some to think his help is restricted to a few, but it is concentration on ways of service and love in the world that he has "chosen." In that active effort to practice his love lies our salvation. We are always his "chosen one" if we love and live in his way.

21–27. "And then, if anyone says to you, 'Look, here is the Christ,' or 'Look, there,' you shall not believe it. For there will arise false Christs and false prophets, who will give signs and wonders to deceive, if possible, those he has chosen. But watch out for yourselves, for I have warned you of it all. But in those days after that distress, the sun will be darkened and the moon will not give her light and the stars of heaven will fall, and the powers in the heavens will be shaken. And then they will see the Son of Man coming in clouds with great power and glory. And then he will send his angels and he will gather together those he has chosen from the four winds, from the lowest of the earth to the highest of heaven."

The heart of true Christianity is in recognizing the nature of Jesus. In him, the love of God was brought down into the truth we use in this world, so that its only life is from that love. All the truth we know and use has no other meaning than that. It is the way love comes into the world to help and save others. This true "Christ," the love of God in all truth, is not always the way religion is seen. Truth can be used to judge others, to prove that we can have what we want, to make our outward life apparently good but in reality a way to get what we want from others. But the Christ is the Messiah, that is, the anointed one. It is truth anointed with the love of God. We must beware of many powers of selfishness that use the truth and so masquerade as "Christs." They produce many schemes that seem to promise good to all, while at the same time allowing us to indulge our selfishness, and they always prophesy a millennium for us personally. There are no shortcuts that are going to change us or bring our influence into the world. There is only the way of love anointing the truth. We must be careful to hold fast to the inner assurance of Jesus' love as the only way of understanding life, and not be deceived by any manipulation of his purpose.

Once we realize the nature of such false Christs in our mind, we shall see that they blot out the real source of light and understanding in human affairs. It needs the "sun" of love from God to see his purposes with others and show our part. It needs that love reflected from the "moon" of our faith to sustain us in darker times. It needs the knowledge he has given us of that love to shine like "stars" and guide us home. But sun, moon, and stars are completely darkened if the heart of our life is taking for ourselves. Such devastation shows the danger of life once the power of heaven fails with us.

When we see and acknowledge this disaster as the only consequence of selfishness, we can at last realize the saving power of Jesus. Then, at last, "the Son of Man" comes. Jesus uses that title for his work on earth for men and women. By living out our life and resisting all the stress and temptation we face, Jesus brought the love of God into the truth we use in this world. All this truth we have from God's Word is like clouds of heaven to us. It reveals him and his purposes at the same time that it clouds them with the practicalities of this world. When we read the Word, we enter the clouds that reveal him. But we must not forget that he is alive in them, that he has filled them with his divine love by using them in our world, that he has come in those clouds. When we read the Word, he is that near to us, alive in what we read. When we live by it, he is filling it with the whole love of God for humankind.

He makes a second coming to us if we read his Word in this spirit and use it for the purposes of his love. Two thousand years ago at a point in time he came on earth to take the power to help us, but in the clouds of the Word of God he makes a second coming with all that power to us individually. There is truly great power in this coming, for it really is the presence of his love gifted to us to enlighten and strengthen us. There could be no greater glory for our lives. Many have interpreted his coming to them as giving them power to declare new doctrines and impose new disciplines. It cannot be so. The coming is in the clouds of the Word of God. It enlightens and directs us by that truth, but now with the power of unselfish love. This it is that will gather up all our mind for his service, from the most earthly service to the highest heavenly inspiration, and from all four quarters of our life—from the cold of our reasoning to the warmth of our understanding, from the shadows of our mundane actions to the rising love of our hearts.

28–32. "But learn a parable from the fig tree. When its branch has begun to grow and produces leaves, you know that summer is near. In the same way, when you see these things happening you will know it is near, at the very door. In truth, I tell you this generation will in no way have vanished until all this has happened. Heaven and earth will pass away, but my words will never pass away. But no one knows that day or hour, not even the angels in heaven, not the Son, but only the Father."

The symbol for this new state is the fig tree. In Mark 11:12–14, we saw the fig tree used for a failure by men and women, when their earthly lives had all the leaves of knowledge about how to live the life of love, but they produced no fruit of true service in their lives. That fig tree withered away. Now we have a new growth of life. The new beginning is in our life lived in this world, but now we live it from love, and all the "leaves" we grow breathe in the spirit of the Lord. We shall know the change has come when our life is powered by Jesus' love and not our own selfishness. And when that happens, we shall see our ideas grow out of love. Our way of thinking will be quite new. One way of judging where our Christianity has gotten to is to look at the thoughts and ideas that fill our mind and see if they all grow out of a love to help others. When they are growing like that, we are coming into a season of Jesus' love, with all its warmth and harvests of good.

Many think that any real change in us means the destruction of all revelation from God in the past. They look for a new basis for religion other than Scripture given for past generations. But such things do not pass away. The love of God spoke in those revelations; and, although the state of humanity meant that he must hide his message in the practices and history of that time, it was still his love speaking. That does not pass away. The "heaven and earth" that people imagined in past ages do pass away when their inadequacy is seen, but "his words" of divine revelation remain to serve every generation.

Although Jesus has indicated the state that will bring this great change, the judgment of when this new state is reached is not one that anyone can know, not even if their state is angelic. Nor can the living truth from God's love that Jesus brought—"the Son"—know that "day or hour." All such judgment would be from reason, thought, ideas, even illumination of the mind. But the fundamental thing about this great change is the love that motivates it. That is the love of God, and only he, the true Father who gives each of us love and life, could define the change that occurs. We are so used to judging by reason and rationality that we are liable to forget how primary is love and how fundamental it is in any judgment of change in a human soul.

> *33–37. Beware! Watch and pray, for you do not know when is that time. It is like a man going away, leaving his house, and giving his slaves responsibilities and to each one his work, and warning the doorkeeper to watch. So watch, for you do not know when the master of the house will come—in the evening, at midnight, at dawn, or in the morning—*

unless coming suddenly he finds you sleeping. And what I say to you, I say to everyone, 'Watch!'"

Every one of us has the feeling that we have been left alone to cope with life. Often we feel we would like to know and feel the very presence of God in us, replacing the uncertain responsibility we exercise. Certainly, we would like to know the time when we will be saved from our selfishness. But life does not have a terminus when all is done. It is a continual living for God. The whole point of our creation was so that God could give to us his life and his joy in loving, as if it were our own. That can only be so if we have the real power to choose what we do with our life. So each of us has to be alive to the need for God's truth in us to be powered by his love. To "watch" is to be aware of the truth in all our life and to choose its way of love. Each of us has a "door" into our minds by which affection comes into our thinking and planning. To watch that door is stressed particularly, for it is easy for selfishness to enter instead of love. To "pray" is to consider our life in the light of God's way.

We have been left with our duties in the world, and we need to keep the truth at work from love in them. To fail in that is to fall asleep and dream life away for ourselves. When things become more obscure and our new day of Christian life has an "evening," when things are dark and difficult at "midnight," when the love of Jesus "dawns" on us again, and in the "morning" when our Christian life seems renewed, in every state we must be awake to the truth and its purpose of love. The Lord is really "coming" at every moment, for he is with us whether we feel near to him or not. We need to watch for him and work with him throughout our life.

THE HISTORICAL <u>PAROUSIA</u> OR
SECOND COMING

Although this commentary is concerned with our personal state and its changes, it is hardly possible to leave this chapter without some comment on the Second Coming that so many have looked for down the centuries. Paul's epistles show that, even in the first century, some abandoned the disciplined Christian life in anticipation of a sudden transformation. Early Christians saw the Roman wars with the Jews and the destruction of the Jewish temple as the signs mentioned in this chapter. Later generations took any and every violent cataclysm in human affairs as the sign of the end, from the fall of Rome to each contemporary war. But there never was any second coming after the distress. Indeed, it is impossible to see how these passages in the gospel can be fulfilled in earthly terms. What we have seen here destroys all idea of a historical sequence. The wars and disasters, the destruction and escape have to do with real things of the mind. To each individual it happens when the mind is revealed for what it is, and the evil and selfishness within apparent religion and moral life are shown up. Only the breakup of a hypocritical established order in the mind can give the opportunity for divine love to act within the truth. The ability to see this demand of love within the Scripture depends on such an apparent destruction of the mind's status quo.

Fulfillment in a historical sense would presumably need a similar change in the majority of a population, a breakup of false claims to dominance by men and women and a derision of hypocrisy in moral life. We could say that we are in the midst of that. It seems that no other age has so questioned who has the right to rule or has doubted and derided quite as much as this age. But that does not guarantee a second coming and the millennium. Only where the love God brought into the world is accepted and becomes the illumination for human life is there any step forward. Certainly we need the means to understand Scripture and reveal its message of love, as we have tried to see in these pages. Men and women must see this internal sense of love within the Word and use it to change their lives. They must not go to the Bible to find ways of criticizing and judging others, or to search for authority to order the lives of others. They must use it to change their own ways of loving and thinking and planning, for only the choice of individuals to serve and understand by the love of God will make any real change.

Means in the world to think about Scripture and use it correctly from love make it possible for individuals to change. My introduction to this commentary has made it clear that I think they exist at this time. Old hidebound attitudes have broken down, and there is a desire with many to see new light in Scripture. But such a desire does not guarantee that they will. The change only comes by an individual's personal choice to live in love to others. And we have seen already that only our heavenly Father's love knows when that happens. We are accustomed to think of human beings "in bulk" as social groups, communities, and nations. The change we are considering is purely individual. If it comes, will it happen with many or a few, with enough to make a change in the world at large or not? Surely that is God's business and not ours. Our task is to accept the love of Jesus as our life and to work from it in the world. The rest we can leave him to provide.

Chapter Fourteen

SUPPER AND BETRAYAL

We have seen, again and again, that salvation from our selfishness depends on the presence of life from God at our earthly level, on his power to love unselfishly brought into this world in Jesus Christ. We come now to the last steps in this work, which continue into the trial and crucifixion. Throughout an earthly life of some thirty years, Jesus had been fighting the evil in the human mind he had assumed through Mary. The work must have been largely done when he began his ministry, for he had clarity in his teaching and power from God which he could exercise in this world. However, he still needed to carry his work on through the greatest stresses and the deepest emotions this world could ever place on men and women. Then his love would be with them all in all their distress, and the whole of his human be divine. Much work had already been done to reject the human self-love he had taken on, but the deepest level of evil remained to attack him. Perhaps we can grasp this if we think of the danger of any desire for personal control or satisfaction in what he was doing. He could resist that evil only by willingly accepting complete loss of freedom and life, a total rejection of self. As the evil of humanity totally rejected him, he had to oppose it with love, witnessing to the divine way that would not reject men and women and still sought their salvation. His battle of temptation was more lonely and desperate than we can ever know. This deep-rooted human evil still obscured his awareness of the divine love in him, but that same love for every man and woman made his agony beyond any human measure.

At this point, two things must be borne in mind in our reading of Mark's gospel. First, it is a partial description of the end of our Lord's work, so far as it could be seen from outward events. It cannot be complete, for much detail is missing; and, indeed, details vary in the four gospels, as is to be expected in eyewitness accounts. It can only indicate at times the stress and deep emotion within Jesus; and his sometimes enigmatic statements do not and cannot reveal his own understanding of what was happening. Since he was bringing divine love into human living, the work itself could not be expressed in earthly words. Still, the gospel tells us what he has done for us and shows us how complete his love is. The effectiveness of this divine work would be the same whether we knew about it and understood it or not.

Some have thought that the suffering and sacrifice involved is what saved men and women; therefore, a simple assertion of belief in Jesus effects salvation. But redemption was accomplished by providing the power of divine love at our level. Thus, we individually must choose to let that power work in us to change the whole of our lives and replace our selfishness with genuine love for others. Therefore, secondly, the story provides us with a parable of the way the love of Jesus conquers our self-centered nature and endures to save us, as he reminds us when he talks of each one of us "carrying our cross." He enters into each of us with the strength of his love, and this in a way similar to his entering into human life to gain the power to help us. We really do need to understand this process, and the details that are preserved in the story are just those that convey this truth. Such understanding would be useless if we did not believe that Jesus redeemed us. So we need equally to believe in his love for us and to grasp how that love works deeply and personally in us for our salvation.

This last work to redeem us is set at the time of Passover. In the Old Testament, the release of Israel from bondage in Egypt on the night of the Passover expressed the idea of God redeeming man. Israel was escaping from earthly bondage to be the Lord's people. Passover's symbolism teaches the same message of salvation that the gospel records. Differences in detail between the gospels show a synoptic tradition, which Mark sets and Matthew and Luke follow and which differs from the story as John tells it. The synoptics appear to identify the Last Supper with the Passover meal, whereas John synchronizes the death of Jesus on the cross with the killing of the Passover lambs on the day before the Passover, and so the supper is not the Passover. John certainly makes it easier to understand the involvement of the Jewish leaders in the trial and crucifixion, for they could hardly have behaved in that fashion on the day of the Passover. But deciding the exact chronology is not important to the teaching that both gospels draw from the events. Each gospel provides a meaning for us to enlighten our own salvation, while their differences are those to be expected in the memories of eyewitnesses.

1–2. Now the Passover and the feast of unleavened bread were in two days, and the chief priests and the scribes were seeking to get hold of him by cunning so that they could kill him. But they said, "Not at the feast, in case the people make a riot."

The imminence of the Passover created a problem for the authorities. Jerusalem was crowded, for every Jew who could came to have a lamb killed in the temple and to eat the feast in Jerusalem. These crowds were listening to Jesus and appreciating what he said. The authorities knew they would need deceit to get one condemned who taught only brotherly love. They might raise a riot among the crowds, however cunningly they moved; and the Romans would not take kindly to a violent disturbance. So they were content to wait—until Judas gave them an unforeseen opportunity.

The Jewish feasts symbolized the work that Jesus was doing. We can all understand that the lamb eaten at the Passover was a symbol of innocence, but we need to realize what innocence really is. We tend to identify it with infants who do not know how to work for their own ends. A truer meaning is approached when an adult does not seek anything for self, although aware of all the possibilities of personal gain. The love of God is unselfish in the supreme sense, innocent of any thought of self despite his infinite power. God's love seeks only to give the joy of his life to us. This love came into humanity's earthly mind in Jesus, expelling all the desires for self that obsess the human mind. In the truest sense, that love was bringing innocence to men and women.

The feast of unleavened bread symbolizes the other aspect of Jesus' work. At that feast no leaven, or yeast, was allowed in the house or eaten. Yeast works to ferment, whether it is in the dough of leavened bread or in grape juice to make wine. This fermenting symbolizes the way false ideas about the purpose of life clash with the truth in our minds, so that we are forced to realize the real demands of truth. Jesus had gone through great stress, with the result that his way of life and thought had become nothing but the truth of God's way. The ideas that he used now to direct his love were free of such fermenting falsity, just as unleavened bread is free of yeast or leaven. This is the deeper reason that Jesus' passion is linked with the Passover and the feast of unleavened bread.

For us, the gospel's mention of these Jewish feasts summarizes the stress in our personal life. We have our old accepted pattern of a moral life, which our selfishness is able to twist to serve our own purposes. The world appears to demand such moral values, so we use them without acknowledging our real motive, as the priests and scribes claimed holiness but hoped to destroy Jesus by cunning. But a demand is being made on us to accept something totally new. We are asked to "feed on the lamb of God" in a real Passover, by taking his innocent love as our whole life and denying our selfish desires. We are asked to let this control our thinking, so that no fermenting falsity twists ideas to suit ourselves. We are being asked to change our motive for living. Such a change will bring a stress in our life as great as the passion of Jesus.

3–9. And he was in Bethany, at the house of Simon the leper, reclining at table, and a woman came with an alabaster flask of perfume of genuine spikenard, very costly. And breaking the flask she poured the perfume on his head. And some were angry,

muttering among themselves, "Why has this oint-
ment been wasted? It could have been sold for more
than three hundred denarii, to be given to the poor."
And they grumbled at her. But Jesus said, "Let her
alone. Why do you bother her? She did a good thing
to me. For you always have the poor with you, and
you can do good to them whenever you like, but you
do not always have me with you. She did what she
could. She came beforehand to anoint my body for
burial. Indeed, I tell you, wherever this good news is
proclaimed in the whole world, what she has done
shall also be told as a memorial to her."

John's gospel places Jesus at Bethany during the last days, for he avoided staying inside Jerusalem at night, where he might be taken in the absence of the daytime crowds. Whether Simon was a leper who had been healed, we do not know. Those who saw the woman anoint Jesus could concentrate on nothing but the value of the perfumed oil and its waste. Spikenard, or nard, was an aromatic oil made from a perennial plant of the valerian family. It was imported from India and was very valuable. Three hundred denarii was as much as a laborer might earn in a year's work. Such aromatic oils were sealed in perfume flasks, generally referred to as "alabasters," regardless of the material they were made from.

Jesus was the Christ, the Messiah, "the anointed one." The woman's action in anointing him with the perfumed oil declared him the Savior. It was an outward sign of what was happening in his inner life, for in him the love of God was pouring down and anointing earthly human life with its divine love. The outcry from those around, that the anointing oil should have been sold, expresses a misunderstanding common to us all. In spiritual things, to be poor is to be without the truth that can enrich our lives. Our feeling is that love is really concerned with improving our understanding of life; it should be "sold and given to the poor." But the true nature of love is that it is a desire to help others. It is a strength to direct our lives in compassion and service. Obviously, it will also enlighten our minds, for "the poor you always have with you, and you can do good to them whenever you like"; but the first purpose of God's love when it anoints life is to bring to it a new power, a new drive and direction. For Jesus, burial meant resurrection, and the anointing is for a burial that is a resurrection of a new presence of God's love in the world. His purpose was not merely to enlarge humankind's understanding of things, but to provide us with a new drive of love in our lives.

We can easily make this same mistake when we try to receive Jesus' saving love into our lives. We can concentrate on the greater understanding we can gain of his purpose in the world and of the way men and women behave; but his purpose is to change the reason we are living, to put a new will behind all we want to do. The "poor" will be satisfied and our understanding will increase, but that is something that improves all the while. What changes everything is acknowledging that the love Jesus has brought is the only power in our life, bringing about a complete resurrection into a new life. It changes, not parts of our understanding, but the whole reason that we are living.

Once we grasp this, we can see why Jesus said this woman's action would be told as a memorial to her wherever the good news was proclaimed. It is not a remembrance of an earthly woman, for we do not know her name. It is the remembrance of the whole purpose of Jesus' work that rests, not just on instructing us, but on giving us a new unselfish love from him to fill all our lives.

10–11. And Judas Iscariot, one of the twelve, went off to the chief priests, to betray him to them. And when they had heard him, they were delighted, and promised to give him money. And he looked for a convenient moment to betray him.

Now, for the first time, Judas Iscariot becomes important in the story. Iscariot probably means "a man of Kerioth"; if that is so, he was from the south, whereas the other disciples seem to be from Galilee in the north. His motive in betraying Jesus has led to a great deal of speculation, including the suggestion that he was trying to force Jesus' hand and make him show his power by bringing about a confrontation with the authorities. We shall never know Judas' thoughts, but in the gospel story, the only motive given for him is that of greed. He betrayed Jesus for money, for personal gain. The authorities needed the help of one of the twelve, who would know where Jesus went at night when the crowds would not be around to object to his arrest. If they could take him then and fabricate a charge that he had affronted Jewish beliefs, they could hope to get the crowd on their side.

Judas represents the deepest and most tenacious evil in the human mind, which Jesus had to conquer and replace with divine love. At the bottom of all our evil is the basic desire to have things for ourselves, a kind of emotional and mental avarice that cannot bear that our life should not benefit us personally. This "Judas" was contained in the human condition Jesus had taken on in the world, for Jesus needed to resist all our evils and change the whole of human life as we know it. Jesus was replacing this "Judas" of self-wanting with divine life, which is totally unselfish and seeks only to give itself away to others. The deepest torment of spirit was involved in such a change and the suffering of the passion portrays it; yet, without it, human beings would not have new life available for their salvation.

If we seek back into our motivation, we shall find this "Judas" lurking at the bottom of all our planning for life, even when we feel we are thinking only of others. Some thought of what others will think of us, some pride in having been "good enough to do it," underlies even the best things we do. We have to face betrayal by our own private Judas, which would destroy love in our lives because we must have something for ourselves. Only by beginning to live from a totally new life from Jesus can this basic spiritual avarice be rooted out.

> *12–17. And on the first day of Unleavened Bread, when the Passover was killed, his disciples said to him, "Where do you want us to go and make ready for you to eat the Passover?" And he sent two of his disciples, saying to them, "Go into the city, and a man carrying a pitcher of water will meet you. Follow him and, wherever he enters, say to the master of the house, 'The teacher says, where is the guest chamber where I may eat the Passover with my disciples?' And he will show you a large upper room ready furnished. There make ready for us." And his disciples went away and came into the city, and found all as he had said to them. And they prepared the Passover. And when it was evening, he came with the twelve.*

There is a "cloak-and-dagger" flavor to this settling upon a room in which to eat the Passover. It was important that the authorities should not find out where they could take Jesus alone at night, with his disciples but without the protection of interested crowds. Since women did all the water carrying, a man carrying a pitcher of water identified himself without the use of names or locations; and Jesus must have known that the master of the house he entered would cooperate. Since it appears later that Jesus knew of Judas' treachery, the secrecy surrounding the location of the supper may have been largely to prevent Judas' acting until Jesus wished him to. Mark seems to regard this last supper as the Passover, though it is noteworthy that at the meal no reference is made to the special food eaten then. Any meal would have required some preparation, but the Passover required very specific preparation. A lamb had to be obtained and ritually killed and then roasted. Wine, bitter herbs and sauce, and unleavened bread had to be obtained and prepared. The room is described as already equipped with table and couches or cushions for them to recline on as they ate. The original command was to eat the Passover standing, as though in readiness to leave in haste, but by now it was customary to eat it seated.

The hiding of the disciples' destination, so that they did not know it until they arrived, typifies the journey of any disciples of our Lord. We do not know our destination until we reach it, for only the Lord understands the unselfish way of life to which he is leading us. If we knew where we were going, we would never follow, for it means denial of ourselves. We follow an unusual watercarrier who bears, not human ideas, but "the water of everlasting life," the truth of the Word of God. By means of it, the Lord brings us to a state when he can reveal to us how much he wants to feed us with the bread of his life.

Since, as we shall see later, Jesus was to make this meal

a sign of his redeeming life feeding all humankind, it may seem strange to emphasize that the disciples were to prepare it. Yet it is essential that we realize the part we must play in receiving salvation. We cannot manufacture new life for ourselves—only Jesus can give it—but we must be prepared to receive it. We have the freedom to choose what we love in our lives, and only if we are prepared to give up our selfish desires can Jesus enter us with new life. Though the life that gives us the power to choose is God's gift to us, that still makes the act of choice ours. We must choose to make ourselves ready for him to feed us with new life.

> *18–21. And as they were reclining at table and eating, Jesus said, "Truly, I tell you, one of you who is eating with me will betray me." And they began to be distressed and to say to him, one by one, "It isn't me, is it?" and another, "It's surely not me?" But he answered them, "It is one of the twelve who is dipping in the dish with me. Indeed, the Son of Man goes as it has been written of him, but woe to that man by whom the Son of Man is betrayed. It were better for that man if he had never been born."*

This must have been an appalling moment for the twelve apostles, as their panic questions show. They had misunderstood him and at times had failed him, but could hardly grasp that one of them would actually betray him to the Jewish authorities who sought to kill him. Jesus insisted that it was one of those sharing the meal with him and declared it to be a fulfillment of Scripture, presumably Psalm 41:9, which John quotes, "Indeed, my own familiar friend whom I trusted, who eats my bread, has raised up his heel against me." It must have shaken Judas to realize that his treachery was known, though his identity was not revealed.

Despite Jesus' warning, he persisted. John tells us that he left under pretense of buying something. Certainly by the time they went on to Gethsemane, he had slipped away to earn his bribe.

Many find it difficult to understand why Jesus chose Judas to be one of the twelve and ate with him even after he knew him as a traitor. But the apostles had to represent the whole of human life, and that includes the basic greed that lurks beneath all our thoughts and actions. The Peter of our faith, the John of our love for Jesus, the James of our service to others, and all the other facets of our Christian life are coupled together and cannot exist apart. And the Judas of our greed is always there. When we are trying to feed on our Lord's way, it is still there, seeking self-aggrandizement out of loving service, taking merit in things done to be unselfish. Jesus knew this facet within the perverted human nature he had taken on in the world, and he was determined to reject it and replace it with the total unselfishness of divine love. If we think of Judas' torment in his treachery, we should also think of the torment that Jesus knew in himself, knowing this spiritual greed trying to destroy all the unselfish life he had brought into the world.

It is not surprising that the traitor is an intimate friend of Jesus, for he is involved in all our acceptance of Jesus' way. He contaminates our highest aspirations and most loving actions. The divine love, which wants to enter us to be a saving life for us, is aware of this deep-seated treachery in our soul. Jesus intends to make us aware of it and to confront it, so that we know we must abandon our own life and let his life rise up in us. We shall know our Judas in its betrayal of genuine love in our life. Only when we know and understand and abhor the treachery of greed in our best efforts and most loving plans shall we give up our own life and allow the life of Jesus to rise up in us.

Jesus said of the traitor that it would have been "better for him if he had never been born." Certainly Judas must have felt that way later, as he hurled the blood money at the feet of the Jewish leaders and went to hang himself; but the meaning for us is not really concerned with a single man, caught up in events too great for his weak character. It is a true statement about the spiritual avarice at the heart of all of us. It expresses the curse of all men and women. Though we were made to receive God's unselfish life, through our freedom to choose there has been born into the race this basic selfishness. Better if it had never been born! Now a redeeming act of God would save us from it.

> *22–25. And as they were eating, Jesus took a loaf and blessed it and broke it, and gave it to them saying, "Take! Eat! This is my body." And taking the cup and giving thanks, he gave it to them, and they all drank from it. And he said to them, "This is my blood of the new covenant, which is poured out for many. Truly I tell you that I will drink of the fruit of the vine no more, until the day I drink it new in the kingdom of God."*

The Passover was instituted so that the Israelites could remember their salvation from Egyptian bondage. They were to eat the Passover lamb roasted, and with bitter herbs. Now Jesus used this last supper to provide a way for men and women to remember him and his saving power. The sacrament of the Holy Supper consists in the eating of bread and the drinking of wine, as Jesus commanded his disciples that night. Eating together has always been a mark of love and friendship, and we feel any meal unnatural where such sentiments are not present; but Jesus gave a special significance to this meal.

When his work was done, Jesus would have made his humanity into divine unselfish love, and all humankind was to feed on this love instead of selfishness. So he gave the bread as his body, the very substance of himself, which they were all to eat. The redeeming love we feed on and live from is his very presence in us. It was unleavened bread he gave them, free from any contamination of leaven, for the source of all our life has to become his unselfish love, mixed with no selfish desire. Such love has its own wisdom flowing in it. It looks at all men and women and their doings with the eyes of love, and so is wise in living with them. This wisdom has nothing to do with knowledge of fact. That can be little or much. It is the attitude with which love looks at all it sees that makes its wisdom. This lifeblood flowing in divine love is like blood in flesh, carrying the life of the body. All of us will drink in this kind of wisdom with the love of Jesus, and it will make our new covenant of love as we work with him.

The wine symbolizes this wisdom, and that says something of its nature. Wine is made from the fermenting of grape juice by the yeast enzyme on the skin of the grapes. As it works, it changes the natural juice into the exhilarating wine. In Jesus' life he had changed humankind's natural way of thinking into a divine wisdom, a wisdom now free of any ferment of false and evil ways. However, since in Jesus it has been through that process here at our level, it is of a kind that human minds can drink in and use to enlighten them in this world. It has been "fully fermented" in their human condition. Jesus comments that he would not now drink wine until the day he was to "drink it new in the kingdom of God." Once he had fought his last temptation on the cross, he would have renewed totally the thinking of his earthly mind and made it divine wisdom. This is the "new wine" filled with the life of God in which he is present with us now, able to enlighten us if we will let him.

So the supper that the Lord calls us to share with him is a full remembrance of what he has done and how near he is to us with his life. In itself, the outward observance of this sacrament achieves little; but, by recalling the love and wisdom of Jesus so perfectly, it can bring us close to him. Calling us to use only that love and wisdom in our living, it draws us near to him and is a true remembrance of the purpose of our lives.

> *26–31. And when they had sung a hymn, they went out to the Mount of Olives. And Jesus said to them, "All of you will shy away from me this night, for it has been written, 'I will smite the shepherd and the sheep will be scattered abroad.' But after I have risen, I will go before you into Galilee." But Peter said to him, "Even if they all fall away, I will not." And Jesus said to him, "Truly I tell you, this very night before the cock crows twice, you will deny me three times." But he insisted vehemently, "If I have to die with you, still I will never deny you." And they all said the same.*

The Passover feast would end with the singing of Psalms 113–118, hymns of praise with remembrance of the Lord saving Israel. They went then to the Mount of Olives on the east of the city, facing the temple complex, which seems to have been a favorite place for Jesus. Here a second blow fell on the disciples. Not only was the traitor one of them, but Jesus told them that the rest would all desert him that night. How they would scatter when he was captured he quoted from Zechariah 13:7, turning into a statement the command "Smite the shepherd and the sheep will be scattered abroad!" The accompanying promise of his resurrection was lost in their protestations that they would not run away, Peter rashly taking the lead.

The defection of the disciples might seem to denote weakness, but their work in the early church does not suggest that they were cowards. Their failure is here to pinpoint an important and often forgotten aspect of Christian psychology. In the emotional environment of worship, religious instruction, or Christian work together, it is easy to make a declaration of faith in Jesus and his teaching. But for the complete renewal of the spirit that his redeeming demands, there has to be a total realization of what is involved. When alone, we have to face the way our corrupt self reacts to the stress of complete self-denial. Then the loving demand of Jesus is seen as an obstacle to us, rather than an opportunity to serve. (In saying that they will all "shy away" or "fall away" from him, Jesus uses a word that means he will "become an obstacle" to them.) In the disciples' case, physical death was the outcome they dreaded; to the human spirit, it is the dread of abandoning self-wanting, which seems to leave us dead and no longer alive as a person. Only by facing this, and knowing in our terror and weakness what it means, can we really make the choice to be a new man or woman in Jesus Christ.

When we realize that the Good Shepherd is all-powerful in loving others but for that very reason not interested in self-preservation, we can feel that he is stricken and we scatter from his way. Yet we must learn that only love that does not count the cost can always rise and triumph. Jesus involves the promise of resurrection in his talk of our desertion, to emphasize that he offers new life in which we will still feel free though we live only from his spirit. But for the moment our reaction is to assert our power to follow him as we are, without grasping the need for such a vast change in ourselves.

32–42. And they came to a place called Gethsemane, and he said to his disciples, "Sit here, while I pray." And he took Peter, James, and John with him. And he began to be in terror and anguish, and said to them, "My soul is deeply sorrowful, even to death. Stay here and watch." And going forward a little, he fell on the ground and prayed that, if possible, this hour might pass from him. And he said, "Abba, Father, all things are possible to you; take away this cup from me. But not what I want, only what you want." And he came and found them sleeping. And he said to Peter, "Simon, are you asleep? Were you not able to watch one hour? Watch and pray, that you do not enter into temptation. Indeed, the spirit is ready, but the flesh is weak." And going away again, he prayed as he had before. And returning he found them sleeping again, for their eyes were heavy, and they did not know how to answer him. And he came the third time, and said to them, "Sleep on now and take your rest. It is enough; the hour has come. Look, the Son of Man is betrayed into the hands of sinners. Rise, let us go. See, the traitor is drawing near."

Gethsemane means an olive press, presumably made to press out the oil from the olives grown on the hill. It is here the disciples gather, and Jesus takes Peter, James, and John a little further away, as he did at his transfiguration, and then goes on himself to pray. He addresses his prayer first in Aramaic, *Abba*, and then in Greek, *Pater*, and it would seem that this became the custom in the early church, especially in the Lord's Prayer. The drowsiness of the disciples on such an occasion seems strange to us with hindsight; but the hour might well be late, and stress in itself can induce sleep.

The prayer of Jesus in Gethsemane, perhaps more than anything else, enables us to understand how real was his temptation and torment. When we think of the power of divine love coming into him, we may feel that he had such surety that failure and the terror of the hour should have had no effect. But this is to forget that he had taken on the mind of men and women, with all its fears and selfish instincts of preservation. Now he is in the darkness of that mind, and his love is the only strength he has. Like us, he has no surety of the future. When internal stress from human evil did not arise, he could see from the truth with clarity and have all the wisdom of divine love. But once the evil was stirred up for him to fight, he came into the same obscurity we know, so that he had to hold on to his mission of love without any security about the future. If it had not been so, his redeeming presence would not be real in our terror and obscurity.

The desire for self-preservation was part of the humanity that Jesus had taken on. It not only included our fear of pain, suffering, and death, but the fear that we shall not achieve things in the way we want to. Jesus knew from the Scriptures, and had said, that carrying his work into torment and death was the only way he could rise to save humanity. But now that he was fully involved in his teaching and his work with his disciples, it was hard for him to give up that way and take the more cruel way divine love saw was necessary. And he had no surety that men and women would use the work he would do. Ordinary human beings face suffering and death, but they do not do so knowing that it is the only way love can reach others, and fearing that way may fail because men and women will not accept the love brought to them.

Shot through with knowledge of the horrible death that awaited him, Jesus' vision was darkened by the last and deepest evil of the human mind. His prayer shows his torment, but it also shows his trust in God and his deep and unshaken love for the Father. There is a touching remembrance of the nature of that Father in the way he addresses his prayer, using first the Aramaic word *Abba* learned in earliest childhood when love is its whole meaning. He dreads what he must do, but he will still trust in the love of God. We must not equate our stress in temptation with his, for we have less at stake. He knew that he was to redeem the world, not just save himself. The love in him was for the whole human race, and the stress and terror were commensurate, far beyond our knowing. His great cry from the cross, "My God, my God, why have you forsaken me?" shows the terror his love could feel when it feared men and women would not accept the love he offered. We do not have so great a love, and so cannot know so great a terror.

It hardly seems possible that the disciples could sleep while Jesus was wrestling in such a torment of love; but as disciples, we are always liable to fall asleep in the midst of the Lord's efforts to save us. The life of earthly activity and worldly motives seems so real to us that we are asleep to a more loving purpose to life. Such sleep is our constant problem. We need to watch and pray for spiritual motives all the while; otherwise, we shall find ourselves constantly dropping into the sleep of merely earthly life. Jesus' words to Peter apply to us all. Even when we strive hard to keep our Christianity awake, the constant invasion of the world's standards and merely natural behavior tends to "send us to sleep" again. While the spirit is willing, the flesh is still weak.

> *43–49. And immediately while he was still speaking, Judas, one of the twelve, came with a great crowd with swords and clubs from the chief priests and scribes and elders. Now, the traitor had given them a sign, saying, "Whoever I kiss is the one. Seize him and take him away securely." And when he came, he went up to him immediately and said to him, "Rabbi, Rabbi," and kissed him lovingly. And they laid hands on him and seized him. But one of those standing by drew a sword and struck at the high priest's slave and cut off his ear. And Jesus said to them, "Are you come out with swords and clubs to take me as though I were a bandit? Daily I was in the temple with you teaching, and you did not take me. But this is so that the Scriptures may be fulfilled."*

The crowd that arrived with Judas was not like those who daily thronged about Jesus. It consisted of followers of the Jewish authorities. The groups forming the Sanhedrin or ruling council are listed here. The term "chief priests" or "high priests" refers to the senior priestly officials: the high priest, a priest as "captain of the temple," and his assistants to govern its work and handle its finance. Sometimes laymen helped as treasurers. These were all Sadducees. The "scribes" on the other hand were largely of the Pharisees and also had considerable influence. The "elders" refer to representatives of the old aristocratic and priestly families who still maintained some authority in the council. The crowd, no doubt including temple guards, came to secure the man the traitor indicated.

At Passover many people might be camped out on the hill, and the authorities needed the knowledge Judas had of Jesus' customary behavior to identify the group. In the darkness, some sign was necessary to identify Jesus amid the group of disciples, and Judas chose to kiss him. Whether the fact that he did it so ardently was to prevent any early alarm, we do not know; it certainly increases our revulsion. Luke 22:38 implies that two of the disciples were armed with swords, although Jesus clearly intended no resistance. John 18:10 tells us that Peter struck the slave and that Jesus healed the injury.

There is no clear indication which Scripture is said to be fulfilled at this point. Isaiah 53:12 has been suggested, although other treacheries with a kiss, such as Joab's killing Amasa while kissing him, 2 Samuel 20:9–10, might be in mind. It is probably better to regard Jesus' life as the fulfillment of the whole purpose of Scripture. The Jews regarded the whole of the Old Testament as a prophecy of the coming of the Messiah, though they looked only for outward signs that agreed with particular passages. Since the Old Testament was a divine revelation, it could not but express the work that Jesus was doing on earth, and that filled it all with its real meaning. Whenever Jesus refers to the Scripture, he accepts the attitude around him, but he points to the deeper meaning that expresses his divine work.

Jesus challenges the hurried clandestine arrest as being quite unnecessary but submits to it. It highlights for us the fact that evil does not attack the Lord in our mind while he is teaching us the truth. It is when we are alone, in the darkness of our own decisions, that the treachery of our selfishness suddenly appears to bind his power. We often tend to look for the stress in our understanding of what Jesus wants, but he is not attacked in our minds while we are just learning truth. It is in decisions of life, in what we want to do, that the presence of Jesus can suddenly be attacked. And it is not the blatant evils that betray us, for those would make us despised by our fellows, and so we avoid them; but it is from our discipleship that the attack comes. Our selfishness uses the good we do as a source of pride and aggrandizement, and so binds to itself any real power of love in our lives. Jesus is betrayed in us by the loving kiss of our apparent obedience, which misuses Christian life for the purposes of the self.

The single blow struck is significant in itself. It cuts off the ear of a slave or servant of the high priest. We have seen that to hear is to obey, and the servant is marked as one who does not obey. The high priest's household should have preserved the holy worship of God, but now it has acted against God's love at work to save humankind. This marked the rejection of Jesus' way of love by the religion of the day; but in our hearts and minds it shows our apparent religion working for our selfishness, and not hearing the true religion of love. Jesus rejects the use of violence and submits to capture, recognizing that the only way love can triumph is by showing its nature in the face of hatred and then leaving humankind to choose to accept the ways of love.

50–52. And they all ran away and left him. And a certain young man was following him, naked save for a linen cloth wrapped round him; and the young men seized him, but he got away naked leaving them holding the linen cloth.

It seems remarkable that, when all the disciples are flee-ing, the adventure of one young man, who we were not aware was in Gethsemane, suddenly takes pride of place. The other gospels do not mention him. It leads to the idea that there was something personal for the writer in this in-cident. We know that the disciples met in "the house of Mary the mother of John, whose surname was Mark," Acts 12:12, and it seems likely that they met there this night. One can imagine Mark at home suddenly awake to treach-ery and running to the garden with a warning, having no time to do more than wrap a linen cloth round him. That was his salvation, for when pursuers tried to grab him, they caught hold of the cloth and he wriggled out of it. This is, perhaps, his personal reminiscence added to what he heard from Peter.

Whoever it refers to, and in whatever way the record of the incident came into Mark's gospel, divine providence has used it to summarize the complete downfall of the dis-ciples. When evil and selfishness challenge us and bind the power of Jesus, all we have of Christian belief and commit-ment flees away. Under this stress, nothing of faith or love or service seems so important as being selfishly in control of our lives. When we react in this fashion, even the last garment of our onetime Christianity is stripped away. The very knowledge of truth we clothed ourselves in from the Gospels we abandon to the grasp of our selfishness. We are willing to wriggle out of even the direct commands of Scripture, since they contradict the selfish way we decide to live.

53–54. And they led Jesus away to the high priest, and all the chief priests and elders and scribes assem-bled. And Peter followed him at a distance into the

high priest's courtyard, and sat with the officers,
warming himself in the firelight.

There is something pathetic in Peter, afraid to declare
himself yet following on, hiding himself in the crowd in
the courtyard and warming himself in the glow of their
fire. It presents us with a very good image of our own state
of mind. We cannot completely ignore his future in us nor
yet can we accept the demand to follow Jesus. Faith is not
just a list of truths that we believe, but an attitude of mind
that wants to live by them. Now we stand outside warming
ourselves at the fire of self-interest and letting that illumine
our life. Yet though we abandon our discipleship, the
knowledge of the truth still remains and holds us, tor-
mented, at a distance from our original ideals.

55–59. And the chief priests and the whole San-
hedrin sought testimony against Jesus to put him to
death, and they found none. For many bore false
witness against him, but their statements did not
agree. And some stood up and witnessed falsely
against him, saying, "We heard him say, 'I will de-
stroy this temple made with hands, and in three days
I will build another not made with hands.'" But still
their testimony was not identical.

Probably we are not to think of this gathering of the
Sanhedrin as an official trial. If it had been, judging by
later Jewish statements in the Mishnah, many illegalities
would have existed. Trial could not take place by night; the
whole process was too hurried; the judges sought for the
witnesses; questioning by the judge, which was out of
order, culminated in a demand for a confession, which was
forbidden; and the sentence was pronounced without

proper delay. Such rules may be later invention, but they must have some roots in earlier practice. However, this meeting was probably an examination of Jesus to find grounds on which to charge him before the Roman authority, as John describes it. The Jews had no authority at this time to try anyone for any grave offense, but had to present all such cases to the Roman procurator to try. Nevertheless, the injustice of the examination is obvious, for the spirit of Jewish justice should have been adhered to. The hatred with which the authorities regarded Jesus made the trial nothing more than a means to achieve his destruction.

At first, no charge could be made to stick, for the Mosaic law demanded the testimony of two witnesses, who must agree absolutely (Deuteronomy 17:6, 19:15). The one accusation of which we are told was a clever distortion of fact. Jesus had never threatened to destroy the temple himself, but had said that, when it was destroyed, he would raise up a temple in three days, by which he meant his resurrected body (John 2:19–21). Mark 13:2 also foretells the destruction of the temple. But even here the witnesses did not give identical evidence.

The law that required the evidence of two witnesses with identical evidence is not just a useful precaution for judges. It expresses a fundamental characteristic of genuine religious life. There are two aspects to such life: the commands of truth that faith understands, and the will to obey and use them that is the heart of a truly good life. Unless the desire is present to use the truth we know, there is no true religion. One can quote truth to condemn one's fellows, to support one's own selfish ambitions. It is not a true witness unless it is being used to bring love and service into the world. Since Jesus united love and truth in himself, any attack on him could not make those two witnesses agree against him. The distorted accusation made expresses how our selfishness sees Jesus. He is the one destroying the temple of our worship. We see him taking away the selfish way we use our religion, and we cannot believe that he can make a new life arise for us.

> *60–64. And the high priest stood up in the middle of them and questioned Jesus, saying, "Why do you not answer these accusations?" But he was silent and answered nothing. Again the high priest questioned him, asking, "Are you the Christ, the son of the blessed one?" And Jesus said, "I am. And you shall see the Son of Man sitting at the right hand of power, and coming in the clouds of heaven." And the high priest tore his garments and said, "What more need have we of witnesses? You heard the blasphemy. How does it seem to you?" And they all condemned him as deserving death.*

Mark nowhere gives the name of the high priest, Caiaphas, as the other gospels do. His tearing of his garments at the blasphemy is according to custom, denoting the devastation of such a sin. However, the accusation of blasphemy is not easy to understand. To claim to be the Messiah was not in itself a blasphemy, and other claimants were not so accused. The high priest's question uses a circumlocution to avoid saying the divine name, which was forbidden to a Jew, but it means "Are you the Messiah, the son of Jehovah?" A Jew would not identify the Messiah with the son of God in this specific fashion, and the question possibly contains the claim of Jesus, made clear in John's gospel, that he was divine. This, indeed, the high priest could recognize as blasphemy. That "all" condemned him shows that this was no full official meeting of the

Council, for Nicodemus or Joseph of Arimathea and others would surely have dissented. The punishment for blasphemy was death by stoning (Leviticus 24:16), but the Jews had no right to try anyone for a capital offense, and Pilate was hardly likely to accept this charge as such anyway. Jesus' claim to be the Messiah was, therefore, presented to Pilate as rebellion against Rome, a charge he could not ignore. The term "Son of Man" is one used only by Jesus for himself. It was used in Hebrew poetry for "man," and Aramaic has a similar use in prose. There is no reason to believe that the term was used of the Messiah at this time, and it would seem to be a phrase chosen by Jesus to express his complete involvement in the human situation, while declaring his special purpose there.

In view of the many promises in the Old Testament that God would redeem his people, it may seem strange that Jesus' claim to be doing exactly that should be regarded as blasphemy. The Jewish leaders, however, saw clearly that the kind of kingdom Jesus was bringing would rob them of their power over the people. This is the way in which selfishness always sees the coming of God. The demand to love others destroys our habit of using religion to keep a personal grip on our lives and satisfy our own love of dominion. To become simply the servant of all is unthinkable. To such a self-centered attitude of mind, God is something that invests us with authority and power, which we can then use for ourselves. The kind of God that shows in Jesus' coming destroys that notion, and so it is a blasphemy to the selfishness and evil in us. The action of the high priest now has a terrible irony. Blasphemy against God had always been marked by tearing the priestly clothes, because the heart of religion is clothed in truths about God and any blasphemy against his power tears such ideas apart. But now it was the high priest himself who was tearing up all the truth about God and his way of redemption, and his torn robes showed his own perverseness, not that of the innocent Jesus.

Jesus' declaration emphasizes that he has come down into our human condition to make it divine, for he is "the Son of Man" and has taken "the right hand of power." Because men and women are selfish, the power of love could only be brought back into their lives by God bringing divine power into earthly life. This power of the divine human on earth, he declares, comes "with the clouds of heaven," for it is only in the clouds of truth revealed to us by God that we can see him. Jesus lived his life by these truths and filled them with divine love in this world. We can now use the same truths and let his love work in them, so that we shall know his power in ourselves. To our selfishness, that is the extreme blasphemy, for such a coming denies our selfish rights in life.

65. And some began to spit on him; and to blindfold him and hit him and then say, "Prophesy!" And the officers hit him with the flat of their hands.

The release of anger in violence is a sorry thing, and the abuse of Jesus demeans his attackers, not him. Luke 22:63 ascribes the violence to those who held Jesus, but here any in the assembly could have taken part. Isaiah 50:6 and 53:3 are called to mind here, and the language has echoes of the Greek version of those passages. Spitting on anyone is still a sign that he is despised. Prophecy is really to teach truth, but they took it in its common meaning and made game of it, asking him to prophesy who hit him.

Once the redeeming love of God is rejected, all the truth about life that stems from it is despised. Instead of being a prophecy of the true state of human life, it becomes a thing to play with and diminish for our own ends. Nor is such an attack merely an intellectual refutation of tenets of faith; until God guides us to understand properly, that can always happen. This attack springs from anger against the Lord's demand that we live by his way of life. Faith is not denied because it is not understood. It is denied because it has made a claim to our life.

> *66–72. And Peter was in the courtyard below. And one of the maids of the high priest came and saw him warming himself and studied him and said, "And you were with the Nazarene Jesus." But he denied it, saying, "I neither know nor understand what you are talking about." And he went out into the porch, and a cock crowed. And the maid, seeing him again, began to say to those standing around, "This is one of them." And again he denied it. And again after a little while, those standing around said to Peter, "Indeed, you are one of them, for you are a Galilean, as your accent shows." But he began to curse and swear, "I do not know this man of whom you speak." And the second time a cock crew. And Peter remembered that Jesus had said to him, "Before the cock crows twice, you will deny me three times." And facing up to it, he wept.*

It has been suggested that the "cockcrow" here is the *gallicinium*, the Roman army call for the last watch of the night. Jesus uses the term in 13:35, where he lists the watches of the night. There is no reason that here it should not have been a cock crowing. Assertions by some scholars that none were allowed to be kept in Jerusalem at that time are probably unsound. Only Mark has the cock crow twice.

If Peter is the original source of the material, it may well be a detail that has been lost in the other records. We do not know what marked a Galilean accent in the Aramaic Peter would be speaking, but Galilee had developed separately, at times with many foreign immigrants, and was still separated from the south by the Samaritans. Such circumstances lead to wide differences in accents.

Peter's denials show us the way we realize what our faith involves. It was easy enough for Peter to declare that he would never abandon Jesus, but now he was face to face with the consequences of such a resolution. It is easy enough for us to declare that we have a faith and that we follow Jesus, until we are left face to face with the demands of that faith. The crowd of selfish desires that throng our mind ask if we really mean to be with Jesus, to be totally unselfish, and we deny because we cannot bear to abandon all our selfishness. Because we have declared our faith and made it part of our life, the pressure will not go away. At another place in our life, again comes the challenge, and again. Because we have accepted the truth, it is as though we "think with that accent," and we cannot get away from the constant challenge to it from our self-love. Each time the stress increases, as we realize what our denial means, until finally we curse the demand on us and are forsworn in denying Jesus' demands. At that moment we finally realize what our faith truly means to us, and it is at that moment the cock crows for a new day, a new life, a new birth into using Jesus' love. Now we remember all we were told of our weakness, because we grieve over losing Jesus' love from our hearts. It is then he can work in us again, not just from ideas we find interesting, but from a love that lets us see the needs of others and strengthens us to serve them.

The pressure upon Peter, his fear of the hatred and

death around him, seems a cruel reward for someone who had tried to follow his Lord. If it had no purpose, it would indeed be cruel. It comes about simply because Peter does want to follow Jesus. That desire can only be fulfilled if he can know and feel what it really involves. And the only way for him to grasp that is if he can experience this devastation of denial. Only when we have seen what faith really asks of us, only when we realize how much our self-love denies such love for others, only when we have despaired of our own power to be true, can we let the Lord into our hearts to be our Savior. As yet there is no comfort for Peter. He will have to see more of what divine love will do for others before he will find it resurrected with power in his own life. But without this great grief of knowing his own weakness and selfishness, that could never happen. The same is true for us. Until we can know and admit our fear of being un-selfish and giving away our whole life, we cannot know God's presence in us.

Chapter Fifteen

PILATE AND CRUCIFIXION

Now the authority of Rome is drawn into the condemnation of Jesus. Since Archelaus ceased to be ruler of Judea in 6 A.D., it had been administered as a Roman province under procurators. Pontius Pilate had been appointed in 26 by Sejanus, who as prefect of Rome under the Emperor Tiberius was given authority to appoint such officials. His policy was opposed to the Jews, and Pilate at first tried to ride roughshod over their religious feelings by carrying the imperial insignia into Jerusalem; but he was forced by their religious fervor to give way. In 31 A.D., Tiberius removed Sejanus and had him executed for treachery, bringing his ruthless policy to an end and ordering more considerate treatment of the Jews. It may be that Pilate showed this change in policy by collaborating with the Jewish authorities now, if the crucifixion can be dated in the year 33. But such a late date depends on the death of John the Baptist being associated with the Nabataean War, consequent on Herod Antipas putting away his Arab wife to marry Herodias. Reckoning from Jesus' birth in 4 B.C., a ministry of three years beginning when he was about thirty would make 29 or 30 a more probable date for the crucifixion, and Sejanus would still be in power. In either case, there was no fundamental change in Pilate's nature, for in 36 A.D. he was removed from office after brutally suppressing a Samaritan demonstration. There are many legends about Pilate, as one might expect, but history knows nothing further about him. The procurator took care to be in Jerusalem at the great feasts, apparently as an official gesture but actually to be on hand should there be trouble, since these were the most likely occasions for riots.

So far we have been concerned with the conflict with the religious authorities, and seen how it reveals our own weaknesses in faith. Now the civil authorities are drawn into the conflict, and we have a new aspect of our lives to consider. We must all live a practical earthly life, performing some use to others, obeying the civil authority of our place and time, and fitting into the pattern of our community. This is clearly the provenance of Rome, the civil authority. In the Roman governor, we see the control of our outward life, and this alone has ultimate power. The way we live with our fellows is the final judgment of our character, and so the horror of our selfishness is now released there in the utmost cruelty and hatred directed against the love of God.

If our religious conviction is to have any power, it must carry with it the control of our earthly life with others. Thus, Roman authority is seen as the ultimate judge of Jesus. However, this natural control of our lives is unable to escape the persuasion of our religious ideas. There is a good deal of common sense in civil judgment when it is left to itself. It can recognize the foolishness of selfishness and greed in the community, and any civil power has to appeal to honesty, social justice, and so on. It is this that accounts for Pilate's apparent sympathy with Jesus in the gospel. Left to itself, our civil judgment of outward affairs would come to a balanced, if not very perceptive, judgment. But it is never left to itself. The decisions we have made about what we want to do with our lives, whether to be God's servants or our own selfish rulers, affect fundamentally the way we govern our outward lives. Once our religion is "self first," it treats any effort to put God first as a destructive force in life, asserting that it will destroy the outward fabric of our natural life by claiming to be king.

At this point, it becomes even more obvious that we are tracing a double thread of meaning in the gospel. There is the work of Jesus on earth, in which the divine love of God is entering into the whole human we use in this world. We have reached a stage when this is forcing out the evil of humanity at its deepest level and is in conflict with self-love that uses the horror of torture and pain to gain its own way. We watch how love uses its power to reject the evil, but not to destroy humanity. But if this is the way Jesus had to bring divine love to us, it is also the road we must tread in conquering our own evil in his power. We must pass through a similar rejection by our selfishness, as we use the power of love Jesus brought us. We look at our own spiritual torment and rejection by the world of evil, and in it can know some faint image of Jesus' divine work.

1–5. And immediately in the morning the chief priests with the elders and scribes and the whole Sanhedrin took counsel, and bound Jesus and took him away to deliver him to Pilate. And Pilate asked him, "Are you the king of the Jews?" And he answered, "You say so." And the chief priests accused him vehemently. And Pilate again questioned him, saying, "Will you not answer? See how many things they witness against you." But Jesus still said nothing, so that Pilate marveled.

Perhaps this morning assembly was at last a formal meeting of the council to decide what action to take. The Jewish authority had no power, save in very minor matters. If Jesus was to be executed, the Roman procurator must order it. The chief priests knew that their religious charges would not sway Roman justice, so Jesus' supposed claim to be the Messiah was now treated as one of rebellion against Rome on the grounds that he was thereby claiming to be king of the Jews. It placed Pilate in an awkward position, for although he might know that he was being used by the Jewish authorities, Tiberius Caesar would be sensitive to any charge that Pilate was not suppressing rebellion. John tells of the private conversation between Jesus and Pilate, and makes Pilate's sympathy with the prisoner understandable; but the more summary account here still leaves us in no doubt that Pilate was impressed by Jesus' quiet dignity in face of the frantic accusations and really wished to free him.

Pilate found it strange that Jesus made no attempt to answer the charges brought against him, but the decision as to the nature of our life is made at a deeper level than civil affairs. Love is a way of approaching life. It will use the things of the world to serve others in the social structure of a community, but it does not argue at that level. The decision is made at a deeper religious level and then carried out in civil life. The battle is with the chief priests; Jesus does not answer to Pilate.

We must be careful to observe the same distinction. We

must make our decision to use our life for others and then carry that into every moral and civil problem that besets our lives. We cannot make this fundamental decision by balancing arguments from merely civil affairs. That would leave us drifting with every difficulty and every change of opinion. The way we choose to use our lives, our "religious intention," operates into our life in the community. If it is a decision, like that of the chief priests, to maintain our own grip on life for our own ends, then we shall look for our own advantage and protect ourselves in every situation. If we choose the way of Jesus, we shall look always for the good of others and for ways to serve them. We all have to use the structure of the community in which we live but, within that, the way we decide to use our life will direct our efforts.

> *6–11. Now at the feast he released to them one prisoner of their choice. And there was one called Barabbas held with his accomplices; and they had rebelled, committing murder in the riot. And the crowd began yelling to him to do as he always did for them. But Pilate answered them, saying, "Shall I release to you the king of the Jews?" For he knew that the chief priests had only charged him out of malice. But the chief priests incited the crowd to ask rather that he would release Barabbas.*

There is no other record of the custom of releasing a prisoner at the feast, but it may well have been a custom of short duration. Pilate's recognition of the chief priests' motive causes him to try to free Jesus by the custom, but the priests get the crowd on their side. No doubt the crowd who came with Judas to take Jesus and others like them were involved; but mobs are notoriously fickle, and it may well be that the crowds who listened to Jesus teaching now preferred a murderer to him. We have no knowledge of Barabbas other than the gospel gives. Agitation against Rome was rife among the more extreme sects of the Jews and culminated eventually in 64 A.D. in the rebellion that was to destroy them and their temple. Clearly the action of Barabbas was violent and had involved killing someone.

For us, the crowd is the crowd of motives and decisions that make up our everyday life. Without any directing force, they become a mob swayed by the impulse of the moment. If they accepted Jesus, they could be directed by feelings of love and service, but the power of self-love that prevents his rule stirs them into destructive ways. Murder is to take a man's life, and spiritual murder is to kill the love that should be the life of anyone. Barabbas is the selfishness that riots through our everyday life and murders any love in it. If we leave our everyday life without the guidance of love, it will become a mob crying out for such selfishness in our every deed. We recognize such forces when the civil life of a community is suddenly torn apart by rioting and looting, but we know that the forces of self-love are constantly at work in a community, even when they are concealed within legal fictions and accepted practices. They have their origin in the personal decisions we make to use our outward lives for ourselves, and very different forces would be at work if we chose to love and serve others. Each of us cries out for Jesus or Barabbas in our life.

12–15. And Pilate then asked them, "What do you want me to do to him whom you call king of the Jews?" And again they yelled out, "Crucify him." And Pilate said to them, "Then what evil has he done?" But they yelled even more, "Crucify him."

Then Pilate, wanting to satisfy the crowd, released Barabbas to them; and having scourged Jesus, he handed him over to be crucified.

The crowd yells for the Roman method of execution by crucifixion, presumably because they are appealing to a Roman judge. The offense of blasphemy with which the high priest had charged Jesus was punishable with death by stoning, but any pretense of religious law is now abandoned, and the removal of Jesus becomes more important than its reason. Pilate's efforts to help Jesus only lead to greater vehemence from the crowd, who refuses Jesus as its king and, though providing no evidence of evil he has done, demand his death. What we know of Pilate shows him very willing to bully people, but in the face of strong opposition from others, liable to give way. The command to scourge Jesus does not imply any further condemnation of him. It was the custom to scourge anyone who was to be crucified. The beating was most severe, administered with a whip whose cords were loaded with lead.

Many suffered the pain of scourging and crucifixion, some with minds full of regret for criminal acts, some with minds bewildered and resenting injustice, some with snarling hatred that justice had halted their evil. We need to look more deeply into Jesus' mind to realize the nature of his torment. In these last stages of temptation on earth, he could not know the surety of divine vision. He had to fight in the same obscurity as men and women, though with full awareness of his mission. He had endured extreme temptation to fight human evil and conquered it to bring saving life on earth. Yet he heard those he came to save scream for his destruction. Would they ever use what he had done and learn to love? His disciples had run away.

Would anyone ever use the strength he had brought on earth to conquer evil? He knew from the truth that this was the way to redeem men and women, but their reaction to the work was this mob that yelled for his destruction and this whip that brought a screaming agony. The agony in his mind is beyond our knowing, and far more terrible to him than his physical agony.

We must not separate Jesus' work to save us from his agony of mind and body. His was not an experience isolated in his divinity. To work, it had to know pain and suffering from the world's cruelty. He saw the individual faces in the mob, and watched in horror as they rejected his love and howled for his destruction. He felt the torture they wanted to inflict, while still trying to save them from such hatred. In a maelstrom of evil, cruelty, and pain, he held to his purpose while they derided him.

There is a constant effort in evil to beat any way of love into subjection. The scourging of Jesus shows the power of evil trying to mutilate his true witness. We ourselves are aware of our selfishness scourging the true way of life. We know arguments that we cannot work in this world by Christian love, persuasions that we must meet lies by twisting the truth, constant urges to use the world's greed because that is the only way the world works, and fear of the distress and pain that Christian life can find in the world. These are the perversions of truth that try to beat love into compliance. Our agony is not so extreme, for we have only our own salvation at stake; but it is still torment, and mercifully there are few of us for whom it involves physical torture as well.

16–20. And the soldiers led him away inside the courtyard of the Governor's palace, and called to-

gether all their company. And they clothed him in purple, and plaited a crown of thorns and put it on him. And they began to salute him with "Hail, King of the Jews!" And they hit his head with a reed and spat on him, and bowing down paid homage to him. And when they had mocked him, they took the purple cloak off him and put his own clothes on him, and led him out to crucify him.

The word used for the governor's palace is *praetorium*, which originally meant "the general's tent," and so the headquarters of a camp and eventually the palace. Its military origin may well still cling to the word here, implying that the troops were quartered at the governor's residence. That would suggest the fortress called Antonia, rather than Herod's palace in the city. Strictly, the word "company" indicates a cohort, several hundred men, and what follows is typical brutal horseplay by soldiers. Romans would deride any Jew setting up as a king, and this is the point of their mocking "Hail, King of the Jews," a parody of their salute to the Roman emperor, *Ave, Caesar Imperator,* "Hail, Emperor Caesar." Matthew 27:28 is careful to call the cloak "scarlet," for it was presumably one of the soldiers' cloaks, but Mark calls it the royal "purple," since that is what it was meant to represent. Any one of a dozen species of thorny plants common in Jerusalem could have been used for the crown, which may have recalled the crown with radiant spikes that the emperor wears on coins of the period. Matthew is careful to say that the reed was intended as a scepter, but Mark stresses the abuse with it.

Jesus is the real king of our lives, and to mock him in this way shows how his kingdom is regarded. Our selfishness provides its own clothing of distorted ideas, and evil twists its own crown of cruelty in life. Any power to control our greed is seen weak as a reed. Any seeming respect of ways to help others is really a pretense to get our own way, a mockery that despises any divine purpose trying to rule our life. Jesus had made love a king in this world and had brought its divine power to men and women to be with them forever. But if they despised love and rejected it, it would still have no power to save them. Their mockery of him left a sharper wound than the thorns of the crown, for he loved them totally and knew only mocking rejection of his love.

Whenever we allow our self to control our life, we mock the love of Jesus in the same fashion. One simple way to realize what it means is to ask ourselves what the Lord thinks of our behavior, what pain he feels when we use our strength to hurt others, what pity he feels when we mock his love with self-serving greed and hatred. The horseplay of a group of soldiers is very like the cruelty that comes into our life when we are carried away by accustomed greed and accept the thoughtless behavior of the world. To be accepted into some of the social practices that rule there can easily involve us in a mockery of the love that should rule our lives.

> *21–26. And Simon, a Cyrenian, the father of Alexander and Rufus, who passed by coming from a field, they compelled to carry his cross. And they brought him to a place called Golgotha, which means "the place of a skull." And they gave him wine mixed with myrrh, but he did not drink it. And they crucified him, and divided up his clothes and cast lots to decide who should have which part. And it was the third hour and they crucified him. And the*

description of his offense was written up: "The King of the Jews."

We know nothing of Simon; he may have made the long journey from west of Egypt to come to Jerusalem for the feast. Clearly, though, Alexander and Rufus were well known to the first readers of the gospel and served to identify Simon. Whether he was working or whether the mention of a field is to locate his impressment outside the city walls, we do not know. John 19:17 says that Jesus carried the cross, but he was likely to collapse eventually from the effects of the scourging. "The third hour" would be reckoned from dawn at 6 A.M., and so is 9 o'clock; but it must be remembered that only the advent of clocks made possible accurate timing, and this and the succeeding time references refer rather to the four watches into which the day was divided.

The evangelists and other authors, along with relics of the period, provide some details of the process of crucifixion. Those to be crucified were made to carry the crosspiece of the cross to the place of execution. The upright stakes were already in place. Once there, the offender was stripped of his clothes, which became the property of his executioners, a group of four soldiers, or quaternion. His hands were nailed or bound on to the crosspiece, which was then raised up and fastened at the top, or near to the top, of the stake. There was a support to take some of the weight of the body, and the feet were bound or nailed to the upright. The statement of his offense, which had been hanging round his neck, was now nailed to the cross. The position of the body hanging from the arms placed great and continuous strain on the muscles of the arms and trunk of the victim. The condemned was then left to die of shock, hunger, thirst, and exposure; death might take more than a day. Cicero calls it the most cruel and frightful of punishments. Places of execution were public, for crucifixion was meant to terrify others into submission; and so Golgotha was probably alongside one of the roads into the city, but we do not know where. "The place of a skull" implies that it was an accustomed place for executions. The offering of wine mixed with myrrh was probably to dull the senses, although elsewhere frankincense is said to be used for the purpose. Psalm 22:16–18 is brought to mind here: "They have pierced my hands and my feet. . . . They divide my garments among them, and for my clothing they cast lots." John quotes from the Psalm.

The killing of Jesus showed the total rejection of his power and his way. Many others suffered the physical pain of his death, but the spiritual torment of watching men and women reject the love he brought was his alone. He was regarded as a criminal for attempting to change their evil, selfish lives. Loving parents know this kind of agony in seeing a child reject them and debase and destroy his or her life; but the love that suffered in Jesus was divine love for the whole human race. It is no accident that he is said to be offered wine, as he had given his disciples to drink at the supper. Then it had represented his vision of life, true wisdom. Now it is mixed with bitter myrrh to show the worldly ambitions and natural lusts, which contaminate the way we look at the world. This he could not take. This was not his wise way, but only the travesty men and women make of truth, so as to use it to get their own way with others.

We all have a cross on which to crucify our Lord. It is the selfish heart of our being, the feeling that we matter first, our fundamental assumption that life was provided to satisfy our desires. Against this, the unselfish love of God is nailed down, totally helpless and slowly dying. Not one of us will escape the agony of realizing this crucifixion of life on our self-interest. Until we realize just what our selfish wanting does to God's gift of love, we shall not be able to reject our self-love, so that true love can be resurrected in us. Step by step, we shall see how our selfishness strips away the clothing of truth Jesus has provided. We argue for our own way by demanding that others obey the commandments to help and serve us. We insist on the community obeying righteous laws, so that we can keep our comfortable life in it. We even excuse our evils by arguing that we cannot do any better because another must save us. This is to cast lots for the particular piece of truth that gets us our own way for the moment, while we destroy the whole meaning of truth in the process, just what the soldiers did to Jesus' clothes.

> *27–32. And they crucified two robbers with him, one at his right hand and the other at his left, and the Scripture was fulfilled that says, "He was counted among the criminals." And those passing by abused him, tossing their heads and saying, "Ah, you who destroy the temple and rebuild it in three days, save yourself and come down from the cross." And in the same way the chief priests with the scribes laughed among themselves and said, "He saved others. He cannot save himself! Let this Christ the king of Israel come down now from the cross, that we may see it and believe!" And those crucified with him upbraided him.*

The two robbers had presumably been condemned earlier. The Scripture recalled is Isaiah 53:12, and Psalm

22:6–8 is recalled in the derision of Jesus. "Those passing by" suggests a main road into the city with its passing throng, but the chief priests and scribes, and no doubt others of the crowd, remained to gloat over the one they had condemned. Luke, relying possibly on a closer witness, tells us one of the robbers was repentant.

Humanity in its selfishness sees Jesus as a criminal, a danger to society. To an evil society, the spirit of love is dangerous. Our assessment of redeeming love is not a matter of take it or leave it. Rather it is a matter of love it or hate it. There is no neutral way. Divine love will break apart any selfish community by its demands for unselfish service from real affection. Selfishness will destroy love as a criminal element endangering its position. We must choose. The power of divine love can only be brought to bear if we accept and use it.

If the way divine love works is not wanted, it is not understood, and it is derided as powerless. Jesus brought love into our lives, but he also wanted us to choose it. None of the power of love could be imposed on human beings. If that love were rejected, it would hang on that cross and die. With enough power, we can compel someone to obey a set of rules, but we cannot compel anyone to love others; that requires a willingness to accept and use affection. The derision of Jesus expresses this point. He had spoken of providing a real "temple" for humanity, and he had accomplished it by bringing divine love into the world, but he could not force men and women to accept him. He could save others because he loved them, but he could not save himself because they would not accept his love. The real ruler of life is the love from which it is lived, and Jesus provided that love. But this was not a kingship that could enforce its rule; it was a rule that had to be wanted.

If we can grasp this idea, we can see clearly God's action in us and in the world around. We tend to want a power that will do things regardless of what others want, but basically that is selfish. Love wants others to join with it, not to be subservient to it. In our own lives, we could not use a Savior who would climb down from the cross of our selfishness against our will, who would exert power over us to change us. I know that sometimes in desperation we feel like asking God to take us over and get rid of our self-love in arbitrary fashion, but really we know it would never work. Jesus can provide all the power of love we need, but we will have to choose to use it. The same rule applies when we want to get something done in the world. Nothing lasting can be achieved by forcing others to be good. We have to show them that we want change because we love them, and we want their good, not our own. And we have to let them see that, for us, the most important thing is their choosing to cooperate in any change for the better. Today, Christians are often derided as "soft" because they seek to persuade people by example rather than force them by power, but this is the only way to change the character of people and so achieve lasting benefit. And it requires a truly firm and determined character to carry it through against all the apparent odds.

33–36. And at the sixth hour darkness came over all the land until the ninth hour. And at the ninth hour Jesus cried out with a loud voice, "Eloi, Eloi, lamma sabachthani?" which means "My God, my God, why have you forsaken me?" And, hearing it, some of those standing by said, "Listen, he calls for Elijah," and ran and filled a sponge with vinegar and put it on a reed and gave it to him to drink, saying, "Let him alone. Let us see if Elijah will come to take him down."

Jesus' cry is the opening of Psalm 22, transliterated from the Aramaic. Matthew transliterates the first word from the Hebrew, which makes more understandable the confusion of Elijah with the word for "my God," *Eli.* Jesus was accustomed to read the Scripture in the synagogues and would probably have quoted it in Hebrew, though others might remember it in the Aramaic vernacular. The vinegar given to Jesus would be the sour wine that the soldiers drank. Some in the crowd were anxious to keep him alive in his agony, so that they could see if Elijah would appear, and so they quenched his thirst.

The cry from the cross is perhaps the most terrifying thing in Scripture. It is the first verse of Psalm 22, which speaks of him abandoned and alone. He had learned the Psalm as a child, and understood it as a man, but now he was experiencing its horror in his very self. All that his love had worked for and wanted to give the human race was despised and hated. His life hung failed and useless to help anyone. Love's power had abandoned him and he was utterly forsaken. Jesus was the love of God brought into this world and lived out in a human mind, and he cries out in despair that God has abandoned him, indicating that he has despaired of the work he was sent to do. He does not see that his work will achieve anything, because men and women will not accept his love into their lives. At this point his temptation had reached the extreme, for he was left to hold to his love for humankind while he felt it had all been in vain. He had now no surety from insight to comfort him, no sense of God's presence with power. He was left to love men and women for no reason whatever—

except that he loved them. Because his love held on, it brought the divine presence into the last level of our torment. It rooted out selfishness from its last stronghold of fear and despair. Even while he despaired of his work, he triumphed.

The darkness in which this last act was played out, whatever its natural cause, clearly represents the state of humanity at this time. There was no light in the human mind, no understanding shed from divine love. And this is our own experience in the depth of temptation. This is the abyss when love must hold on without light or achievement. His cry was to God, but it was misunderstood as calling to Elijah. This is the mistake the world makes. Jesus calls to the love of God to remedy the world's despair, but selfish men and women think it must be simply a cry to the austere restriction of Elijah. Selfishness thinks a method, a pattern of denial, is all that is calling to us; but it is love that is stretched out to us, and only love will help the world.

Jesus' cry of despair brought the offer of vinegar to drink, which again expresses the state of humankind. Wine represents true wisdom, but when wine is left open to the air, it sours to vinegar. Generation after generation had soured the wisdom of God by using it in their selfishness, until all its true ideas of love had been destroyed. People used it now to control each other, to argue for their own esteem. Nothing was left of its real purpose to show men and women the life of love. Now each generation was taught this way and could see the truth only as this complete falsity of its meaning. Strangely enough (as John makes clear), Jesus can accept this. When the wine of wisdom was mingled with myrrh, and its obvious use for evil was there, it was unacceptable. But people who have never had anything but false ideas are acceptable to the Lord, if they themselves do no evil. None of us can know the truth without some false and wrong ideas clinging to it. In us, the wine of life has soured to the vinegar of false ideas. Some of us may feel we understand very little at all. But if we are willing to work from love for others, our intent makes us acceptable, and in time the false notions can be put right.

> *37–41. And Jesus uttered a loud cry and died. And the curtain of the temple was torn in two from top to bottom. And the centurion who stood on duty in front of him, when he saw him cry out and die, said, "This man was indeed a son of God." And there were also women looking on from a distance, including Mary Magdalene, Mary the mother of James the Less and Joses, and Salome, who had followed him in Galilee and served him, and many other women who had come up with him to Jerusalem.*

The curtain meant here is the veil that hung in the temple between the outer Holy Place where, lighted by the lampstand, the priests daily burned incense and offered the bread of the presence, and the inner Holy of Holies, which was in total darkness, where the Ark of the Covenant had been until it was looted by the Babylonians. Tearing that veil opened up access to the innermost and holiest part of the temple. The quarternion at an execution was under the command of a centurion, and here he is mentioned for the first time. His comment recognizes Jesus' nature from his behavior but should not be understood to imply the recognition that he was divine. Luke records the centurion's comment as, "This was a righteous man," which is what it really implies. We become aware now of a body of women who had followed Jesus in Galilee, as had the men who were his disciples. Among them three are picked out by name. Luke 8:1–3 tells us that Jesus had cast seven devils out of Mary of Magdala. Matthew 27:56 suggests that Salome was Zebedee's wife. James the Less and Joses cannot be identified now, but were presumably well-enough known to the first readers of the gospel to identify their mother. John records a different group, including Mary Magdalene but adding Jesus' mother, her sister, and Mary, the wife of Clopas. Some of these may refer to the same women, though those who followed from Galilee were clearly many. However, the presence of his mother and the record of Jesus consigning her to the care of John is not recorded in Mark.

The message of the gospel is that Jesus tore aside the veil between God and humankind. As John says, "No man has seen God at any time. The only-begotten son who is in the bosom of the Father, he has made him known." The human quality of God had never been realized before, nor that this quality was love and all the wisdom it brought. God had created the human race, cared and provided for it, but had never before been manifest at the earthly level of life. In Jesus, we have a way of thinking about God who, in his creative power, is beyond our understanding. We have seen God's love where we must live, showing compassion and a love that enlightens life and makes its meaning clear. But the work in Jesus is greater than that, for he brought the power of the divine itself into our level of mind. It means that, when we try to live as he commands, we are not distanced from him, but have his own power of love ready to act in us and replace our old selfishness. It was inevitable that God would find a way to be with humanity and help people in their selfishness. The whole of the Old Testament foretells it and, indeed, religions across the world have some concept of a savior God. It was necessary for God to wait until all the evil that might beset men and women was manifest. Yet the delay was not from lack of urgent love but so that when he came to tear aside the veil between God and humanity, the work could be complete and make his power of love available to all, in all times and places.

The recognition of Jesus' quality by the Roman centurion shows that unbiased civil power recognizes the nature of love in everyday life. It does not understand its divine origin, but it sees the power it has in the life of a community and acknowledges that it works from another source than mere social pressures. It comes to see in it, as the centurion had in Jesus, forgiveness of others and a willingness to endure on their behalf without looking for worldly power or reward. It is important that Christians maintain such a witness in the world, not asking for civil power but earning its respect by bringing compassion, forgiveness, and a willingness to sacrifice self for the good of others. Because women are in some cultures more honest and open than men in showing affection and love, they are often used in the Scripture to show such qualities. Here they remain and watch from a distance when the disciples, learners and teachers of the good news, are scattered. When understanding of our role can no longer cope, we are still left with affection for Jesus' way of love, although we are too frightened of the consequences to stay and use it to control our life. Such affection is at a distance because we have not been faithful to Jesus' way; but, nonetheless, in our despair it plays a part to draw us back.

42–47. And since evening had now come, because it was the preparation (that is, the day before the Sab-

bath), Joseph of Arimathaea, a distinguished coun-
cillor who was himself waiting for the kingdom of
God, had the courage to go in to Pilate and ask for
the body of Jesus. And Pilate was surprised that he
was dead already, and he called the centurion and
asked if he had indeed died. And when the centurion
confirmed it, he granted the body to Joseph. And he
bought a linen cloth, and took him down and
wrapped him in it. And he laid him in a tomb cut
out of the rock, and rolled a stone across the entrance
to the tomb. And Mary Magdalene and Mary the
mother of Joses saw where he was laid.

The Jewish day began at evening, and it would shortly
be the Sabbath when nothing could be done. There was
also the command in Deuteronomy 21:22–23, that no
body executed should be left overnight on the tree. We
have no more knowledge of Joseph of Arimathaea than is
here. He presumably came from a place called Ramathaim,
but there are at least two places of that name. He is unknown in the early Christian church, and it has been suggested that his action may merely have been that of a
devout Pharisee to fulfill the command of Deuteronomy;
Jews took great care to bury even strangers. However, to
have associated himself with one condemned by his council
and accused of rebellion against the Roman state was very
bold and is said specifically to have taken courage; so it
would seem rather that he acted from conviction. Although
a member of the council, Matthew asserts that he was also
a disciple of Jesus.

Most of those crucified took a longer time to die of exposure; but Jesus was under enormous inner stress, as we
have seen, and this may have hastened his death. From the

time of Augustus, bodies had been granted to friends and relatives for burial. Nevertheless, the burial was hurried, for no spices were used. The fact that a linen burial cloth could be bought suggests again that Mark was incorrect in thinking that this day was the Passover, when such a transaction was unlikely. The customary Jewish tomb was used, hewn out of rock and with a stone to seal the entrance. John tells us it was new, and Matthew adds that it was Joseph's own tomb.

There are two sides to burial in a tomb. From this world it seems to be an end, but from the next world of life after death it is seen as a beginning. So the burial of Jesus means the putting off of the things of this world in which he had done his work and the putting on of his divine power at the resurrection, which would also resurrect men and women into a new way of life. That a "Joseph" performed this burial stresses the point for, in the Hebrew Scriptures, the name Joseph is said to refer to taking away and to adding, as Rachel says in Genesis 30:23–24. Since the resurrection was to follow, details of the burial of Jesus might seem superfluous, but such a reaction misinterprets the nature of Jesus' work, which had to be performed in this world. It had to bring divine love into truth while it worked in the quality and details of this life, so that it would be available to men and women. When we choose to use the truth, the love of God is powerful in it, because in Jesus he brought it there. The life lived here formed the divine human that was to be eternally present, and it cannot be forgotten.

Nonetheless, the nature of the burial still conveyed the rejection Jesus had known. Pilate, the power of worldly things that condemned Jesus' love to death, authorized the release of the body, satisfied that he had killed love as a way of life. Joseph replaced the clothing that had been stripped from Jesus with a linen cloth, just as the devout, mourning for a power they have not used, can still wrap it up in the truth they learn and discuss. The tomb, with the stone rolled across its mouth, typifies the way we still roll a stone of false arguments in front of any possibility of using love in our lives.

Chapter Sixteen

RESURRECTION

The resurrection of Jesus is far more than just the disappearance of his earthly body and his ability to appear to those who believed in him. We have seen that he came on earth anointed with the love of God, so as to bring its power into every facet of earthly human life. Once that work was done, he had made the earthly human plane of life divine, one with God. This is what is called "the Son," because although it is the one love of God, it has been brought down by that creative love that is "the Father" into the life of this world and remains in it forever. As the gospel says, the Father and the Son are one (John 10:30; 17:11), for divine love is always the same, whatever it is doing. But the divine in the human enables us to see how it acts and to know its compassion and redeeming love, which is beyond our knowing when it creates universes. More, it brought divine love into the truth we use to govern our lives, and so brings God himself into our endeavors, Immanuel, "God with us." This divine presence in the human remains always for all men and women. It means that they can call on its power of love when they are willing to live by it.

This union of God with humankind comes about because of the work of Jesus. In this life, he brought the divine love of God into the truth we use to understand and control our lives. So when, like the women in this chapter, we come with affection, looking for the truth we love but thinking it is just dead and powerless, we find it powerful beyond our understanding. The truth we must use has been glorified by the love of God and is risen into power. Jesus told us that he would always be with us, and he is always present in the truth we use because he used it too. He is not just an example of a way of thinking and an external life we can copy. He has brought his divine power to be in that way of truth. If we use an idea of truth from affection, he brings his risen power of love into it, and we begin to see with something of his perception and have power to live by that truth. His risen power in the truth we use here never becomes our own. We choose to let it work, and as he said, he is in us and we are in him; but we never possess this power as our own. Our lack of knowledge, our misunderstanding of what we do know, the selfish tendencies we still have not conquered, all of these restrict what we can see and feel. And if we could make all these things perfect, we would still be dependent on God for the life that enables us to choose his way. However, though we do not use all the power Jesus brought, what we do use brings him alive in our lives.

1–5. And when the Sabbath was over, Mary Magdalene and Mary the mother of James and Salome bought spices that they might come and anoint him.

And very early on the first day of the week, they came to the tomb at sunrise. And they asked each other, "Who will roll away the stone for us from the entrance to the tomb?" And looking up they saw that the stone had been rolled away, though it was very large. And entering the tomb, they saw a young man clothed in a white robe sitting on the right-hand side, and they were filled with awe.

During the Sabbath, nothing could be done. Having begun at 6 P.M. on the Friday, it ended at 6 P.M. on the Saturday. It would seem that the women then bought spices so as to be able to come to the tomb early on the Sunday. John 19:39 says that Joseph and Nicodemus used spices when they buried the body. Either the women did not know this or wished to supplement it, or we have a confusion because of hearsay and not observation. The women in their haste either forgot about the stone or were willing to look for help to move the stone when they got to the tomb. The young man is clearly an angel, who Revelation 7:9 tells us would be robed in white.

Jesus was anointed before his death by the woman in Bethany, and we saw then that it was a recognition that he was the Messiah, anointed with the love of God on earth. The women's intention to anoint his body shows the same acceptance of him, but now in grief that his kingship is lost. We saw at the burial that the great stone blocking the tomb is the symbol of humankind's false use of the knowledge of truth, by which they seal in God's love and get their own way and control others. The women have the desire to remove this, but feel they do not have the power. We are in much the same position when we realize how much we misuse truth. We feel helpless to break our selfish wanting that makes it happen. But the stone is already rolled away in the power that Jesus brought on earth. If we have the desire to change, like the women, the power has been brought into this world to enable us to do so. We, too, shall come to a new dawn in our lives when we choose to accept Jesus' way. That power brings us a new messenger, the truth alive with Jesus' love.

The human appearance of the messenger is important. It reminds us that life in this world continues into the spiritual world, which is not inhabited by alien beings but by men and women who have lived in this world. More importantly, it shows us something of the nature of a messenger of truth. We are liable to think of truth as being the same as knowledge, just a series of ideas to explain and analyze our relation to God. This makes it abstract and not human; but in reality, truth is the living affection that is contained in those ideas. Knowledge of ideas is simply a pattern of thinking, which can be quite detached from the personality of the thinker and so have no power to comprehend the living reality intended. Indeed, anyone may use it to attack and destroy its avowed purpose. Truth exists only where the ideas are believed and therefore loved. This makes the complete human nature of love and wisdom together; and this is the human messenger in our life, the angel, which can assure us of the risen power of Jesus.

6–8. But he said to them, "Do not be amazed. You seek Jesus, the Nazarene, who has been crucified. He is risen. He is not here. See the place where they laid him. But go, say to Peter and his disciples that he goes before you into Galilee. There you shall see him, as he said to you." And leaving quickly, they fled

*away from the tomb, trembling and distraught, and
they said nothing to anyone, for they were afraid.*

That the body of Jesus vanished from the tomb is
stressed in the Gospels. Matthew adds that a guard was put
on the tomb and still it vanished, while John describes the
burial cloths left behind in such a way as to emphasize that
the body had simply left them, and they had not been un-
rolled from the body. Mark is content with the simple assertion that the body had gone. We can hardly expect to
understand completely what happened. When Jesus had
fully glorified the natural level of life with divine life, he
was present there but could no longer be restricted to a
particular space or time. The physical structure of his body
was so restricted, since it was made of matter, and so it will
have dissipated in the presence of this new divine life. But
the whole emphasis of the Gospel is that the divine life
Jesus brought was still present in all humankind's living in
this world. It is present in all our earthly life, down to our
sensations, for Jesus told his disciples, "Handle me and see,
for a spirit has not flesh and bones as you see me have"
(Luke 24:39). Clearly he could act upon the senses and in-
teract with the physical world as he showed by eating, but
he was not restricted by the physical body to one place or
one time. This emphasizes that his presence with us exists
down to the lowest level of life that we can use, leaving
apart only insensible matter in space and time. This is
quite different to human beings who, when they die, put
off the sensation and action of this world and rise in a spiritual body in the spiritual world. We will consider later
how Jesus appears and how he is present with us.

The assertion that Jesus goes before his disciples into
Galilee to meet them there seems strange, in view of his

appearances to them in Jerusalem; but it is not exclusive, and it is necessary to make a spiritual point to us. Jesus showed his conquest of this world's selfishness in Galilee first, and we saw then that it stands for the rough and tumble of our natural life in this world. It was only there that Jesus could gain power for us. The reference to that level of life is strengthened by calling him "the Nazarene." It is only in that rough and tumble of everyday life that we shall accept and know his love. We need to "go into Galilee" if we are to see our risen Lord and truly use his power.

The gospel does not appear to continue smoothly from this point into the following verse, and the style becomes unlike Mark. We saw in the introduction that the end of this gospel appears to be a summary, which may be by another writer because of the difference in style. It may have been composed when it was realized that the original had lost its conclusion, or had never been finished beyond the message received at the empty tomb. (For the details on this, please refer to the introduction, which also explains why here I deal with the text as being provided by the Lord and therefore having meaning for us, despite the possibility of multiple authors.)

9–11. But he rose early on the first day of the week, and appeared first to Mary Magdalene, from whom he had cast out seven devils. She went and told it to the ones who had followed him, who were grieving and weeping. But when they heard that he was alive and had been seen by her, they would not believe it.

Luke 24:9–11 shows similarities with this, but it is probably a brief summary of what was well known. The statement links clumsily to what has gone before; and the identification of Mary Magdalene (who has already been mentioned in this chapter) by the description in Luke 8:2 seems to indicate a new and unrelated beginning.

All the gospels have this theme, that the disciples found it difficult to accept that Jesus had risen. It pervades this ending to Mark. All Jesus' assertions of his divine nature and his work on earth never seem to have been grasped even by those closest to him; it follows, therefore, that they could not at first grasp the idea of the resurrection. By its very nature, it is difficult for all of us. We may think we have some idea of the love of God; but his work in sending that love into human life reveals its nature in astounding reality. With each man or woman he creates, he has a personal relationship so deep it will endure anything to make it work. We can only grasp such a love if we are of a nature that can comprehend it. If we truly want a relationship with such love, we must accept its unselfish nature in ourselves. Only using such love makes it understandable. This is the real obstacle to accepting the resurrection. Much is made of the apparent difficulties of God's appearing in his own creation and establishing a presence there; but once we grasp his nature as love, the creation becomes his way of sharing it, and his actions ensure that he does so.

The fate of the earthly body of Jesus is often made an incomprehensible mystery because it is discussed apart from his purpose. He put on a human life in this world so as to bring divine love into it. He could not do that without eventually putting off the fallen nature he assumed, which he did step by step, replacing it with divine love at each level. When the body had served its purpose, that too was put off, and so had no more existence than the various aspects of thought and feeling that he had dispensed with. Just as in those cases, he acquired a divine presence at that level in its place. The nature of that presence becomes clear from his appearances. He appeared where it would help belief, and he appeared in whatever way was most useful to those he was trying to help.

12–13. And after this, he appeared to two of them in a different form, as they were going into the country. And they came and told it to the rest, but they did not believe them either.

This suggests the story in Luke 24:13–35, in which Jesus appears to two disciples walking away from Jerusalem, but in such a guise that they do not recognize him until he breaks bread for them. However, the conclusion to that story shows the disciples assured of the resurrection by an appearance to Simon, whereas here they do not yet believe. Again we have a summary of a well-known story, but not drawn directly from the other gospel. The summary is so abbreviated that the phrase "in a different form" could refer to the appearance being different from that shown to Mary, but it seems rather that it refers to a form in which the two disciples did not recognize him in the story.

It is necessary to think out clearly what happened when Jesus appeared to anyone. No created person could grasp the divine nature, and so the actual presence of the Lord could not appear, since it would include his relation with all human beings for all time. What could appear was his relationship with an individual in the form in which he or she could receive his presence. If his presence was not believed in, his appearance might not be recognized. This is the reason his appearance was often not recognized at first and then, with developing reception, could be recognized. Appearances to physical sense were necessary at the beginning to confirm the faith of the first disciples, but these could not continue without removing humankind's freedom to choose its way. So, for us, the Lord appears in ideas and feelings at our natural level, which enable us to grasp his nature in our life. These too will change as we develop and perceive more clearly and deeply the nature of his love for us, but the reality of his presence is always the same. The sphere we live in is also the sphere in which God's life is present, and it is always ready for our salvation.

14. Afterwards he appeared to the eleven when they were at table, and reproached them for their unbelief and hard hearts, because they did not believe those who had seen him risen.

This is hardly a summary of John 20:19–29, nor yet of Luke 24:36–42. It is more an independent reminder of well-known incidents. It is well to remember that what is recorded in the other gospels is not all that may have been current orally, and therefore available to make up this conclusion to the gospel.

Jesus' reproach is offered to us all, for self-love prevents our belief in the Lord's presence. It makes it impossible for us to believe in the work of redemption the Lord has done for us, for selfishness means that we see our own purpose in the world and cannot see his loving purpose for us. A "hard heart" cannot believe in the risen power of love because it does not want to use that love. While we want the world to serve us and achieve our own purposes, we cannot believe in the risen Lord. It may well be that part of our mind is convinced that the Lord's presence is there to act into our life and save us, but other pressures emphasize our apparent need of this world's kind of behavior and with a "hard heart" refuse wholehearted belief. It is necessary for us to see that this is the result of selfishness active in us and not a mere dispute in our reasoning. It is something for which the Lord in his love reproaches us and pleads with us to change. Nothing is more important than to admit our need of the Lord's presence and to choose to let him act in all our life.

> *15–18. And he said to them, "Go into all the world, and proclaim the good news to the whole creation. He that believes and is baptized shall be saved, but he that does not believe shall be condemned. And these signs will accompany those who believe: in my name they shall cast out devils; they shall speak with new tongues; they shall take up serpents; and if they drink anything poisonous, it shall not harm them; they shall lay their hands upon the sick, and they will be well."*

Matthew 28:19, Luke 24:47, and Acts 1:8 have similar charges to the disciples to begin their missionary work. The signs that will accompany them appear only here, but are similar to those mentioned as occurring in various places in Acts of the Apostles and the gospels, with the exception of drinking poison, which appears again only in the early church father Eusebius.

We began the gospel with the assertion that it would declare the good news to us. Now at the end comes the Lord's charge to carry the good news to others. That does not mean that we all need necessarily to become missionaries and teachers of the Word. Our best witness is the life we live. If others see us as honest and true, loving and compassionate, because we believe we should serve the Lord by living that way, they will realize that there is real power in the presence of the Lord Jesus Christ. We do not need to lecture others, still less to reprove them. Like our Lord, we need to show the love and light he has brought into our lives. Our greatest service to our neighbor is in our daily work and our care for others, and there we can fulfill our witness by honest loving service.

The signs to call people to the Lord, performed physically by the disciples in the beginning, show us the things we must do spiritually to carry his message. We have seen that baptism means to wash the mind clean with the truth we love. Anything in our life that can be so cleansed becomes part of our Christian self, but anything that cannot receive such a baptism is condemned and must be rejected. While we hold to our faith, we shall be able to cast out "devils" of selfishness and lust in the strength of compassion and love from the Lord. We shall begin to speak with "a new tongue," speaking from the truth and understanding life from its viewpoint. There will be a great deal of earthly reasoning crawling on the ground like serpents, but we can pick such things up without any harm, for we can enlighten them with ideas of truth. If we should drink the poison brew of some human reasoning that secretly opposes the way of truth, we shall not be harmed by it, for we shall be working from love and eventually shall see the harm in such reasoning. These are the signs that follow those who witness the truth. Throughout the spread of Christianity, there has been an effort to provide physical signs that would prove the truth of the good news, but such effects only served a purpose at the beginning. Once given time to use the power Jesus brought into earthly life, everyone's personal life can provide these real signs of his presence, the real confirmation of its genuine power.

19–20. So after saying this to them, the Lord was taken up into heaven, and sat at the right hand of

God. And they went out and preached everywhere, the Lord working with them and confirming the message by signs that followed it. Amen.

The concept of the Lord's being at the right hand of God occurs in several places. The right hand is used in the Scriptures to express power, and God exercises his power with men and women through the human nature he took in the world and glorified with the divine love itself. We must be careful not to think that the Lord's being taken up into heaven removes him from his contact with us. He assured us that he would be with us always. Heaven, as he reminded us, is in the midst of us, for heaven is not a place but a state of life in which love works in the world. True, such is the state of those who accept the Lord's life and pass into the spiritual world, but this quality of life is present too with all those who accept and use the Lord's love here.

The coming of divine love into this sphere of human life is a reality that works with all men and women, whether they know about it or not. It is the source of unselfish affection with everyone, whatever their knowledge or belief. The Gospel enables us, like the disciples, to know and use and rejoice about that work of God, which redeemed all humankind. It also enables each of us personally to understand how this love from God can work in us for our salvation. For so wonderful a gift, thanks be to God!

All the foregoing is what I see in Mark's gospel when I read it and think about it, seeking a personal message from God for my life. As I said at the beginning of this book, what I have written is only an example to illustrate a "person-to-person" way to read the gospel and listen to the Lord's Word. May we all find the Lord near to us as we read, and may we rejoice in his way of love and service.

About the Author

Paul V. Vickers is a retired minister of the General Conference of the New Church. He was ordained from the New Church College, Woodford Green, London, in 1944, and that same year received a degree in physics and pure mathematics from London University.

After eleven years as a pastor in Birmingham and London, he spent sixteen years as principal of the New Church College, raising educational standards and opening up new approaches to pastoral work. Then, he became minister of the New Church in Bournemouth and also served as chaplain to the town's mayor. Illness forced his retirement in 1990; since then, he has resumed his writing.

Among his previous publications are *Person to Person to the Lord Jesus Christ* (1970), *God-Talk and Man-Talk* (1970), and *Living with God* (1996).

Rev. Vickers currently lives in Bournemouth with his wife Nita.

True Christian Religion, Two Volumes.
JOHN C. AGER, TRANS.

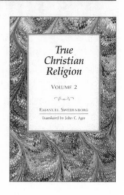

Published in 1771, *True Christian Religion* is Swedenborg's final major work. Derived from his intense spiritual experiences, it is a comprehensive, revealed theological system, intended to resolve dilemmas that had confused and divided Christians for centuries. Present here are Swedenborg's unique perspectives on the Trinity, the Bible, the faith/works controversy, human nature and spiritual growth, the sacraments, and the true nature of the church. 0-87785-295-2, 2-vol. set $19.95; 0-87785-292-8, vol. 1, pb, $11.95; 0-87785-294-4, vol. 2, pb, $11.95

Heaven and Hell, Divine Love and Wisdom, Divine Providence: Three-Volume Boxed Set
JOHN C. AGER & WILLIAM F. WUNSCH, TRANS.

Three volumes of Swedenborg's best-known works are offered in a slipcase format. *Heaven and Hell* describes the wonders of the world of spirits. *Divine Love and Wisdom* shows the spiritual structure and operation of the universe. *Divine Providence* explains God's care of humanity and articulates the way to redemption. 0-87785-282-0, pb in slipcase, $39.95

Heavenly Secrets
(Volume 1 of Arcana Coelestia)
EMANUEL SWEDENBORG
JOHN CLOWES, TRANS.

A detailed exposition of the internal meaning of Genesis, verse by verse, from Creation through Noah. 0-87785-214-6, pb, $11.95

Heaven and Hell
EMANUEL SWEDENBORG/GEORGE F. DOLE, TRANS.

"*Heaven and Hell* is the best introduction to Swedenborg because it has the quality of a compressed image of all his theological works."
— Colin Wilson

Heaven and Hell, the most important of Swedenborg's works, fully describes the spiritual realm and explains its meaning and relationship to our lives in the material world. Dole's easy-to-read translation from the original Latin makes Swedenborg's experiences accessible to all. Well-delineated chapters help readers explore their questions. 0-87785-153-0, pb, $10.95

Divine Love and Wisdom
EMANUEL SWEDENBORG/GEORGE F. DOLE, TRANS.

Outlines God's purpose in creating the natural universe, examining the means, structure, method, and goal of creation. A metaphysical base for a coherent, holistic existence.
0-87785-129-8, pb, $9.95

Divine Providence
EMANUEL SWEDENBORG/W. F. WUNSCH, TRANS.

Shows how divine nature governs human life and creation. Describes individual human freedom as inherent in creation, empowered by a God-given ability to understand and decide.
0-87785-061-5, pb, $9.95

"There are things that can be known, and then understood, if only the mind enjoys them; for pleasure brings light with it because it stems from love. For people who love matters of divine and heavenly wisdom, a light shines from heaven, and they have enlightenment."
— *Heaven and Hell* ¶ 265